Effigy hung from the flagpole at Mansfield High School on Thursday, August 30, 1956. The figure remained in place until September 4. Another effigy, hung on August 31, remained above the school's main entrance for several more days.

DESEGREGATING TEXAS SCHOOLS:
Eisenhower, Shivers, and the Crisis at Mansfield High

Robyn Duff Ladino

UNIVERSITY OF TEXAS PRESS, AUSTIN

Cover photo/frontispiece courtesy of *Fort Worth Star-Telegram*
Photograph Collection, Special Collections Division,
The University of Texas at Arlington Libraries.

Copyright © 1996 by the University of Texas Press
All rights reserved
Printed in the United States of America
First edition, 1996

Requests for permission to reproduce material from this work
should be sent to Permissions, University of Texas Press,
P.O. Box 7819, Austin, TX 78713-7819.

♾ The paper used in this publication meets the minimum
requirements of American National Standard for Information
Sciences—Permanence of Paper for Printed Library Materials,
ANSI Z39.48-1984.

Library of Congress Cataloging-in-Publication Data

Ladino, Robyn Duff, 1954–
    Desegregating Texas schools : Eisenhower, Shivers, and the
crisis at Mansfield High / Robyn Duff Ladino. — 1st ed.
        p.   cm.
    Includes bibliographical references and index.
    ISBN 0-292-74691-1 (alk. paper). —ISBN 0-292-74692-X
(alk. paper)
    1. School integration—United States—Case studies.
2. School integration—Texas—Case studies.   3. Mansfield
High School (Mansfield, Tex.).   4. Shivers, Allan, 1907–   .
5. Eisenhower, Dwight D. (Dwight David), 1890–1969.
I. Title.
LC214.2.L33   1996
370.19'342—dc20   96-12112

This book is dedicated to my loving family,
Tony, Marie, and Beth.

Contents

Foreword

This study of the Mansfield, Texas, school desegregation crisis in 1956 fills an important niche in the history of the civil rights movement and in the history of southern public education. By exploring carefully the relationship between school desegregation and politics, both state and national, the author helps explain the slow progress in integrating public education during the years immediately after the Brown decisions. That analysis of the politics of school desegregation clarifies why Mansfield, despite a failure to desegregate, did not become a focal point of national attention and debate as did Little Rock, Arkansas, in the following year.

From reading this account of events in Mansfield and those related to its school desegregation case, one is also reminded of the important role states of the Border South played in the early efforts to integrate public education. Too often the later struggles to desegregate public accommodations and to regain voting rights in the Deep South drew attention away from states like Texas. Because some cities and towns in the Border South integrated earlier with less resistance, the slowness of overall change, even in these states, has sometimes been ignored.

The efforts of African American parents in Mansfield and black attorneys in Texas, who sought better education for a younger generation, also provide important examples of courage in trying to achieve positive and peaceful change. Their actions seem even more impressive because they faced emotional and sometimes threatening efforts to maintain a segregated and unequal system of public education.

This account of the Mansfield school crisis will immediately stand as one of the few in-depth analyses of desegregation in Texas public education. It also offers insight into the debate about whether Dwight Eisenhower provided active or passive leadership as president. Furthermore it contributes to a fuller understanding of Allan Shivers, who sought to maintain his popularity as governor amid other political controversies by opposing school integration in Texas. Finally, this book should have a long-term value as a stimulant to the writing of further and much-needed studies of public education at the state and local levels and especially of school desegregation for communities large and small across Texas and the nation.

Alwyn Barr

Acknowledgments

I am truly thankful and fortunate to have had the opportunity to work under the guidance and supervision of Dr. Peter L. Petersen, my thesis committee chairman and graduate advisor at West Texas A&M University. His caring encouragement, patient support, and constructive criticism helped me put forth my best effort in researching and writing my master's thesis, which is the basis for this book. Dr. Petersen never wavered in his confidence in this project as I worked through the transition from thesis to manuscript. I could not have asked for a greater mentor. By his example, his students are better historians and educators.

I would like to thank Dr. Frederick W. Rathjen for his kind, steadfast guidance as my first advisor. His office door was always open to his students, and his kind words boosted many spirits. His support throughout the process of publication has been heartwarming to me. He never left my many questions unanswered.

I am indebted to my editor, Theresa J. May, for her unfailing guidance during the revisions to the manuscript. Her optimistic outlook and encouragement made my tasks more simple.

I appreciate the beneficial suggestions and cheerful enthusiasm of Dr. Darrell Munsell and Dr. Duane Guy, members of my thesis committee. I am also thankful to Dr. Bruce Brasington for his interest and sound suggestions.

I am grateful to Dr. Paul Scheips for his recommendation to look into the crisis at Mansfield, Texas. I would like to thank Dr. Michael Lowery Gillette for his helpful advice during my research. My appreciation is extended to Thomas Branigar at the Eisenhower Library and Claudia Anderson at the Johnson Library for their counsel in my probe for information. Helen Butsch and Jean Rick, at the Cornette Library, West Texas A&M University, were instrumental in directing me through the interlibrary research process. I would like to offer my gratitude to Beryl S. Gibson,

Mansfield Historical Society; Berta Patterson, Mansfield Public Library; Kathryn Howard, Mansfield city secretary; Annette White, Mansfield Independent School District; and Jerry Ebansberger, editor of the *Mansfield News Mirror,* for their assistance and recommendations. I am indebted to those interviewed as cited in the endnotes. This manuscript would not have been possible without their recollections. I appreciate the grant and support from the Killgore Research Committee.

I treasure Herbert Brownell's correspondence. I am deeply touched by his straightforward and sincere answers on his role in the Eisenhower administration.

I wish to thank my parents for instilling in me a profound regard for racial equality. I am indebted to my daughter, Marie, for her suggestions and help in proofreading and formatting. I would like to thank my daughter, Beth, for her aid in organizing the bibliography. I cherish my daughters' patience and love. To my husband, Tony, thank you for believing in me when I did not always believe in myself. I am exceptionally grateful to Tony for his assistance, strength, and confidence in my ability.

Introduction

By the late 1940s, African Americans in the South were experiencing changes within their segregated communities that inspired a struggle to dissolve the color line on all fronts. Integrated education became a focal point in their efforts for civil rights.

White segregationists in the South believed the traditional caste system represented social customs that should remain an integral part of their lifestyle. To them segregation was a noble cause. When the mandates of *Brown I* and *Brown II* were handed down, segregationists found it incomprehensible that integration was the law of the land. Texas Governor Allan Shivers sided with the southern white segregationists. Using segregation as a tool to strengthen his political machine, Shivers consistently espoused state's rights and the doctrine of interposition.

During this time, President Dwight Eisenhower resisted endorsing the Supreme Court mandates on school integration. Publicly, throughout his first term, he remained uncommitted and indifferent toward the growing national civil rights movement.

In 1955 and 1956, incidents in Mansfield, Texas, forced the civil rights positions of national, state, and local elements to the forefront of the country's conscience. Many facets of the racial problems facing the United States became apparent in Mansfield as African Americans, struggling for school integration, collided with officials at all levels who clung to the established traditions of the southern caste system. Events in Mansfield revolved around a school integration case brought by the relatives of three African American teenagers hoping to integrate Mansfield High School. The resulting crisis exposed the diversity of views on civil rights in the United States, and Mansfield became a microcosm of the nation's struggle over school integration. The crisis at Mansfield marked a significant milestone on the pathway to equality in the United States.

Mansfield could have been the "Little Rock" of a year later, but its national impact was subdued at the state and national levels by powerful politics. Shivers held a unique and strong political position as a Democratic governor supporting President Eisenhower. Shivers also controlled the Texas Rangers, a group incomparable to any in Governor Orval Faubus' Arkansas.

The crisis at Mansfield High School has never been told in its entirety until now. I document as closely as possible exactly what occurred as the events unfolded. My sincere commitment was to "tell it like it happened" because so many family tales and legends were passed down over the last forty years throughout Tarrant County, Texas. These stories relate one-sided, distorted recollections. Many nonprimary residents and family members of those involved in the crisis recall misconstrued accounts. In several areas, I established the record no one has pieced together until this research. I deliberately wrote the story based on collaborated testimony rather than embellished hearsay. After concluding a nine-month search for primary participants and contacting dozens of residents in and around the Mansfield, Fort Worth–Dallas, and Austin areas, I conscientiously used oral histories of primary participants willing and able to be interviewed. In many instances, the "key" sources are deceased, mentally or physically incapacitated, not available, or could not be tracked down. Several responded that the crisis was so long ago, and so scarred Mansfield's history, that they chose to remain quiet.

The Mansfield crisis was a significant pathway to equality. I have labeled the events in Mansfield a microcosm of the social changes gripping the United States in the 1950s because this small town, on the fringe of southern culture, portrayed the contrasts of what blacks and whites held in their hearts and minds. For the African American community in Mansfield, there would be no turning back. The steps forward might be slow and small, and there might be many stumbles, but inch by inch the path was forged by courageous African Americans, and in time it led to equality.

DESEGREGATING TEXAS SCHOOLS

1. Pathway to Equality: The Determination to Change

In the late 1940s, African Americans in the South witnessed and experienced changes within their segregated communities that inspired a struggle to dissolve the color line on all fronts, especially education. Since 1896, when the United States Supreme Court upheld "separate but equal" in *Plessy v. Ferguson*, the civil rights of African Americans were tightly confined behind racial barriers. Education, employment, transportation, accommodations, and all social aspects of living in the southern United States were tied to a strict code of segregation. During the next fifty years, the practice of segregation became an undeniably ingrained institution in the South.[1]

The changing attitudes within black sections of southern towns evolved from an expanding awareness of economic, technological, and social advances within U.S. society that were bypassing blacks because of their oppressed conditions within the traditional southern caste system. The goal of this system was to keep blacks at the lowest point on the scale of humankind.[2] An African American scholar interviewed by Robert Penn Warren explained, "It's not so much what the Negro wants as what he doesn't want. The main point is not that he has poor facilities. It is that he must endure a constant assault on his ego. He is denied human dignity."[3] As second-class citizens, blacks struggled daily under a system-imposed inferiority complex.

Throughout the United States, African Americans began to realize that education was the key to equality. Nowhere was this understood more than in the seventeen border and southern states and the District of Columbia, where inequitable dual systems of public education stood firmly fixed as a constant reminder to all of the inadequacies and injustices of "separate but equal." Many southern black community leaders readily agreed that fully integrated school systems would allow their children a better chance at breaking out of the oppressive caste system to attain equal rights and status as citizens of the United States.[4] During this time, Harry Golden, the editor of the *Carolina Israelite,* wrote:

> We must remember that economic equality for the Negro race of the South is still a very long way off; so let us bear in mind that self-esteem . . . comes also with education. . . . at this moment in the history of the American Negro there remains only one course of action—the true wisdom—there must be nothing short of a stampede of the Negroes of the South into the classrooms of America. There is no other way.[5]

The caste system began to erode in the same way it was instituted, through legal litigation.

The subdued apathy of a large number of whites throughout the country toward the southern blacks' predicament began a revision after World War II. In areas throughout the United States, including the South, many whites began to acknowledge the degrading living conditions of their fellow black citizens. It became unfashionable, outdated, and immoral to be openly prejudiced.[6] Many Americans heard of, read, and discussed Gunnar Myrdal's *An American Dilemma.* Published in 1944, it defined the blatant inequalities forced upon African Americans and examined racism as a social disease. Myrdal wrote of an anticipated transformation within U.S. society:

> If this book gives a more complete record than is up to now available of American shortcomings in [race relations], I hope . . . that it also accounts more completely for the mutability in relations, the hope for great improvements in the near future and particularly, the dominant role of ideals in the social dynamics of America. . . . *not since Reconstruction has there been more reason to anticipate fundamental changes in American race relations, changes which will involve a development toward the American ideals.*[7]

A Swedish economist, Myrdal worked with a team of social scientists supported by the Carnegie Corporation to dissect the problem of racism in the United States. Examining the "moral dilemma" as both a black and a white enigma, Myrdal referred to "the Negro problem" as "the ever-raging conflict." Studies such as Myrdal's reinforced the growing notion among many white and most black citizens that the time for direct action against the caste system must begin with an attack on "separate but equal."[8]

In the South, this notion slowly began to take the shape of a civil rights movement in the homes and churches of the black communities. Black Texans felt this drive as strongly as blacks in Alabama and Mississippi. Texas, because of its size and geographical diversity, was sectioned racially and economically. The majority of black Texans lived in the northeastern and central eastern counties. These counties, because of migration patterns and topography, had developed a southern agrarian economic system based primarily on the cotton crop. Historically, slavery had supported this crop, and by the twentieth century, sharecropping held many blacks to the land.[9]

By the early 1950s, the small town of Mansfield, in Tarrant County, Texas, included an estimated 1,450 citizens of which 350 were black. Situated approximately fifteen miles southeast of Fort Worth, this hamlet was on the fringe of what was known as the Deep South. Mansfield was a picturesque, well-kept, quiet town. Running north and south, U.S. Highway 287 was Main Street through the town, and it was intersected by Broad Street. Most stores and businesses were found on Main Street, with several branching off east and west on Broad Street. White residential areas developed around this central intersection and to the east of Main Street.[10]

Migrating from the southeastern United States, Scotch-Irish settlers came to this area a century before, establishing a gristmill on Walnut Creek. Many of the settlers brought African slaves with them to work the land. By 1856 Julian Feild and his partner, Ralph S. Man, bought 540 acres of land including the gristmill. In 1860 they founded their own steam-powered gristmill that eventually became the center of the town named Mansfeild. The name was later changed to Mansfield. In 1861 Texas seceded from the United States, becoming a part of the Confederacy. The cornmeal and flour from the Mansfield mill became important contributions of the Texas commodities sent east for the Confederate cause.[11]

After the Civil War, the town grew steadily and was a well-known trade center in Texas. Most of the former slaves remaining in the area became sharecroppers or farm laborers. The educational opportunities in Mansfield also brought the town notoriety. In 1867 the Mansfield Male and Female College was founded on East Broad Street. In 1901 the Mansfield Academy was established followed by the creation of the Mansfield Independent School District in 1909.[12]

In the early twentieth century, Mansfield continued to prosper economically. Several businesses built stores and offices on Main Street. This growth continued until the 1930s, when the Depression devastated the agricultural centers of the United States. Another contribution to the slowdown in prosperity was the growing urbanization of the South. For several years after World War II, Mansfield's growth stagnated because of the draw of opportunities to the bigger neighboring cities of Dallas and Fort Worth. At this time, both the white and black residents of the town had to accept the changing status of their community.[13]

The black section of town was situated off Main Street to the west on West Broad Street. A hill and an open field created a definite break in the town's development before entering the rows of smaller, simpler homes occupied by black families. Many blacks lived further out in the country as sharecroppers on larger farms owned by whites. The black church, Bethlehem Baptist Church, and the elementary school, Mansfield Colored School, stood within the small, closely knit community approximately two and one-half miles from Main Street.[14]

In the late 1940s, Mansfield's African American residents lived under a tightly structured caste system. The races were segregated in the churches, school system, and all social activities within the town. Only white citizens held municipal offices. All white-collar jobs in Mansfield were limited to whites. Blacks employed in the town worked for low wages as laborers or in service-oriented jobs such as maids, cooks, janitors, and groundskeepers. Many blacks worked as sharecroppers and farmhands in the outlying large farms owned by white families. Those seeking better employment opportunities, especially in factories and industries, commuted to Fort Worth and Dallas.[15]

Black families were permitted to shop on Main Street, but rarely were they seen east of this street. Many young black men congregated in the alley on the west side of Main Street behind the local cafe, but were never allowed in the front door. To be served in the restaurants in town, blacks had to enter through the back doors off the alleys and often ate in the kitchens. Certain eating establishments banned blacks completely. The segregated system was so entrenched in the community that a barbecue drive-in owned by a black resident on the edge of Mansfield divided eating areas by race. The two grocery stores on Main Street allowed black clientele, and one accepted credit until the crops were harvested.[16]

Black and white children were allowed to play together around the outskirts of the town. As a young black child living near

Mansfield, Floyd Moody recalled playing in the open fields around the town with two white boys during his childhood:

> On Saturday mornings we used to get together, run, play stick horse together. . . . It's ironic because at that point there was no color. . . . I didn't see Charles and Wesley [Seeton] as white. . . . We wasn't taught that way as black children. . . . It was only when we tried to do what they done that I noticed a difference. If we were together he'd walk in the cafe to get a hamburger, I couldn't. . . . We had to sit in the back, in the kitchen.[17]

The racial code that existed in Mansfield allowed black and white children to play together under certain restrictions. When the children grew into young adults, the color line became much more noticeable. The associations of mixed race dating were strictly forbidden. As adults, the races were acceptably civil to each other, but there remained an obvious separation ethic. The African Americans held their own gatherings in their section of town, while the white residents congregated at events in the main area of Mansfield. Race relations in Mansfield were defined as "good" by the white citizens, but the black community felt oppressed because these "good" relations were based on doing "what the white man said."[18] In an editorial from the *Mansfield News*, the segregationist attitude of the era was clearly expressed: "We are not against the Negro, but we are against social equality. We think the Negroes are making great strides in improving their race and commend them for it, as long as they stick to their race."[19] By the late 1940s, African Americans throughout the South began questioning this type of proclamation. As constitutionally equal citizens, they believed they were entitled to better treatment than that defined by the established racial stigmas.[20]

During this time, members of Mansfield's black community began to question their conditions within the town. Sermons, services, and meetings held in Bethlehem Baptist Church, under the guidance of the Reverend L. E. Billingslea, initiated the exchange of newly forming ideas to change the status quo for their children's future. Some adults found these discussions upsetting, remembering from their childhood the activities of the Ku Klux Klan in Tarrant County. Others believed that the time to join the budding national civil rights movement had arrived in Mansfield. Although the black community remained closely knit, this controversy continued for many years.[21]

African American leaders within the Mansfield neighborhood

proved to be both progressive and determined. A branch of the National Association for the Advancement of Colored People (NAACP) was founded in Mansfield in 1950. Most of the black residents became members during the early part of the decade. Those that chose not to join remained sympathetic and interested in the NAACP objectives. As a leader in the community, T. M. Moody was outspoken and knowledgeable. Employed by the federal government as a civilian, Moody worked in a large warehouse outside of Mansfield for a quartermaster. In the early 1950s, as the military integrated, Moody experienced a different social standard at his job than in Mansfield. Because of his experiences, Moody brought new ideas back to his community.[22] Floyd Moody described his uncle: "T. M. was somewhat the leader of the community. . . . He always brought [ideas] back to us that maybe we didn't have time to go out and to search out for ourselves."[23] The black community "looked up to him" even if at times they did not agree with his ideas. He was known as an "instigator" and a progressive planner.[24]

In the late 1940s, T. M. Moody was selected to serve as a "subtrustee" for the black elementary school in Mansfield. The white elected board members allowed several black men to act as communicants between the black community and the Mansfield School Board on matters pertaining to Mansfield Colored School. During the early 1950s, T. M. Moody became the president of the Mansfield branch of the NAACP. He also served as the chairman of the Board of Deacons and the superintendent of the Sunday school at Bethlehem Baptist Church. Through these commitments, especially with the NAACP, Moody began to realize that he must move his community forward in the emerging civil rights movement and seek out changes that he was not sure either the black or white residents in Mansfield were ready to accept. He directed most of his energy toward improving the deplorable conditions of the black elementary school.[25]

In 1950 the Mansfield Colored School consisted of two long shabby barracks-style buildings placed lengthwise, side by side, on a plot of land off West Broad Street. There was no electricity, running water, or plumbing. Only one teacher was hired for grades one through eight. Water was hauled in milk cans from Ben Lewis' well one-quarter of a mile north of the school by the teacher with the help of students. Two outhouses sat several feet north of the buildings. There was very little equipment, no flagpole, no fence around the playground, and no school bus.[26]

Black children in the ninth through twelfth grades had no school in Mansfield. They traveled by bus to downtown Fort Worth to attend the only two Negro secondary schools in an area encompassing several counties. Ninth graders went to James E. Guinn School then transferred to I. M. Terrell High School. Black teenagers in Mansfield would walk to Main Street from their homes in the early morning to catch the 7:15 Trailways bus that traveled into downtown Fort Worth. Then, to get to the high school, students had to walk approximately twenty blocks. School dismissal was at 3:30 P.M., but the Trailways bus did not leave the station until 5:30. These students would not return to their homes until well into the evening. After-school activities were extremely difficult because transportation after the 5:30 P.M. bus was almost impossible to arrange. Students who engaged in after-school sports and clubs often did not get home until after 9:00 P.M.[27]

T. M. Moody, John F. Lawson, Mark Moody, and others over the years, acting as "subtrustees," continually requested educational improvements in facilities and equipment for the black students in Mansfield. In the early 1950s, many of their requests were turned down, but several were accepted. The school board acquired a twenty-four passenger school bus for the black elementary students, trading it in for a larger model in 1951. A new elementary school for the black community was built on the same land as the old school buildings. This four-room school was opened in 1954 with two teachers. A new well was dug in front of the school on the playground, and rest rooms were added inside the building. By summer 1954, water coolers, chalk boards, lockers, typing tables, new door locks, and a remodeled library were included in the additions to the black elementary school. The only improvement for the African American high school students was the decision of school board trustees to issue paid bus passes to cover the fare to the black secondary schools in Fort Worth.[28]

Even with the improvements of the early 1950s, T. M. Moody, John F. Lawson, and several other members of the black community became disillusioned and frustrated because so often what they believed was necessary for the education and welfare of black students was turned down. They struggled with the Mansfield School Board on numerous occasions when requests were denied for specific improvements that would help equalize the dual school system. Often they sat and watched as motions carried for additions and improvements to the white schools in Mansfield.[29] In 1953 a new elementary school opened, splitting the white students between this school, later named Erma Nash Elementary School, and Mansfield High School. The new school contained seventeen classrooms and, in addition to twelve teachers, employed a full-time coach and a music teacher. In September 1953, the local newspaper stated, "The new changes, improvements, and additions serve as a reminder that Mansfield Marches On In The Field Of Education, which is so vital to keeping the spirit of democracy alive in our United States of America."[30]

The United States Supreme Court decided in 1954 and 1955 to end school segregation everywhere in the United States at all levels.[31] Since the late 1940s, African Americans across the nation, such as T. M. Moody, John F. Lawson, and the Reverend L. E. Billingslea, watched the United States Court system slowly dismantle "separate but equal." They educated themselves and others to the significance of the numerous school integration cases and their mandates. They studied the role played by the NAACP in unraveling the injustices brought against them as U.S. citizens and were proud to be active members of the association. These men saw the 1954 and 1955 Supreme Court decisions as a foundation to change the conditions to which their children had been confined for so long.[32]

On August 17, 1954, at a called meeting, the black subtrustees presented a petition to the school board requesting immediate integration of the Mansfield public schools. Although this petition was not mentioned in the school board minutes, it was reviewed and denied. On August 18, 1954, the first of two letters sent by the school board to T. M. Moody asserted:

> The problem of desegregation does not rest within the jurisdiction of our local school board. Our school system is State wide and as a board we are obligated to perform the duties so given us by law and as of this date the law and our instruction regarding same given to us from the State officials is to continue with our dual school system just as we have in the past.
>
> These obligations and laws we will follow until we have been so instructed to do otherwise.[33]

The second letter, sent the same day, stated:

> Here after when the colored trustees of the colored school have anything to present to the local School Board that it be so done in writing and it be so done in due time so that it may be taken up only in regular school board meetings.[34]

T. M. Moody knew he had the Supreme Court decision behind him in his push for desegregation. He remained patient yet determined to change the course of education in Mansfield. For Moody, his fellow subtrustees, and many of the black families in Mansfield, this was only the beginning. Although some progress had been made by 1955, the Mansfield school system for African American students remained separate and definitely unequal.[35]

2. The Dismantlement of "Separate but Equal"

After World War II, African Americans made integrated education the focal point of their efforts for civil rights. This commitment developed over the next several years into a master plan to break the racial barriers that controlled their lives. African American veterans held new hope that the democracy they fought so hard for across the seas could be attained for their race on the homefront. They hoped that the final days of battle in Europe, when some combat lines were integrated, would set a precedent after their homecoming in the employment lines and public school lunch lines.[1]

On June 29, 1947, President Harry S. Truman addressed the National Association for the Advancement of Colored People's Thirty-Eighth Annual Convention in front of the Lincoln Memorial and firmly stated:

> We can no longer afford the luxury of a leisurely attack upon prejudice and discrimination. There is much that state and local governments can do in providing positive safeguards for civil rights. . . . we cannot, any longer await the growth of a will to action in the slowest state or the most backward community. Our national government must show the way.[2]

Most African Americans agreed with Truman and the veterans. After the war, there was no turning back. The struggle to affirm themselves as full citizens under the laws and privileges of the United States Constitution was at hand. They believed that if their united country fought against Hitler's evil and unjust Nazi Germany, certainly it would recognize the inequalities at home.[3]

Truman signed two orders that strengthened African Americans' beliefs that the time to advance and improve their conditions had arrived. On December 5, 1946, Executive Order 9808 established the President's Committee on Civil Rights. By late 1947, members of this committee released a report titled *To Secure These Rights.* In it they asserted that certain essential rights must be attained for all citizens. These included equal privileges under the law, the guarantee of security and safety, freedom of expression, and equal opportunity.[4] On July 26, 1948, Truman signed Executive Order 9981 establishing the Committee on Equality of Treatment and Opportunity in the Armed Forces. This committee would move slowly toward implementing integration in all branches of the armed forces.[5] Equal rights among the civilian population in the United States proved to be much more difficult to obtain, particularly in the South. The color line that had slightly faded during military duty in the war proved stronger than ever before as black families were reunited in the Deep South.[6]

A majority of the southern black population held great hope that the years ahead would be prosperous and promising. The wartime economy had improved the income and standard of living of most U.S. citizens, including blacks. Industries had developed and grown in all areas of the United States. Yet African Americans found many of their aspirations for less prejudiced attitudes dashed when they sought equal salaries, fair housing, and higher education. The racial injustices were felt keenly in the South, where the postwar agricultural economy was rapidly shrinking, forcing competition for jobs within the growing urban centers. Southern suburban neighborhoods and schools springing up outside growing metropolitan centers admitted only white families.[7]

Southern blacks confronted choices: migrate to the North in the hope of improving their status and standard of living; move into the expanding southern cities where industries and blue-collar businesses were creating a large market for unskilled and service-oriented occupations but neighborhoods, housing, and schools for their families were substandard; remain in their small-town communities and accept their position in the existing traditional southern segregated system; or choose to stay in these same communities with the determination to change their conditions for the better, seeking equal rights for themselves and their children.[8]

For many African American families choosing to remain in their small communities, the determination to change the status quo grew stronger with each passing year. One step they took toward aiding their communities was to join the local branch of the National Association for the Advancement of Colored People. Most African Americans understood the importance of the NAACP and its commitment to equal justice under the law. Founded in 1910, its objectives were:

To promote equality of rights and eradicate caste or race prejudice among the citizens of the United States; to advance the
interest of colored citizens; to secure for them impartial suf-
frage; and to increase their opportunities for securing justice in
courts, education for their children, employment according to
their ability; and complete equality before the law.[9]

These objectives were the same as those taught in the homes and
preached in the churches of most African Americans. As the 1940s
closed, NAACP members took a more active role within their
branches and contributed readily to the funds of the local area
chapters and national organization, in particular, the Legal Defense and Educational Fund.[10]

Established in 1939, the Legal Defense and Educational Fund
was developed and directed by Thurgood Marshall with the guidance of Walter White, executive secretary of the NAACP. The
Fund's responsibilities revolved around legal research and litigation to secure the objectives of the NAACP. Marshall was a devoted civil rights attorney, skilled in preparing and delivering
cases. Over the next fifteen years, he put together a team of equally
skilled professionals from Yale, Harvard, and Columbia Universities. He also had several devoted faculty members from Howard
University on call for duty and advice when needed. They included
James Nabrit Jr., William H. Hastie, Spottswood W. Robinson III,
Robert Ming, and George Edward Hayes. These men were noted for
their thoroughness and precision.[11] Marshall explained his admira-
tion for his colleagues and staff: "I never hesitated to pick other
people's brains. . . . After awhile you'd get to know who was best at
what kind of thing." [12] Herbert Hill, NAACP labor affairs director,
reminisced about Marshall, "He was a very courageous figure. . . .
He would travel to the courthouses of the South, and folks would
come for miles, some of them on muleback or horseback, to see
'the nigger lawyer' who stood up in white men's courtrooms." [13]
Along with his professional staff, Marshall employed a number of
loyal research assistants and a skilled technical support staff.[14]

The Fund was incorporated into a separate foundation from the
NAACP. Therefore, it could legally receive tax deductible dona-
tions. Raising funds toward litigation costs became very important
because the number of cases handled increased dramatically after
the war. Black veterans, ready to use their G.I. benefits, were
turned away from overcrowded integrated colleges and universities.
Their alternative was to attempt to seek admission in currently
segregated schools in the South. For many this proved frustrating
and demoralizing.[15]

By the late 1940s, after analyzing the state of the nation, all those involved with the Fund agreed that the time had come to pool their skills, talents, and resources and to begin the push toward eliminating segregation in higher education. Under Marshall's leadership, the Fund decided to pursue, through the judicial system, the desegregation of tax-supported universities at the graduate level. The Fund initiated a plan to help students gain admission to institutions of higher learning. With the help of local chapter attorneys, many discrimination cases were brought to district, state, and federal courts. Three cases associated with education and one involving transportation and accommodations set the precedent for the final push to abolish "separate but equal" not only at the undergraduate and graduate levels but throughout the entire public school system.[16]

In 1948 Marshall argued the case for Ada Lois Sipuel, in *Sipuel v. Oklahoma State Board of Regents*.[17] Sipuel was an outstanding black student who had been rejected by the law school at the University of Oklahoma because of her race. Using the precedent set in 1938, in *Missouri ex rel. Gaines v. Canada*, when the Supreme Court decided that if a state furnished higher education for white students it must provide the same for black students, Marshall's brief to the Court affirmed, "Classifications and distinctions based on race and color have no moral or legal validity in our society." He began to dismantle "separate but equal" as defined by the 1896 Court and argued:

> Segregation in public education helps to preserve a caste system which is based upon race and color. It is designed and intended to perpetuate the slave tradition. . . . Equality, even if the term be limited to a comparison of physical facilities, is and can never be achieved. . . . the terms "separate" and "equal" can not be used conjunctively in a situation of this kind; there can be no separate equality.[18]

The Court presented a unanimous opinion that the University of Oklahoma could not deny Sipuel a higher education in its law school. And further, she must receive an education that would conform "with the equal protection clause of the Fourteenth Amendment, and must provide it for her at the same time it provides such education for members of any other group." The decision was remanded for implementation to the lower courts where it remained at different levels within the court system for several months, even returning to the Supreme Court because the mandate had not been fulfilled. The Court reaffirmed its opinion and reminded the plaintiff that desegregation was not the issue if the school provided an education for her. Sipuel was finally admitted to the University of Oklahoma School of Law in 1949.[19]

In February 1946, Heman Marion Sweatt applied to the University of Texas Law School at Austin. Sweatt, a mail carrier in Houston, was rejected because he was black by the university president, Theophilus Painter. The NAACP saw this as a clear opportunity to strike out against segregation. The organization stepped in to help Sweatt by filing a petition in district court to force the university and its president to admit Sweatt to the law school. In *Sweatt v. Painter*, the district court accepted Sweatt as qualified to attend the law school, but allowed Texas six months to establish a black law school equal to the law school at the University of Texas. The state set up a temporary law school in Houston in a building that housed the offices of two attorneys assigned to teach any black students accepted to the new program. The Texas state legislature, under State Bill 140, allocated funds to begin improvements at the existing Houston College for Negroes. Three million dollars was set aside to establish the Texas State University for Negroes in place of the college. The plans included a new law school within the new university. During this time, Sweatt refused to attend the makeshift law school in the attorneys' offices in Houston and again petitioned the district court for assistance and remedy. This court upheld the state's efforts and gave Sweatt no choice but to turn to the Texas Court of Civil Appeals for relief.[20]

The Texas state legislature, anticipating the appeal, discontinued the basement law school in Houston and established a second basement school in downtown Austin near the University of Texas. The state of Texas insisted the second school was better equipped than the first. The Civil Appeals Court asked the district court to examine the new school and judge its quality. Sweatt remained steadfast; he would not attend an inferior school.[21]

The president of the University of Texas student body called for a rally supporting Marshall's endeavors and Sweatt's admission. Two thousand students attended. Sweatt was amazed when two hundred university students formally established their own chapter of the NAACP on campus. It was the only all-white chapter in the country.[22]

In May 1947, Marshall, with the help of fellow lawyers James Nabrit Jr., W. J. Durham, and Ulysses Simpson Tate argued *Sweatt v. Painter* in the district court of Travis County, Texas. State Attorney General Price Daniel represented Texas. The district court confirmed the state's conviction and accepted the separate facility as adequate. Sweatt again refused to attend the inferior school and, with the assistance and counsel of Marshall, turned to the United States Supreme Court.[23]

In 1948 a third case involving higher education, *McLaurin v. Oklahoma State Regents* began to unfold at the University of Oklahoma. George McLaurin was refused entrance to the graduate school of education. With the aid of the Fund, McLaurin went to a special three-judge United States District Court for help. In late September 1948, the court agreed that McLaurin must be granted admittance. At this time, the Oklahoma state legislature stepped in and insisted that, according to state law, McLaurin must be physically segregated from white students during his time on campus. He was forced to sit in separate rooms adjoining his classrooms, study at a specific reserved table hidden away at the library, and sit alone in a separate area of the cafeteria after the white students had finished their meals.[24]

Returning to the district court, Marshall argued on behalf of McLaurin. The unequal and separate treatment forced upon McLaurin was demeaning and produced "a badge of inferiority which had affected his relationship, both to his fellow students and to his professors, . . ." The court denied issuing an injunction for changes in McLaurin's conditions. He too decided to take his case to the Supreme Court.[25]

Henderson v. United States was another important case litigated for the cause of abolishing "separate but equal."[26] Filed by Alpha Phi Alpha, a black fraternity, on behalf of Elmer Henderson, it initiated a case against the Southern Railroad Company because of segregated dining facilities on their trains. This case was brought before the United States Supreme Court for resolution at the same time the *Sweatt* and *McLaurin* cases were heard. The Fund filed a brief of amicus curiae, as a friend of the court, but did not represent Henderson.[27]

The presentation of the three cases to the Supreme Court during the same session was very significant. Each case brought a unique attack on different aspects of the *Plessy* decision.[28] Marshall's brief in the *Sweatt* case assailed the inequalities of segregated education. Under Marshall's direction, a committee of 187 law professors from across the nation came together to file a brief of amicus curiae attacking the legality of "separate but equal" because of the impossibility of true equality with separation. The professors wrote, "As soon as laws make a right of responsibility dependent solely on race, they violate the Fourteenth Amendment."[29] Under the *McLaurin* case, Marshall and his staff calculated a plan to strike at the constitutionality of "separate." Because McLaurin was admitted to the University of Oklahoma under strict rules of segregation, Marshall attacked the conditions under which McLaurin lived on campus. These conditions, contended Marshall, brought about inferior feelings that were psychologically demeaning and depressing.[30] In the *Henderson* case, a direct assault was made on the practice of segregation in transportation and accommodations.[31]

On June 5, 1950, the Supreme Court handed down opinions in all three cases. In each case, the Court decided unanimously to order all segregation practices forced upon the plaintiffs to end immediately. To avoid the question of the constitutionality of "separate but equal," the court had carefully stated its decisions within the framework set down in *Plessy v. Ferguson*.[32] In the *Sweatt* case, Chief Justice Fred M. Vinson explained the court's opinion: "Broader issues have been urged for our consideration, but we adhere to the principle of deciding constitutional questions only in the context of the particular case before the court."[33] These three decisions significantly weakened "separate but equal," even though they existed within the bounds of *Plessy*. The outcome of these cases allowed thousands of African American students legal entry into institutions of higher learning throughout the country with the exception of South Carolina, Georgia, Alabama, Florida, and Mississippi. These states adamantly denied compliance.[34]

With the latest Supreme Court decisions, Marshall and his staff knew they could turn all their efforts toward complete elimination of segregation in the public schools. At the end of June 1950, a convention was held in the New York offices of the Fund. Forty-three lawyers and fourteen state and branch presidents, including Nabrit, Robinson, Ming, and Tate attended the meetings designated as think tanks to develop the plan for the final assault on "separate but equal." Marshall explained to his constituents that arguments in all educational segregation cases must from now on

> be aimed at obtaining education on a non-segregated basis and that no relief other than that will be acceptable. . . . all lawyers operating under such rule will urge their client[s] and the branches of the Association involved to insist on this final relief.[35]

Marshall requested that this statement be adopted by the national offices of the NAACP. The board of directors for the association accepted this objective as policy, thereby ending all "gradualistic" notions.[36]

Over the next two years, Marshall and his staff, working with and supported by lawyers throughout the United States, initiated cases directly challenging the inequitable conditions of segregated elementary and secondary schools. Charging that disparity existed in facilities, equipment, staff experience and qualifications, school texts, busing, and attendance requirements, the lawyers engaged in a frontal attack on dual public school systems. In addition, they argued that no "equalization plan" could remove the stigma of inferiority felt by the black students' enforced separation. The Fund's lawyers were joined by well-respected social scientists in a carefully plotted program to examine and expose psychological damages experienced by segregated black students.[37]

By fall 1952, five cases directly challenging school segregation on all levels and the legality of "separate but equal" in *Plessy v. Ferguson* reached the United States Supreme Court. The cases, officially recorded as *Oliver Brown et al. v. Board of Education of Topeka, Shawnee County, Kansas, et al.; Harry Briggs, Jr. et al. v. R. W. Elliott et al.; Dorothy E. Davis et al. v. County School Board of Prince Edward County, Virginia, et al.; Ethel Louis Belton, et al. v. Francis B. Gebhart et al.;* and *Spottswood Thomas Bolling, et al. v. C. Melvin Sharpe, et al.,* were pooled together by the Court because of their similarities and became known under one common title, *Brown v. Board of Education.*[38] The Court had to resolve the question of the validity of the *Plessy* decision. Could it stand up in the shadow of the "equal protection" clause in the Fourteenth Amendment?[39] This amendment declared:

> No state shall make or enforce any law which shall abridge the privileges or immunities of citizens of the United States; nor shall any state deprive any person of life, liberty or property, without due process of law; nor deny to any person within its jurisdiction the equal protection of the laws.[40]

Oral arguments in the cases were heard by the Court on December 9–11, 1952. Using legal precedents set in forty-six previous cases and relying heavily on the premises set in the *Sipuel, Sweatt, McLaurin,* and *Henderson* cases, Marshall and seven prominent attorneys from the Fund represented all the plaintiffs attacking "separate" as illegal according to the Fourteenth Amendment. In his presentation, Marshall explained, "Segregation of Negroes as practiced here is universally understood as imposing on them a badge of inferiority."[41] His argument was bolstered by an amicus curiae brief filed by the United States Attorney General James McGranery that supported the unconstitutionality of segregation.[42] A group of social scientists also submitted a document upholding the plaintiffs' contentions titled "The Effects of Segregation and the Consequences of Desegregation: A Social Science Statement." These men stated that forced segregation socially and psychologically damaged both whites and blacks.[43]

John W. Davis represented South Carolina and acted as the coordinating lawyer for the defense team. Davis was a presidential candidate in 1924, past solicitor general, and former ambassador to Great Britain. In each case, the defendants attempted to resolve the question of equality with the implementation of particular measures within their respective school systems, while continuing to maintain separate facilities. The defense argued that segregation was constitutionally correct and that states had the right to enact and enforce their own laws in regard to equal protection of their citizens. Davis and the defense team consistently emphasized the legality of allowing decisions on segregation to be left to state and local governments.[44]

Six months later, on June 8, 1953, the Supreme Court announced that reargument for purposes of clarification would be heard on October 12. Five specific questions were asked by the Court. Answers to the questions were prepared by both sides for presentation. The questions requested thought-provoking responses on the intentions of the authors of the Fourteenth Amendment including: their position on segregation, the interpretations of the ratifying state legislatures on the implications of the amendment, and the responsibilities of the Court in clarifying and implementing the terms of the amendment. Also at this time, an invitation was extended to United States Attorney General Herbert Brownell to file an amicus curiae brief for the reargument phase of the trial.[45]

Reargument was postponed until December 5, 1953, giving Marshall valuable extra time in preparing a final brief. In September 1953, approximately 125 prominent social scientists attended a national conference conducted by the Fund in New York City. These professionals came from across the United States to discuss the best strategy for answering the Court's questions. Included in the group were historians, constitutional lawyers, sociologists, psychologists, political scientists, and educators. The conference lasted three days, but most of the attendees continued to work as volunteers long after the formal meetings concluded. Four men, in particular, stood out for their dedication and expertise: Alfred H. Kelly, a noted constitutional historian and professor at Wayne State University; Howard J. Graham, law librarian for the Los Angeles County Bar Association and an expert on the political and historical ramifications of the Fourteenth Amendment; Horace M. Bond, president of Lincoln University and an authority on African American history; and John P. Frank, a professor of law at Yale University.[46] These men, their colleagues, and the Fund's determined lawyers and research team developed a 235-page reargument brief. Filed on December 5, 1953, it stated, in part, the "separate but equal" doctrine

> stands mirrored today as the faulty conception of an era dominated by provincialism, by intense emotionalism in race relations . . . and by the preaching of a doctrine of racial superiority that contradicted the basic concept upon which our society was founded. Twentieth century America, fighting racism at home and abroad, has rejected the race views of *Plessy v. Ferguson* because we have come to the realization that such views obviously tend to preserve not the strength but the weakness of our heritage.[47]

Oral reargument lasted three days beginning on December 7, 1953. The states' defense claimed that only Congress held the power to change the Fourteenth Amendment. The Court's responsibilities, they argued, remained in the boundaries of interpretation. Established by the Court in the *Plessy* case, "separate but equal" was solidly accepted and practiced in a large section of the United States and therefore should not be changed. The defense asserted that because Congress had created the Fourteenth Amendment while maintaining segregated schools in the District of Columbia, and several of the ratifying states also operated dual school systems during this time, segregation was acceptable under the guidelines of the amendment.[48]

Once again, as director-counselor for the plaintiffs, Marshall declared segregation was unconstitutional because the framers of the Fourteenth Amendment truly intended to abolish all caste systems with the equal protection clause. He reiterated the idea that segregation practiced in school systems condemned African American children to lifelong inferiority complexes, therefore ending any hope of equal citizenship and continuing the establishment of "Black Codes." The only reason, Marshall submitted, for the segregated "Black Codes"

> is an inherent determination that the people who were formerly in slavery, regardless of anything else, shall be kept as near that stage as possible, and now is the time, we submit, that this

Court should make clear that that is not what our Constitution stands for.[49]

After a five-month wait, the United States Supreme Court handed down two unanimous decisions that would change the course of civil rights in the United States. The concise but clear opinions of the Court declared segregation in public education unconstitutional. These 1954 mandates became known as *Brown I*. Chief Justice Earl Warren delivered the opinions of the Court stating in part:

> In approaching this problem, we cannot turn the clock back to 1868 when the Amendment was adopted, or even to 1896 when Plessy v. Ferguson was written. We must consider public education in the light of its full development and its present place in American life throughout the Nation. Only in this way can it be determined if segregation deprives these plaintiffs of the equal protection of the laws. Today, education is perhaps the most important function of state and local governments. . . . [education] is the very foundation of good citizenship. . . . it is a principal instrument in awakening the child to cultural values. In preparing him for later professional training, and in helping him to adjust normally to his environment. . . . We conclude that in the field of public education the doctrine of "separate but equal" has no place. Separate educational facilities are inherently unequal.[50]

The Court also ordered the cases returned to the docket for further argument on implementation of the decision.[51]

Once again, the Court invited the United States attorney general to submit an amicus curiae brief. Attorney generals from all the states affected by the decision to end dual school systems were also invited to submit a brief as friend of the Court. These invitations also extended to oral arguments. During the week of April 11, 1955, the Court heard from the parties in the cases, the solicitor general of the United States, and representatives from six state governments.[52]

On May 31, 1955, Chief Justice Warren read the opinion of the Court, which became known as *Brown II*, firmly stating under clear terms the 1954 decision, "All provisions of federal, state or local law requiring or permitting such discrimination must yield to [the 1954] principal." The statement continued, acknowledging the local school districts, not the courts, would bear most of the responsibility of desegregation, "School authorities have the primary responsibility for elucidating, assessing, and solving these problems; . . ." The lower courts were called upon for coordination and enforcement:

> Courts will have to consider whether the action of school authorities constitutes good faith implementation of the governing constitutional principles. Because of their proximity to local conditions and the possible need for further hearings, the courts which originally heard these cases can best perform this judicial appraisal. Accordingly, we believe it appropriate to remand the cases to those courts. . . .
>
> While giving weight to . . . public and private considerations, the courts will require that the defendants make a prompt and reasonable start toward full compliance with our May 17, 1954, ruling. The burden rests upon the defendants to establish that such time is necessary in the public interest and is consistent with good faith compliance at the earliest practicable date.[53]

Remanding the cases to lower district courts, and circuit courts of appeal if needed, for primary implementation and enforcement of desegregation, the justices delivered a phrase that would be interpreted as one of the most ambiguous statements ever made by the Supreme Court, ". . . to admit to public schools on a racially nondiscriminatory basis with all deliberate speed the parties to these cases." The words "with all deliberate speed" handed the segregationists a victory. These four words, combined with the assignment of enforcement to lower courts, were quickly adapted by southern segregated school systems to mean, "go slow," "stall," "delay," and in the most conservative sense "never."[54]

In the June–July 1955 issue of the *Crisis*, Marshall and Roy Wilkins, executive secretary of the NAACP, collaborated on an article titled "Interpretation of the Supreme Court Decision and the NAACP Program." In it they explained:

> The [Court's] opinion . . . gives us the necessary legal weapons to bring about compliance in areas of the South which openly flout the mandate of the Supreme Court. . . .
>
> We know that the highest court did not (a) set a deadline date for either the beginning or the completion of desegregation . . . and (b) [did not] outline a definite plan by which desegregation

must proceed and by which lower courts might judge the efforts of local school boards toward compliance. . . . Not having done this, what did the Courts do? . . .

Armed with the powers embodied in the language of the Court's opinion, we look confidently toward the future. We stand ready with qualified experts in public education and community organization to cooperate with any and all school boards willing to work toward desegregation.

We always realized that there are those who would defy the ruling and others who would drag their feet no matter what language the Supreme Court used. We now have the weapons to make them accept the highest court's affirmation of true American principles. This we shall do. We shall not rest until we have ended second-class education for all Americans.[55]

Lawyers interested in handling civil rights cases studied the new mandates, planning their strategies with enthusiasm. Marshall commented optimistically, "The decision was a good one. . . . We can be sure that desegregation will take place throughout the United States—tomorrow in some places, the day after in others, and many, many moons hence in some, but it will come eventually to all."[56] Although disappointed in the vagueness of "with all deliberate speed" in *Brown II*, these lawyers realized the law of the land was now on their side.[57]

Educators, lawyers, and social scientists presented theories on the best methods to desegregate. In late 1955, Herbert Hill, labor secretary for the NAACP, and Jack Greenberg, assistant counsel with the Fund, published one strategy in *Citizen's Guide to Desegregation: A Study of Social and Legal Change in American Life.* Chapter 13, titled "What Can Citizens Do?," offered steps to take toward successful desegregation including: state the law; analyze the "workability" of desegregation; "prepare" both races within the community; include the black residents in the decisions; obtain a "clear statement" from the school board supplemented with a desegregation plan and timetable if possible; obtain support from the residents, both black and white, for the school boards' proposals. Part 2 of the chapter emphasized "Principles of School Integration." This section gave practical directives to ensure compliance and avoid circumvention of the law. Black communities across the South geared up for the desegregation process to begin. When local school boards did not act quickly to end their dual school systems, many black leaders took matters into their own hands.[58]

In January 1955, L. Clifford Davis, a young African American lawyer from Arkansas, relocated permanently to Fort Worth, Texas. Davis was an experienced civil rights attorney, having filed several "equalization law suits" that included school cases in Arkansas in the early 1950s. Born in Little River County, Arkansas, the son of a farmer, Davis attended segregated schools in Wilton and Ashdown. Buses were provided for the white students of the county, but the black families had to arrange for their own transportation throughout their children's school years. After high school, Davis went to live in Little Rock in a home his family kept there so that their children could further their educations. In 1945 he graduated from Philander Smith College.[59]

In the fall of 1945, Davis entered Howard University Law School. After one year, he left to attend Atlanta University to pursue studies in economics. Returning to Howard University in 1947, Davis combined his interests, studying business law. His timing for attending Howard University allowed him to study under, and associate with, several of the most dedicated and prestigious civil rights law professors in the United States. These men, including James Nabrit, William H. Hastie, Leon A. Ransom, Spottswood Robinson, Robert Ming, and George Edward Hayes, instilled in Davis a deep commitment to "equalizing" the law. He found their fortitude, intelligence, and aspirations inspirational.[60]

After graduating in 1949, Davis joined W. Harold Flowers in law practice in Pine Bluff, Arkansas. Flowers was the president of the NAACP State Conference of Branches in Arkansas. Filing lawsuits for civil rights became their predominant practice. One particular school case filed by Davis on June 20, 1952, well before the decisions of *Brown I* and *Brown II*, was titled *Alvin J. Matthews et al. v. R. W. Launius, President, etc. and Beardon School District No. 53 of Ouachita County, Arkansas*.[61] The plaintiffs sought "a declaratory judgement declaring Section 80-509, Ark. Stats. [state statute for segregated schools], to be unconstitutional," and also a clear decision "that the policy of denying equal facilities to school children of the Negro race is unconstitutional." The case was continued pending the United States Supreme Court decisions of 1954 and 1955. The opinion was remanded on October 4, 1955, declaring:

> The defendants and their successors in office shall make a prompt and reasonable start towards the effectuation of the transition to a racially non-discriminatory school system as required by the ruling of the Supreme Court . . . by its order of May 17, 1954; . . . the defendants . . . report to this court not later than the beginning of the next school year, the progress

that has been made and the plans that they have to effectuate the transition . . . to a racially non-discriminatory school system.[62]

The judgment required the case to be continued into the next regular term for consideration of the school system's plan and timetable for compliance. They added, "The court will consider the adequacy of such plans and determine whether further time is necessary in the public interest and is consistent with . . . the constitutional requirements at the earliest practicable date."[63] As the lawyer for plaintiffs in several other "equalization suits," Davis quickly became an experienced and articulate civil rights attorney. NAACP directors and Fund representatives throughout the South, including Texas, knew of his hard work and commitment to civil rights.[64]

In September 1952, Davis moved to Waco, Texas, and taught business courses at Paul Quinn College for two years. In 1954 he made the decision to leave Waco and practice law full-time in Fort Worth.[65]

In January 1955, Davis became one of only three African American attorneys practicing law in the Fort Worth area, and the only one handling civil rights litigation. Judge Joseph E. Estes admitted Davis into practice in the Northern District of Texas. He became an active member of the Fort Worth branch of the NAACP, representing his area at state conferences. The NAACP Southwest Regional Offices in Dallas recognized Davis as an excellent attorney and accepted invitations from him to assist in civil rights cases. The regional director of the NAACP and an area lawyer for the Fund, Ulysses Simpson Tate, had heard of Davis' work in Arkansas and readily accepted requests by Davis to contribute to pending cases involving the area's black communities.[66] Davis stated, "A part of the educational program [of the Fund] is to try to show people . . . areas of discrimination and how to try to go about . . . correcting them." Explaining how plaintiffs accepted responsibility for initiating a case and dispelling the rumored theory that the NAACP sought out clients, Davis recalled:

As far as going and looking for somebody [a plaintiff], I don't think there was any instance where somebody really went out and looked for somebody. . . . In discussions you'd talk about things, employment, discrimination, this and that and the other, housing and all the rest of it, and how we might go about trying to . . . get relief from it, and somebody would say this or that . . . and then the question [would] come, would you be willing to try to help correct it? And if that person was willing to help correct it. . . . The first thing you get is a contract of employment so that you establish the attorney-client relationship and in the . . . contract you put a provision in there that you may invite other lawyers to assist. So the other lawyer comes in at my invitation. So he has . . . no direct tie to the client. He may not even know him. A lawyer, . . . somebody a little more expert in that particular area than you are, . . . you invite them to assist you or counsel with you. Doctors do it all the time. That's why you get a specialist.[67]

Cases assisted by the regional office were reported to the national offices in New York City. The Fund received reports on all school cases pending under the assistance of the regional NAACP lawyers.[68]

Davis accepted clients he felt were denied "equal justice under the law." On many occasions, he was called an "agitator," an "instigator," and an "outsider" stirring up trouble in communities he only visited.[69] He saw it very differently. Davis believed in the integrity of the black community and the strength of its residents. He also knew these people realized their predicament and were ready to challenge the status quo. Davis believed white southerners saw the black man in their own way:

They think, "That poor man doesn't have sense enough to say, 'Something's wrong with this.'" You see how deep the roots are in their thinking. They just can't understand it. This [black] man might say, "This ain't fair. This ain't right. Ain't got no business doing dis!" [The whites thought] if you can't say it with a Harvard accent, [you] can't think enough to say this is not right.[70]

In 1955 Davis saw practices within the segregated school systems in Fort Worth and the surrounding towns that he knew were blatantly illegal.[71]

3. The Creed of Segregation and States' Rights in the South with an Emphasis on Texas

Part 1: The Southern Move to Resist

The United States Supreme Court decision of 1954, in *Brown I*, was examined with dismayed caution and suspicion by millions of southern whites who solidly stood up for their generations of segregated lifestyle. They thought it incomprehensible to consider that desegregation was now the law of the land. Confused discussions took place among those seeking a definition of what was to become of the racial and social structure they had always accepted. The South, from Virginia through East Texas, was a diverse group of independent states verging economically on great industrial advancement by the mid-twentieth century. Yet, these states continually clung to sectional definitions such as genteel, traditional, laid-back, and old-fashioned. Insisting the South was a unique and cultured area within the United States, most white southerners admitted proudly that they were different: different in the sense of what had developed from their past. A social standard of racial hierarchy and segregation, they believed, was a healthy and honored tradition among both races of the South.[1] In 1957 James J. Kilpatrick, editor of the *Richmond News-Leader* wrote:

> The case for the South cannot be set down . . . in any book or essay: It has to be lived and sensed and felt; it is an amalgam of smiles, hopes, fears of the Southerner's life, a mosaic of countless fleeting impressions and experiences. The South, . . . is a state of mind; . . .[2]

Later, Kilpatrick elaborated:

> There remains a great and well-understood meaning simply in *the* South; there is, in fact, a sense of oneness here, an identity,

a sharing, and this quality makes the South unique. . . . The Confederacy was, as a matter of law, a state in being; but it was first of all, and still is, what so many observers have termed it: a state of mind. And running through this state of mind, now loose as basting thread, now knotted as twine, now strong and stubborn as wire, coloring the whole fabric of our lives, is this inescapable awareness: the consciousness of the Negro.[3]

These southerners were convinced that segregation was a noble cause. Protecting their customs and traditions was a sacred duty. They justified their attitudes toward African Americans with paternalism. Guy B. Johnson, a segregationist, wrote:

> Segregation is a benevolent and philanthropic institution which "protects" the interests of the Negro, which mediates to him the wisdom and virtues of white society, which gives him a chance to develop "in his own way" under his own leaders in his own institutions. . . . he is stirred up by "outsiders," Communists, the NAACP or other subversives.[4]

By the 1950s, white southern segregationists, in general, held several ideologies in common: an apprehension of change and a deep respect for the status quo; a determination to maintain the South as a separate region tied to the earth and not to the new technologies and industries moving in from the North; a fierce resolution to govern and be governed locally; a committed stand for states' rights; a background of honor and reverence for the lost Confederacy; a distrust for authoritative federal laws and regulations; a hatred of Communism to the point of paranoia; an adamant conviction of white superiority; and a deep-rooted fear of racial amalgamation. These factors controlled the lifestyles and attitudes of a large majority of the southern white population.[5] On July 12, 1954, the American Institute of Public Opinion released results from a national poll examining the reaction to the *Brown I* decision. In the South, 71 percent disapproved the decision, 24 percent approved, and 5 percent were undecided. These results began to change through the summer and fall months toward an increasingly higher percentage of disapproval.[6]

Enhanced by the United States Supreme Court's 1955 implementation ruling in *Brown II*, the southern opposition intensified.[7] Several elements contributed to the hardening line toward noncompliance of the desegregation ruling. In May 1954, Circuit Judge Tom P. Brady introduced the idea of organized resistance in a speech presented to a large group of white citizens in Greenwood, Mississippi. From this speech, Brady published a pamphlet, *Black Monday*, outlining the ways and means of organized defiance of integration. Predicting what was about to unfold throughout the South, Brady declared, "When a law transgresses . . . moral and ethical sanctions and standards . . . invariably strife, bloodshed and revolution follow in the wake of its attempted enforcement."[8] After Brady's speech, local businessmen and politicians met to discuss a plan to defend and promote white supremacy.[9]

By late July 1954, a newly formed organization emerged from the meetings held in Mississippi. Established to fight integration legally, the White Citizens' Council held its first official meeting in Indianola, Mississippi. Soon afterward, a headquarters was set up in Winona, Mississippi, the hometown of Robert Patterson, the executive secretary. The idea behind this group was to portray a respectable, law-abiding organization committed to upholding segregation throughout the South using every legal means available. Patterson, as an outspoken leader, proclaimed, "The Southern Negro isn't anxious to end segregation but is being manipulated by the well known NAACP."[10] And later, "We cannot and must not accept this scourge [integration] as inevitable. The people of America must call all of their resources and stand together forever firm against communism and mongrelization."[11]

Within the next two years, as defiance solidified throughout the South, chapters were numbered in the hundreds across the states. The local groups maintained their independence because council headquarters made it clear that each chapter was to operate on a local level and that national leaders were not liable or responsible for the actions of each chapter. Their techniques included mass mailings of pamphlets, newsletters, and flyers. These readily proclaimed, "The CITIZENS' COUNCIL is the South's answer to the mongrelizers. WE SHALL NOT BE INTEGRATED! We are proud of our white blood and our white heritage of sixty centuries."[12]

The White Citizens' Councils concentrated on four main areas to strengthen the resistance against the implementation of the Supreme Court integration rulings. The first area was political activity. After the Supreme Court decision, politicians in the South were very slow to speak out for or against the new mandate. Those that did used caution and moderation. Only those who believed their opinions were clearly synchronized with their communities spoke out against integration. The membership of the White Citizens' Council grew so rapidly after the summer of 1954, that no southern politician could deny its strength and popularity.

Officials at every level of state and local government were asked for a commitment to segregation. A "lobbying" of politicians made it very clear to all those in office that the Citizens' Council was powerful and determined in its quest to defend segregation. As the months went by, more and more elected officials from every southern state, believing they represented a majority of their constituency, condemned the decision for integrated schools.[13] Senator Harry F. Byrd of Virginia coined a title that defined the white segregationists' movement, "massive resistance."[14] Senator Herman Talmadge of Georgia became an outspoken and opinionated leader among the politicians opposing the Supreme Court's decision. Asked if the South would ever accept school integration, Talmadge replied:

> The South will not accept desegregation regardless of what the Supreme Court says or does about it. The Constitution was not intended to be twisted or ignored to meet the changing demands of the times. The Supreme Court ignored the Constitution of the United States. It ignored it when it violated the principle of sovereignty of the States. I think the individual states should be allowed, . . . to maintain local laws that will better support the peace and tranquility of those states. The decision was divisive in that it attempted to pit region against region, and race against race for political profit. It shall be my purpose to utilize every legal means at my disposal to undo it.[15]

As the power and membership of the council became apparent, politicians at all levels of government met at conferences set in several southern states to iron out strategies and tactical plans for noncompliance.[16]

The second area of concentration for council members was recruitment. Only by touching every community would the segregationists be able to build a solid foundation of resistance. By continuous attempts to indoctrinate current members and those nonmembers considered borderline, moderate, and even liberal could they produce enough resistance to keep the cause for states' rights, customary segregation, and the fear of racial mixing at a fever pitch.[17] Indoctrination was carried out through propaganda techniques such as the six-point plan titled "What You Can Do." This plan, outlined in a Houston, Texas, membership application stated:

> Join us. . . . Enlist additional members. Educate your fellow citizens so that we may all stand together. Contact your friends

and relatives in other counties and states and urge them to join. . . . 40,000,000 organized white citizens of the South can defeat this un-constitutional mixing of the races. . . . Let everyone know that you stand for segregation of the races. This nation was founded by White People for White People and if we are worthy of our heritage we must stand up and be counted, UNITED against every effort to mongrelize our people.[18]

The applicants paid a fee of at least two dollars and signed a pledge swearing, "I am a White American citizen, am not now and never have been a member of any communist group or subversive organization. I believe in and will support by every lawful means the principles of racial segregation."[19] Membership lists contained names of men considered to be upstanding southern citizens. These men held political and economic power within their communities and states. The councils benefited from these members' respectability and gained a reputable stand within the South.[20]

A third area to which council members directed their efforts was public opinion. Convincing national newspapers to accept and editorialize the council's viewpoint was considered mandatory in converting the moderates and liberals in the South and the rest of the country. Segregationists were encouraged to write essays, letters, articles, and books promoting their cause. James J. Kilpatrick proved to be a leader among southern "anticompliance journalists."[21] Kilpatrick was convinced that the Supreme Court had violated the Constitution. He was determined to educate the public on the infallibility of states' rights and "the southern case for segregation." On June 1, 1955, an editorial from Kilpatrick's *Richmond News Leader* explained the South's bitterness:

> In May of 1954, that inept fraternity of politicians and professors known as the United States Supreme Court chose to throw away the established law. These nine men repudiated the Constitution, spit upon the Tenth Amendment, and rewrote the fundamental law of this land to suit their own gauzy concepts of sociology. If it be said now that the South is flouting the law, let it be said to the high court, *You taught us how.*[22]

Kilpatrick also wrote about solving the dilemma in the South, "The remedy lies . . . in drastic resistance by the States, as States, to Federal encroachment. . . . The checking and controlling influence of the people, exerted as of old, through their States, can indeed preserve the constitutional structure."[23] The press was a tool the council needed to legitimatize the resistance movement. A majority of the northern media and a number of contemporaries in the South continued throughout these years to denounce the councils and their tactics.[24]

The fourth mode of defiance that the White Citizens' Council promoted was social and economic pressures. White residents who leaned toward compliance or who did not join and work toward the goals of the council were ostracized by council members and their community. Black residents who attempted to use the new Court mandates soon found themselves unemployed, evicted, or threatened. Those that had used credit in their communities found that it was canceled and payment was due immediately. Sharecroppers and farmhands were especially vulnerable to this type of pressure. A council member in Alabama stated:

> The white population of this county controls the money, and this is an advantage that the council will use in a fight to legally maintain complete segregation of the races. We intend to make it difficult, if not impossible, for any negro that advocates desegregation to find and hold a job, get credit or renew a mortgage.[25]

What developed across the South was a blanket control by the council that infiltrated every aspect of local communities.

On January 11, 1956, white supremacists received a boost in confidence from the state of Virginia. The Interposition Act was introduced into the General Assembly for consideration. Three weeks later, it passed the resolution, firmly stating Virginia's commitment to noncompliance of the Supreme Court's rulings in *Brown I* and *Brown II;* states' rights; and the powers to "interpose." Over the next several years, the doctrine of interposition was approved and incorporated into resolutions by most of the southern states.[26]

The theory of interposition established the right of each individual state to interpose itself between the federal government and the state's citizens when the state identified a federal law or court decision to be contrary to the Constitution or harmful to the state's citizens. If the state interposed its rights permanently against the law or decision, nullification would occur. Interposition was declared constitutionally valid by many southerners, based upon their interpretation of the Tenth Amendment. This amendment stipulated that a state retained rights and privileges not granted the federal government. And each sovereign state had the right to interpose its authority between its citizens and the federal government in cases where the central governing power overstepped its area of responsibilities.[27]

The history of interposition in the United States involved four prominent southern politicians: Thomas Jefferson, James Madison, John Tyler, and John C. Calhoun. The first three men were colleagues in the late eighteenth and early nineteenth centuries. In 1798 and 1799, Jefferson authored and introduced the doctrine of interposition in the Kentucky Resolutions. The Virginia Resolutions of 1798 were penned by James Madison with the support and advice of Jefferson and John Tyler. The resolutions were devised to attack the federal government's authorities provided by the Alien and Sedition Acts of 1798. Meetings to discuss the rights and sovereignty of the states and the need for a central government of limited powers were held at Jefferson's home, Monticello. Jefferson's definition of interposition asserted:

> The several states composing the United States of America are not united on the principles of unlimited submission to their general government but that by compact under the style and title of a Constitution . . . delegated to the government certain definite powers, reserving each state to itself, the residuary mass of right to their own self-government, and whensoever the general government assumes undelegated powers, its acts are unauthoritative, null and void.[28]

In the early 1800s, interposition and nullification were used by states several times to assert their authority and exhibit their dissatisfaction with federal statutes and court mandates.

Between 1830 and 1850, Calhoun became widely known as "the Great Nullifier." He was the staunch leader in the political drive for states' rights throughout the middle of the century and one of the first southerners to formally threaten secession. During this time, he wrote *Disquisition on Government,* declaring that a stable government would be retained if the states were allowed to remain independent and were able to give their acceptance or refusal to the central government on matters concerning the individual states. The ultimate use of the doctrine of interposition came with the withdrawal of the southern states from the United States in 1860. The secessions and formation of the Confederate States of America were examples of complete nullification. Throughout U.S. history, however, nullification was never accepted by any Congress, Supreme Court, or president.[29]

Southern segregationists readily accepted their state legislatures' interposition resolutions and felt sustained by the acceptance of their cause by their state governments. They believed the stand for segregation had gained legitimacy.[30]

On March 12, 1956, eighty-two representatives and nineteen senators of the United States Congress from eleven former Confederate states added more fuel to the segregationists' resistance movement by signing "The Declaration of Constitutional Principles," to become popularly known as the Southern Manifesto. Conceived by South Carolina's Senator J. Strom Thurmond, authored by Senator Sam Ervin Jr. of North Carolina and revised by a group of southern members of Congress, the statement declared that the Supreme Court, in its "unwarranted decision" to end segregation in public schools, had usurped the powers of states to govern and control public education. Furthermore, it claimed, "We regard the decision . . . as a clear abuse of judicial power. . . . a trend in the Federal Judiciary undertaking to legislate, in derogation of the authority of Congress, and to encroach upon the reserved rights of the States and the people." The "Manifesto" clearly made defiance socially acceptable in the South.[31] In 1956 a young lawyer from Clinton, Tennessee, summed up the accelerating acceptance of the resistance movement, "What the hell do you expect these people to do when they have ninety some odd congressmen from the South signing a piece of paper [the Southern Manifesto] that says you're a southern hero if you defy the Supreme Court."[32]

During the mid-1950s, several southern state legislatures enacted numerous laws and amendments to circumvent the Court's mandates on school desegregation. A consensus of these legislative measures included pupil placement laws, abolition of public schools, financial aid for students seeking segregation in private schools, curtailment of court decisions on segregation, abolition of compulsory attendance to integrated schools, and nonsupport of integrated schools. Partial compliance, superficial acceptance, and "token" integration supplanted strict segregation in a few states, but gerrymandering of political districts was added to make the compliances minimal. By fall 1956, ninety-five such laws had been enacted in the South with more added rapidly each month. State legislatures also encouraged litigation as a time-consuming measure to slow the integration process.[33]

By 1956, the South was an embittered region. During this time, William Peters, a writer, clarified this feeling:

It is a rare social change that does not bring with it a certain amount of human anguish. . . . For Negroes who see a final realization of lifelong dreams within grasp, it is difficult to escape bitterness at the knowledge that it may not come in time to benefit their children. For whites who see an impending realization of lifelong fears, it is hard to escape something very close to terror.[34]

Neither race intended to back down. The voices of moderation and compromise grew increasingly faint.

Part 2: The Southern Stand in Texas

Texas was a unique southern state. Because of its physical size, historical background, and the diversity of its population, Texas was a sectioned state with regard to the southern resistance movement. In the early 1950s, African Americans made up 13 percent of the Texas population, but 90 percent of those citizens lived in eighty-eight counties in the northeast and east central sections of Texas. These counties were considered a part of the southern United States when measured geographically, politically, socially, and economically.[35] At this time, attitudes on integration differed sectionally. In general, East, Central, and Coastal Texas strongly opposed integration. West Texas held a more liberal attitude, accepting that changes toward integration seemed inevitable.[36] Because West Texas was sparsely populated, Texas state officials and politicians, not tied to specific districts, tended to adopt positions aligned with eastern Texas voters.

In the early 1950s, Governor Allan Shivers developed one of the most powerful political machines in the history of Texas to run the state and the state's dominant Democratic Party. In July 1949, Lieutenant Governor Shivers unexpectedly rose to the state's highest office when Governor Beauford Jester died. Born in 1907, to a poor family in East Texas, Shivers struggled the first half of his life to meet the high goals he had set for himself. As a campus leader at the University of Texas and later as a young ambitious lawyer, Shivers was known for his diligence and fortitude in getting what he wanted. Shivers set his sights on and won an election for state senator at the age of twenty-six. At this time, he was the second youngest state legislator in Texas history. On his thirtieth birthday, he married into the prominent and wealthy Shary family of the Lower Rio Grande Valley. With his wife's social standing, he moved into new and powerful political circles. Shivers gained greater confidence and sought higher goals.[37]

As governor, Shivers became quickly known for his competitive personality. An Austin reporter observed, "Allan has no affection for lost causes. He hates to be beaten, even in a friendly game of gin rummy. He always plays like hell to win."[38] Another colleague commented, "He's so self-sufficient nobody gets really close to him."[39]

By 1952 Shivers was extremely powerful within the state. He continually planned and schemed to get his conservative programs into the resolutions of the state legislature and his influence into the decisions of the state courts. He carefully appointed officials he trusted to carry out his agenda. Shivers consistently sought advice from experts on particular topics, only to turn around and decide independently what was best for Texas. Very few stood in his way. At this time, the Republican Party was so weak in the state that his only competition came from the more moderate and liberal politicians within the Democratic Party.[40]

Ralph W. Yarborough became his strongest and most dedicated opponent. First challenging Shivers for the Democratic nomination for governor in 1952, Yarborough declared, "If I'm going to fight an organized machine, a conspiracy against democracy—then I might as well buck the lead dog." Shivers won on the first ballot.[41]

The governor's reelection brought a unique twist to Texas politics. Shivers and his supporters fought the federal government over ownership and mineral rights of the Texas tidelands off the Gulf Coast. The Democratic nominee for president in 1952, Adlai Stevenson, supported federal ownership. The Republican nominee, Dwight D. Eisenhower, deemed the coastal area and natural resources to belong to the state. After meeting with Stevenson, Shivers realized that Stevenson had no intention of changing his stand on the tidelands. Therefore, Shivers took an unprecedented move in Texas politics and threw all his power and support to Eisenhower. Forming "Democrats for Eisenhower," Shivers gained both parties' nomination for governor and ran unopposed. During these campaigns, Shivers formed a friendly alliance with Eisenhower and the Republicans that would last for several years.[42]

In 1952 conservative John Ben Shepperd was elected Texas attorney general and soon became one of Shivers' strongest supporters. Shepperd had his own political ambitions and believed his goals would be achieved with the help of Shivers and his political machine. Shepperd had never held an elected office before becoming attorney general, but he was appointed secretary of state immediately before his election and earlier had held membership on the State Board of Education and the Texas Economy Commission. All three of these positions were offered by Shivers.[43]

Shepperd was a determined prosecutor, bringing several unrelated controversial investigations to trial across the state. Under his direction, the department conducted lengthy and costly investigations into alleged communist infiltration of trade unions attempting to organize in Texas. During his tenure, the Texas insurance industry almost collapsed because of shoddy management and corruption. His department diligently examined records and interviewed those involved in the troubled industry. Even though it became apparent that Shivers' State Insurance Board had behaved unprofessionally in dealing with the crisis, Shivers remained aloof and purposefully removed from the investigations. Shepperd also took control of a state inquiry into a major veterans' land scandal that eventually brought indictments against twenty people, including the commissioner of the General Land Office. Shivers and Shepperd were both members of the Texas Land Board; therefore, many Texans accepted that they too were part of the scandal. Both adamantly denied any foul play, claiming that they often sent substitutes to the board meetings because of their conflicting schedules. Shivers was clearly implicated in the land scandal and the insurance crisis, but managed to remain on the fringe of the controversies, never officially accused of wrongdoing.[44]

Shivers' opponents believed Shepperd had carefully maneuvered the investigations away from a Shivers connection. Many believed Shepperd and Shivers overstepped their official responsibilities regularly, but because of the power Shivers and the "Shivercrats" held in Texas, very little could be done in the early 1950s to slow this political machine. Clearly, the governor had tight control.[45]

Shivers did not restrict his efforts to state issues. On many occasions, he pushed his position at the national level. After the Supreme Court invited United States Attorney General Herbert Brownell to address the Court in *Brown I*, Shivers wrote directly to President Eisenhower to offer his opinion as a representative of a southern state on the inappropriateness of the Court's invitation. In the July 16, 1953, correspondence Shivers stated:

> I see in this unusual Supreme Court invitation an attempt to embarrass you and your Attorney General. There is nothing more local than the public school system. . . . I assume that the invitation to your Attorney General . . . will be accepted. I trust that he will see the implications involved and advise the Court that this local problem should be decided on the local and state level.[46]

Shivers' warning proved meaningful in defining his future strategy on the issues of segregation and states' rights. At this time, he was unaware that his position, along with that of other influential southern leaders, contributed significantly to the moderate attitude of Eisenhower toward the unfolding integration crisis (see Chapter 4).

Less than a year later, Texas received the Supreme Court's decision on school integration with ambiguous feelings. Again, the sectional differences within the state contributed to the reactions. Shivers' attitude reflected the state's confusion. Within several days after the Court's decision, Shivers made a number of conflicting statements to the press. On May 18, he was quoted in the *Austin American:*

> It will require years to comply with the order for integration of schools.
>
> I hope that it can be worked out so as not to cause damage to the school children and that the children themselves will not be placed at a disadvantage.
>
> Sometimes those who seek reforms go so far that the evils of the reform movement are more onerous than the evils they're trying to remedy. The problems are by no means insurmountable, but are too big to be solved in days or weeks or months. Just saying we abolish segregation doesn't cure it. It doesn't accomplish anything. What is done about enforcing it is the important thing.[47]

Shivers also spoke out against eliminating the state public school system, as threatened by Georgia and South Carolina, explaining, "I hope the people of Texas will—and I believe they will—approach this problem with an effort toward solution rather than saying 'abolish public schools.'"[48] His position was disclosed in newspaper articles throughout the state, and as early as May 18, the realization that the "problem would be more acute in East Texas than in other sections of the state" became very clear. Shivers prophesied, "There is sure to be violent disagreement and condemnation. People will bitterly condemn the Supreme Court in a political year."[49]

On May 24, 1954, Dr. J. W. Edgar, the state commissioner of education, after conferring with Shepperd, sent a letter to all Texas school superintendents informing them that all public schools in the state should continue to operate on a segregated basis for the

1954–1955 school year because the system was still obligated to function under the laws of the Texas state constitution and the statutes of the state legislature. No changes were to be made until the Supreme Court implemented its decree and the state officials studied the problems of compliance. The State Board of Education, composed of twenty-one elected members, supported Dr. Edgar's announcement.[50]

The Roman Catholic school system in Texas began the move toward integration with the 1954–1955 school year. One of the first to open its doors to blacks was the Diocese of San Antonio under the direction of Archbishop Robert E. Lucy. Other parochial school systems soon followed.[51]

By June 1954, Shivers began to take a more defiant stand against the decision. Many observers pointed out that the change in Shivers came at a time when he was in a political battle with Yarborough for the 1954 Democratic nomination for governor in a run-off primary. In a campaign speech on June 21, he elaborated on his convictions:

> All of my instincts, my political philosophy, my experiences and my common sense revolt against this Supreme Court decision. It is an unwarranted invasion of the constitutional rights of the states, . . .
>
> My administration has already told the local school districts that, as far as the state of Texas is concerned, there are no changes to be made.[52]

On segregation, he proclaimed, "We are going to keep the system that we know is best. No law, no court, can wreck what God has made. Nobody can pass a law and change it." Campaign ads reiterated this stand in bold print.[53] Shivers equated Yarborough, the NAACP, the Communist Party, and the CIO as a group with similar goals banded together for his demise. He declared integration would not take place in Texas while he was governor, and he considered Yarborough a "nigger lover."[54]

In turn, Yarborough announced that he was against the "commingling of races in our public schools" and that he promoted equalization programs.[55] Yarborough and his supporters readily pointed out the irony of the governor's campaign promises and the fact that his son attended Saint Edwards High School, the only integrated school in Austin.[56] In his campaign speeches, Yarborough denounced Shivers and the Shivercrats:

To a political machine, the object is power, first, last and always. And principles are just a propaganda device. . . . A democrat tries to win friends. . . . A political machine uses methods which are a tip-off to its goal to destroy opposition, to destroy discussion—to rule by leaving the people no choice.[57]

It was a bitter campaign. Yarborough was convinced that Shivers' segregation platform was strictly a power play.

Shivers won the run-off primary and the election for an unprecedented third term. In September 1954, the Texas Democratic Convention, under the leadership of the governor, adopted a party platform pronouncing the Supreme Court's *Brown I* decision an "unwarranted invasion of states' rights" and resurrected the doctrine of "separate but equal."[58]

In May 1954, the Supreme Court had invited southern states to file briefs and present oral statements as amici curiae in the *Brown II* implementation arguments. Shepperd accepted the invitation and began preparing his presentation in the fall of 1954, declaring, "The Texas segregated school system is unique and most Texas citizens think Texas should be allowed to work out her own problems. We will urge this view in our brief."[59]

On April 13, 1955, Shepperd told the Supreme Court what Texans thought of the "implementation" of desegregation, "Three out of ten [Texans] expected serious trouble, most of the remainder predicted 'more than a little trouble,' and only fifteen percent of all races were optimistic enough to expect a minimum." He later elaborated, "It is clear that any attempt to effect immediate or too-sudden mixture of white and colored pupils, especially if made by an authority outside the individual school district, would be rash, imprudent, and unrealistic."[60] In clarifying the tradition of segregation in Texas, Shepperd explained:

This touches the deepest roots of human emotions. . . . It comes dangerously close to interference in the sacred, inviolable relationship between parent and child and the right of parents to bring up their children in their own customs and beliefs.

Texas does not come here today to argue the cause of other states. . . . It argues only that in Texas, a man-made cataclysm must be made slowly and with wisdom. Our argument may be summed up in eight words, . . . It is our problem—let us solve it.[61]

One solution that Shepperd believed Texas could choose was to legislate noncompliance measures. On April 19, he spoke in San Antonio of the growing need for the state legislature to incorporate into law provisions to protect the existing school system:

> I have reason to believe that the National Association for the Advancement of Colored People is going to make Texas a testing ground for segregation cases. . . . If we do not have a substitute ready . . . we may be forced by the courts to accept immediate integration. If we wait too long, our school legislation is going to be made by federal courts instead of our own legislature.[62]

Shepperd was justified in his comments. Since January, Texans had waited for the legislature to move toward tightening state control on the segregated public school system. That move never came.

On January 11, the Fifty-Fourth Texas Legislature convened with 181 members. Shivers addressed the assembly, recommending, ". . . no change be made in our [segregated] system of public education until—and maybe not then—the Supreme Court gives us its complete mandate."[63] Shivers was insinuating defiance. The legislature met in regular session until June 7 and chose to do nothing.[64]

On May 31, 1955, the Supreme Court issued the implementation decree in *Brown II*. Referring to the Court's opinion to integrate "with all deliberate speed," Shivers released a memorandum to the press, "Preliminary reports indicate that the . . . Court is leaving some discretion to local authorities. I think that is good. I have always advocated that these matters be handled by local agencies of government."[65] Shepperd, asked to comment on the latest decision, answered, "We are, . . . pleased that the Supreme Court recognized the local nature of the question. But in announcing the ruling it did not solve this problem. . . . The Court should say what the law is, not what the law should be."[66] State lawmakers had numerous and varied comments on the implementation mandate, but made no move to present new resolutions into the legislative chambers in its last month in session.[67]

In spring 1955, several state polls measured the reaction of Texas citizens to enforced integration. The *Texas Poll*, directed by Joe Belden, divided Texas into seven regions. Each region was handled by one investigator. Completed surveys were then sent to a central headquarters and processed by a computer. In the spring of 1955, a poll showed 45 percent favored resisting integration, while 35 percent would accept gradual integration, and only 14 percent would accept integration. The results were deceiving because the pollsters did not take sectional differences into consideration. Therefore, it was likely that a large proportion of the 45 percent that favored resistance lived in eastern counties. The polls taken throughout this time were helpful, yet tended to misrepresent the true picture because the resistance movement was based predominantly in the northeast and east central portions of Texas, where the southern caste system was deeply entrenched as an acceptable lifestyle.[68]

By June a number of western and southern school districts in Texas moved toward integration. The number of African American students in these districts was relatively small, and the school boards made plans to open registration for the 1955–1956 school year on an integrated basis. It was also made public that the Friona school district had operated as an integrated system throughout the 1954–1955 school year with eventually five black students attending the previously all white elementary school. Friona received the distinction of being the first system to mix races peacefully. As the 1955–1956 school year began, sixty-three more districts followed Friona's lead with either full integration or a gradual program beginning in September. These districts included El Paso, San Antonio, Kerrville, San Angelo, Denison, Hillsboro, and Harlingen. By the end of the school year, ten additional districts began integration.[69]

The news of integrating districts did not sit well with several factions working within the state. Dissent and dissatisfaction with the Supreme Court's final decree grew throughout the summer. In July the first Texas Citizens' Council organized in Kilgore. Soon after, councils sprang up in Arlington, Beaumont, Dallas, Fort Worth, Galena Park, Houston, La Grange, Mansfield, Marshall, Orange, Texarkana, and Waco. By fall the Citizens' Council had received a state charter. Meeting in November in Dallas, 250 members from twelve chapters representing ten eastern counties formed the Associated Citizens' Council of Texas. Ross Carlton, a Dallas attorney, was elected chairman of the executive committee. Boasting a membership of 20,000 Texans, Carlton and the councils represented passed a motion asking Attorney General Shepperd to investigate the communist influences they believed had infiltrated the NAACP. Carlton claimed, "Negroes have . . . become unwitting and dumb tools of the Communistic propagandists in the NAACP."[70] Other resistance groups emerged, but the Citizens' Council proved to be the strongest.

Ku Klux Klan activity was reported to the Attorney General's

Office in twenty-two counties. Concerning this activity, Shepperd sent a telegram to United States Attorney General Herbert Brownell reporting, "[We] recently fought what we believe was an effort to revive the Ku Klux Klan in Texas, and we will . . . resist any such terrorist organizations, . . . There is not now, and there will not be, a breakdown of state law enforcement in Texas." Although a few Klan chapters reactivated, their presence was kept under a clandestine shroud; whereas, the Citizens' Councils sought publicity and advertised extensively.[71]

On July 27, 1955, Shivers appointed a forty-member Texas Advisory Committee on Segregation in the Public Schools to study the problems that Texas faced from the decision of *Brown I* and *Brown II*. Committee members were biracial and considered ultraconservative. Their responsibilities were to determine whether state legislation was needed in dealing with compulsory attendance and segregation laws; whether both races would be "compelled" to attend a particular school; whether registered pupils could be assigned to particular schools in their best interest and that of the local school district; ways to decentralize school authority; and what the state could do to increase the authority of local school officials and their districts. These duties vaguely masked the true request of the governor. Obviously, members were to work toward legal measures to circumvent the Court's ruling and to prepare a plan to be presented to the state legislature and the State Board of Education at a later date.[72]

On October 12, 1955, Texas segregationists received a blow from the state supreme court. In the case *McKinney v. Blankenship*, it was decided that plaintiffs representing several groups, including chapters of the Citizens' Council, could not be allowed an injunction to stop the Big Springs school district from integrating grades one through six. The Texas Supreme Court ruled that the laws on segregation in the state constitution and statutes were invalidated by the United States Supreme Court school integration mandates.[73] Shivers issued the following press release: "Neither the Texas nor the United States Supreme Court has said that schools must desegregate immediately." In conclusion, he added, "In the light of these decisions, no school district should feel compelled to take hasty or unnecessary action." Clearly, the growing tactic among state officials and local school boards prone to segregation was to stall.[74]

By the beginning of 1956, Shivers knew he had lost his political clout: his administration had been implicated in several scandals since the last election, and the state was sectioned by school integration issues. He understood this was not a good position to be in during a presidential and state election year. Shivers recognized it would be an uphill struggle to run for an unheard-of fourth term, but he was determined to keep the party leadership out of the hands of United States Representative Sam Rayburn and Senator Lyndon Johnson. To succeed in both these endeavors, Shivers concocted a plan to rally conservative white voters behind a platform based on states' rights and interposition. He would be their leader and chief spokesperson, thereby winning their support and retaining his political machine.[75]

In January, Shivers wrote to Governor Thomas B. Stanley of Virginia, requesting a copy of Virginia's interposition resolution that was circulating among state representatives. He planned his moves to use this doctrine to his benefit in stages that would produce the greatest amount of publicity and keep his image and his issues in the limelight.

First, upon receiving the interposition information from Stanley, the governor sent a copy of the material to Will Crews Morris, chairman of the Texas Advisory Committee on Segregation in the Public Schools. In turn, Morris sent each member of the committee a packet of the material to study.

Second, on February 23, he issued a statement carefully outlining the importance of a referendum to allow Texans the opportunity to express their opinions on interposition, states' rights, and a possible amendment to the United States Constitution strengthening the powers and protecting the rights of all states.

Third, on the same day, Shivers sent letters to George Sandlin, chairman of the State Democratic Executive Committee, and Morris, summarizing his plan. In his letter to Sandlin, he wrote:

> It occurs to me that the interposition proposal would be a proper subject for discussion and possible action by resolution at the precinct, county, and state conventions in May. The question there would be . . . whether such a proposition should be placed on the ballot. Eventually, . . . the expression of the voters would be a guide to the Texas Legislature in the preparation of proper interposition resolutions.[76]

Thereby, Shivers could take the credit for its initiation.

Fourth, during February and March, several diverse groups and individuals, including the Citizens' Council, Shepperd, a number of state lawmakers, and organizations presenting signed petitions, repeatedly implored the governor to call a special session of the legislature to address the questions of states' rights, interposition, and the decisions handed down by both the United States Supreme Court and the Texas Supreme Court. Shivers resolved not to call a session because he did not want to diffuse these issues during his campaign. They were too valuable to him.[77]

Finally, on March 1, Shivers gave a public address clarifying a four-point program to strengthen state and local government, and he called for voters to become involved in the process of proposing an amendment to the United States Constitution.[78] Shivers believed he had set up the framework for the leadership role in the Texas Democratic delegation to the national convention, a possible endorsement as Texas' "favorite son candidate," and the possible nomination for a fourth term as governor.[79]

Shivers had overestimated his support and his influence. By March he announced that he would not seek a fourth term. Throughout the spring, it became very clear he was to lose everything. Shivers' political machine began breaking apart as the opposing faction, a coalition of moderate-loyalist-liberal Democrats under the leadership of Rayburn and Johnson, took control.[80]

In mid-April, Shivers and his wife entertained weekend guests at their home near Woodville. The guests were United States Attorney Herbert Brownell, his wife, and Oveta Culp Hobby, a Texan who had served as Eisenhower's secretary of health, education, and welfare from 1953 to 1955. Brownell explained the visit:

> I had worked closely with Governor Shivers and Attorney General (later Senator) Price Daniel in 1952 and 1953 on the Tidelands fight and the legislation. In April 1956 I spoke in Houston to the Inter-American Bar Association and the Houston Bar Association in the course of which I met Shivers who was also on the program at one of the events.[81]

Referring to the weekend as "purely a social visit" and "a family-to-family social event," Brownell recalled:

> It was only later, . . . that I realized that Shivers and LBJ were contesting the chairmanship of the Texas delegation to the Democratic National Convention. So not only did the LBJ faction want to embarrass Shivers for having dinner with a Republican but the Republican Texas State Chairman, Jack Porter, wrote to Eisenhower protesting that I shouldn't be having dinner with a Democrat.[82]

When the news of this visit became public, the coalition opposing Shivers attempted to turn it into a scandal. The press speculated on several subjects the two men "must" have discussed. The topics suggested were: Shivers as a possible running mate for Eisenhower; "dumping" the current vice-president, Richard M. Nixon; opinions and suggestions on federal and state positions on the 1956 Civil Rights Bill; and making a deal on a presidential "hands-off" approach to Texas school integration. There was never any proof of what was discussed in private by the two men. Everything printed was highly conjectured.[83] Brownell asserted, "I never discussed with Shivers or anyone else the possibility that DDE might dump Nixon or put Shivers on the national ticket." Recalling the 1956 Civil Rights Bill, Brownell affirmed, "It is comical to think Shivers would have co-operated with us on a Civil Rights bill in view of his stand, and he was not in fact involved in the formation or presentation of it."[84] Because of this visit, Shivers lost even more ground with the Democratic Party in Texas. The opposing coalition used this as proof that Shivers would again bolt the party for Eisenhower in the presidential election.

In May, Johnson was handed the state's chairmanship to the Democratic National Convention and the presidential nomination as "favorite son." With these defeats, Shivers chose to throw his support to a more moderate candidate, Price Daniel.[85] The Shivercrats were "dying" with only one major cause left, interposition. They clung to this issue throughout the summer and fall.

In March and April, Shivers and Shepperd worked relentlessly to ensure that the interposition referendum would be incorporated into the July primary ballot. To succeed, Shivers and Shepperd created the Texas Referendum Committee, headed by Robert Cargill, an oilman and member of the Association of Citizens' Councils of Texas. This group, with the help of Citizens' Council members, circulated petitions for signatures needed to place three specific proposals on the July primary ballot. The group collected 153,868 names within a month. The proposals asked Democrats to vote "yes" or "no" to:

1) Specific legislation exempting any child from compulsory attendance at integrated schools attended by white persons and Negroes.
2) Specific legislation perfecting state laws against [racial] intermarriage. . . .
3) The use of interposition to halt illegal federal encroachment.[86]

On July 28, 1956, Texas Democrats went to the polls to let their opinions be known. A *Texas Poll* conducted in May showed more Texans were opposed to integration than in 1954 or 1955: 47 percent of those voting favored disobeying or circumventing the laws to preserve segregated schools; 42 percent favored integration gradually or immediately; and 11 percent remained undecided.[87] Several counties, including Harris, Bexar, and Jefferson, refused to place the propositions on their ballots. Shepperd warned these counties that their actions might be illegal. Only Jefferson County reconsidered.[88]

The results of the primary showed a great majority of those voting approved the three measures. The results were:

	For	Against
1. Exemption from attendance	782,693	227,479
2. Ban on intermarriage	798,039	203,871
3. Interposition	772,295	180,427[89]

All three recommendations were adopted into the Democratic Party platform in September.[90] Once again, a very clear picture of the strength of segregation sentiments in Texas was exhibited. A large number of white citizens accepted the Shivercrat notions of interposition, states' rights, and circumvention, possibly noncompliance, of school integration, the law of the land.

In the 1956 political race for the Democratic nomination for governor, moderate Price Daniel and liberal Ralph Yarborough fought a close battle. Other outside candidates were former governor W. Lee "Pappy" O'Daniel and writer and West Texas rancher J. Evetts Haley. The biggest issue of the campaign was segregation, and all four candidates spoke out for continuing the tradition of segregated schools. Explaining the voters' fury against federal authority, Yarborough commented, "Cussing the federal government had already become a favorite occupation in Texas before integration came." Even liberal Yarborough inadvertently alienated several African American organizations, supporters, and the NAACP when he declared he would oppose sending troops into areas to enforce integration. Yarborough recalled:

> I used one expression that I never used again. . . . I said I was opposed to sending in troops to use force to enforce integration. . . . It got so hot for the blacks, they wouldn't defend me . . . The liberals took after me, a bunch of them didn't vote for me.

Enough liberals quit on that, that I would've won without that. [I] shouldn't have said it.[91]

Again, in 1956 as in 1952 and 1954, Yarborough was up against Shivers in this campaign. Even though the governor was not running, he chose to throw his remaining power and the support of what was left of the Shivercrat machine to Daniel. Yarborough felt Daniel used this support to stay out of the "dirty" tricks of the campaign. Yarborough explained, "[Shivers] could be the mean guy . . . and Price Daniel did not have to say a mean thing." Once again during the campaign, Shivers made it known that Yarborough was "a nigger lover." Recalling this phrase, Yarborough elaborated on the racial sentiment in Texas during the 1950s, "He said I was a 'nigger lover.'. . . That [was the] vilest term you could give anybody in Texas at that time, traitor wasn't that bad." Daniel and Yarborough were forced into a face-off in a second primary runoff. The vote was extremely close with Daniel winning by a small margin. Yarborough was convinced Daniel, with the help of Shivers, had stolen the election. Conducting his own investigation, Yarborough became aware of missing, trashed, and destroyed ballots, but he chose not to contest the election because of the high cost involved.[92] Daniel was elected governor. As a previous United States senator, he was one of only five out of twenty-two Texan members in the United States Congress to sign the Southern Manifesto.[93]

In September, Shivers came out in support of Eisenhower. Eisenhower carried Texas by a larger majority of voters than in 1952 (see Chapter 4).[94] The voters of Texas had examined, discussed, and decided the issues in a very turbulent year in Texas politics. The results showed a majority for interposition, states' rights, and circumventing federal authority on the mandates of school integration.

By the opening of school in September, at least one hundred Texas districts had integrated their school systems either completely or under gradual plans. Some surveys believed the number was slightly higher because there was no official count kept. The *Dallas Morning News* reported 500,000 white students and 25,000 black students attending schools within integrated districts at the opening of the school year. The number actually studying in mixed classrooms was dramatically lower: 315,000 white children and 3,380 black children. The difference was due to the gradual programs of integration and schools in segregated neighborhoods that remained one-race schools because of their location.[95] There was no move to integrate in any of the eastern school districts.

Mansfield, Texas, was a small town on the western edge of what was considered the "Deep South." Most of the residents regarded their small community as "southern" by tradition. Segregationists in the town believed customs should be left as they were, including separation of the races. By 1955 and 1956, the serious talk around town centered on the decisions of the Supreme Court to integrate schools, the importance of states' rights, the encroachment of the federal government into Texas state and local responsibilities, and the determination by a large majority of the town's whites to maintain the status quo and keep the school system segregated. The sentiments of many white citizens were explained by Kenneth Pressley, a young white adult residing in Mansfield at the time, "I don't think it was black versus white or white versus black. I think it was resisting change. Resisting being pushed or being told you had to do something."[96] Describing the separation of the races in Mansfield in the 1950s, Pressley recalled, "I was brought up in that time . . . where blacks were supposed to be in one place and whites were supposed to be in another one."[97]

Among the white segregationists in Mansfield, this was the law of the land, and they would do everything in their power to see that it did not change. They believed in the growing southern resistance movement. They had their state and local government officials pledging the same commitments. Their local newspaper editorials agreed.[98] And very few moderates or liberals spoke out in opposition. As the months passed, the few liberal voices grew fainter.

4. Taking a Stand on School Integration: The Dilemma of President Dwight David Eisenhower during His First Term

At the time Dwight David Eisenhower became president of the United States in 1953, the nation was in a social and political turmoil over civil rights and school integration. Eisenhower's stand on these controversial topics was important to those on both sides of the issue. The committed position of the executive branch of the federal government on the side of either the integrationists or the segregationists was considered one of the most significant factors in setting the pace and progression of the struggle for civil rights throughout the country. Eisenhower carefully and consistently took the path of moderation.[1] Nowhere was this cautious restraint more clearly evident than with the events surrounding school integration. Commenting in his memoirs on the Supreme Court's decision in *Brown I*, Eisenhower wrote:

> I believed that if I should express, publicly, either approval or disapproval of a Supreme Court decision in one case, I would be obliged to do so in many, if not all, cases. Inevitably I would eventually be drawn into a public statement of disagreement with some decision, creating a suspicion that my vigor of enforcement would, in such cases, be in doubt.[2]

Throughout his tenure as president he remained inactive and noncommittal. The exception, by his own interpretations of the Supreme Court's decisions in *Brown I* and *Brown II*, occurred in the 1957 Little Rock school integration crisis. Even then, he was slow to respond, and his critics claimed his eventual intercession was too little and too late to defuse the volatile situation at Central High School.[3] Eisenhower's reasoning and understanding of executive powers with regard to school integration baffled and infuriated all sides in the civil rights controversy.

The president's aversion to publicly support the Supreme Court's

decisions proved to be a plus for segregationists. By his own silence, Eisenhower gave the southern resistance movement room to
grow.[4] During Eisenhower's presidency, William Peters wrote:

> [The] absence of a firm stand by the president on what is clearly
> the overriding moral issue in America today has unquestionably
> weakened the position of Southerners, both white and Negro,
> who are working for desegregation of school. . . . It has . . . obvi-
> ously strengthened the hand of die-hard segregationists.[5]

The segregationists wanted more. Citizens and politicians alike,
hoped to persuade Eisenhower to express a sympathetic attitude
toward the southern tradition of segregation. They understood he
was a southerner by birth and many of his friends throughout his
life were from the South. Many segregationists had turned away
from the Democratic Party to vote for Eisenhower in 1952; therefore, they believed he "owed them one."[6]

Moderates and those undecided on the Court's mandates were
disappointed by the president's leadership. They looked to the executive branch for guidance and direction, but received, what they
believed to be, aloof indifference. Questioning why Eisenhower refused to use his powers to support the cause for integration, they
found themselves concerned that the executive branch misunderstood its responsibilities toward promoting and achieving school
integration. A southern moderate during this time, Harry Ashmore, wrote:

> There is no evidence that the Eisenhower administration is gen-
> uinely concerned with the lot of the Negro—none, certainly, in
> the record of the President's flaccid inaction in the quiet time
> after the Supreme Court decision when the moral weight of his
> office might well have headed off the polarization of public
> opinion.[7]

Because Eisenhower was a popular president, a celebrity, and war
hero, people known as "middle-of-the-roaders" on the integration
issues used him as an example to remain out of the controversy.[8]

Integrationists were disgusted by the lack of support from the
White House. They resented deeply Eisenhower's continual refusal
to endorse the Court's decisions on school integration. Eisenhower
referred to "extremists on both sides" of the controversy. Integrationists attempted to uphold the law of the land and balked at

being labeled "extremists."[9] They sought to allow African Americans the freedom to exercise their constitutional rights, while segregationists sought to prevent this. The integrationists grew bitter and resentful at the blatant shortage of executive leadership to promote their cause.[10]

Eisenhower never used his power or presidential position to reprimand those resisting the Court's orders, and many believed Eisenhower's silence was politically motivated. The Republicans were attempting to build broader support in the South and wanted both the white and the black vote. By straddling the issues, Eisenhower could keep both races guessing which side he favored, possibly not alienating either.[11] Southern members of Congress, governors, and state officials spoke out for noncompliance and defiance, using every means of promotion and publicity at hand, while the president never rebuked or condemned their words or actions.[12]

Eisenhower expected those in his administration to uphold his neutral stand. Many did, but there were several, throughout their White House days, who tried to raise Eisenhower's consciousness to their convictions. Special assistant Arthur Larson recalled the differences between the president and himself on racial tensions. "I realized that this man," he stated, "whose views on so many other subjects were easy for me to identify myself with, had views on race relations that to me were distinctly old-fashioned or of another generation, and not a little Southern."[13] One of Eisenhower's speech writers, Emmet John Hughes, struggled with the president on the wording of addresses where references to civil rights were included. Hughes later wrote:

> Our differences on [civil rights] punctuated our reviews of almost every campaign address he made. . . . my own drastically different convictions forced me to question the political hope or moral value of any "Republican philosophy" . . . that failed to reaffirm grave and binding commitment to the authentic spirit of the party at its very creation. . . . through all the preparatory process on almost all speeches, the text on civil rights signaled the playing of a . . . game . . . I toughening every reference, he softening it, I rephrasing upward, he rewording downward.[14]

E. Frederic Morrow was an advisor and administrator for Special Projects in the White House. He was also an African American, and up until this time, one of only a few to work as an administrator under a president. Working for Eisenhower under the prevailing conditions and the president's moderate approach to civil rights, Morrow often found himself in awkward situations. He revealed his feelings in his diary:

> It is my responsibility to explain to white people how Negroes feel on this matter, and by the same token, explain to Negroes the Administration's attitude.
> The time may come when I will find that these two responsibilities are incompatible, and that will mean that I will choose. Knowing myself as I do, I know that I would decide to retire from my present position.[15]

The internal conflicts and bantering over what became the most explosive subject of the era only reinforced the president's determination to remain impartial. He saw his staff's and cabinet's reactions as examples of the emotions running through the nation.[16]

At times, the president let his guard down in private. The moderate stance he took in public never wavered, but occasionally within the White House, he expressed candidly his concerns and opinions. These were rare occurrences, and those closest to him recorded these discrepancies. On May 19, 1954, Eisenhower was asked by a southern reporter if he had anything he wanted to say to the South concerning the Court's decision for integration handed down only two days before. His response, "Not in the slightest." He then explained his attitude, "I am sworn to uphold the constitutional process in this country; and I will obey." The reporter then pointed out that the decision was made with a Republican administration in the White House. Eisenhower snapped, "The Supreme Court, as I understand it, is not under my Administration."[17] The president refused to support or endorse the Court's decision. The White House remained silent.[18] Yet, with "insiders" on several occasions, Eisenhower allowed his concerns to surface. Larson recalled a discussion with the president:

> He stressed repeatedly two themes that were already familiar: he was determined to stay within the bounds of his constitutional powers, and he was determined not to take sides on the merits of the Supreme Court decision. . . . But then [Eisenhower] dropped a bombshell. "As a matter of fact," he said, "I personally think the decision was wrong." It seemed a bombshell to me . . . because President Eisenhower had taken great

care to keep his personal views out of sight, certainly from the public, and even from most of his associates.[19]

A second episode was described in Hughes' memoirs. He quoted the president as telling him:

> I am convinced that the Supreme Court decision *set back* progress in the South *at least fifteen years.* . . . It's very well to talk about school integration—if you remember you may be also talking about social disintegration. Feelings are deep on this, especially where children are involved. . . . We can't de-mand *perfection* in these moral questions. All we can do is keep working toward a goal and keep it high. And the fellow who tries to tell me that you can do these things by *force* is just plain *nuts.*[20]

On August 14, 1956, Ann Whitman, the president's personal secre-tary, recorded in her office diary a discussion between Eisenhower and herself:

> [He] said that the troubles brought about by the Supreme Court decision were the most important problem facing the govern-ment, domestically, today. I asked the President what alterna-tive course the Supreme Court could have adopted. He thought that perhaps they could have demanded that segregation be eliminated in graduate schools, later on colleges, later in high schools, as a means of overcoming the passionate and inbred attitudes that they developed over generations.[21]

On another occasion, in mid-August 1956, the president tele-phoned the attorney general, Herbert Brownell, to reiterate his demands concerning the wording of the 1956 Republican plat-form. In records kept by Whitman, the call was acknowledged and summarized:

> [The president's] quarrel was with efforts to insert the words "The Eisenhower Administration . . . and the Republican Party" have supported the Supreme Court" [*sic*] in the desegregation business. He wanted the words "Eisenhower Administration" deleted. . . . The President asked him to talk to Bush and Dirk-sen and if they did not come around, he would refuse to "go to San Francisco."

The President said that . . . he was between the compulsion
of duty on one side, and his firm conviction, on the other, that
because of the Supreme Court's ruling, the whole issue had
been set back badly.[22]

The private opinions of the president concerning school integration were clear and consistent, although they differed markedly
with those he expressed in public. Many asked why? What was
the reasoning behind Eisenhower's consistent public display of
moderation?

President Eisenhower had his own personal reasons and strategies for remaining as neutral as possible on the issues of civil rights
and school integration throughout several of the most tumultuous
years in race relations in United States history. In March 1956,
Eisenhower wrote the Reverend Billy Graham and firmly stated his
stance on the highly charged racial issues, "I shall always, as a
matter of conviction and as a champion of real, as opposed to spu-
rious, progress, remain a moderate."[23] Three factors contributed to
the formation of the president's strategy: his own personality traits
and philosophies pertaining to race relations; his definition of the
responsibilities and limitations of the executive branch of the federal government and its relationship to the other federal branches
and the states; and his interpretation of the Supreme Court's school
integration decree of 1954 and the implementation and enforcement decree of 1955.[24] These factors combined to solidify Eisenhower's unwavering stand.

Eisenhower's philosophy and convictions on race relations centered around his conclusion that integration could not be forced on
the South by judicial, legislative, or executive actions. He believed
changes would eventually occur by instituting a gradual approach
with a broad timetable. He understood that the move toward ending segregation was inevitable and had no problem with it. His
conflict came between weighing the importance of the civil rights
movement and the sacredness of states' rights under the Constitution.[25] His convictions were affirmed by his press secretary, James
Hagerty:

[Eisenhower] didn't have a segregationist mind or a segregationist bone in his body. . . . before [the Supreme Court's] decision
came down, . . . he was unalterably opposed to the federal government telling local districts and local school systems what
they should or should not do. . . . Once the Supreme Court
acted, it was his immediate reaction that this is the law of the

land and this must be carried out. . . . segregation was repug-
nant to him, and was completely alien to everything he believed in. . . . he had some doubt in his own mind what in the
devil the Supreme Court meant by "all deliberate speed." [26]

By his own traits, Eisenhower was cautious, unwavering, and
diligently against extremes. In July 1954, he wrote, "I think that
the critical problem of our time is to find and stay on the path that
marks the way of logic between conflicting arguments advanced by
extremists on both sides of almost every economic, political and
international problem that arises." [27] Many believed that these
characteristics made him a World War II hero, but throughout his
presidency, they were interpreted as "indifference." He had many
southern friends over his years in the military, and his own up-
bringing was flavored with southern attitudes. He kept in touch
with many of these longtime friends throughout his presidency,
sympathizing with their concerns over integration. Combining his
own personality characteristics with the southern influences in
his life, Eisenhower developed a concrete fear of the chaos and violence that might occur if the civil rights movement and the southern resistance movement were not kept in check. He believed it
was his duty to keep the peace by taking a position in the middle. [28]

Eisenhower executed the duties and responsibilities of the executive branch of the federal government under rigid guidelines and
limitations according to his definition of the Constitution. He
practiced a strict regime of respect for "separation of powers" and
states' rights. He did not believe the White House and the presidency should be used as a national "soap box"; therefore, he remained determined not to lead "crusades of a moral, humanitar-
ian, or civil rights nature." [29]

He had very little legal training and did not always understand
the laws of the land until tutored. Because of his lack of political
experience and his many years overseas serving in the military, he
lacked the expertise to understand the era's complex racial and do-
mestic issues. These shortcomings intensified Eisenhower's need
to limit the scope of his office. The executive office was so powerful as construed by the Constitution, believed Eisenhower, that in-
terpreting responsibilities beyond this could be dangerous to the
balance between branches of the federal government and between
federal and state governments. [30]

In 1955 the Supreme Court remanded the management and enforcement of school integration to the lower federal district courts,
and if needed, the federal circuit courts of appeal. The decision put

the execution of integration in the hands of local and circuit court judges. Eisenhower and the Justice Department accepted the rulings and placed the responsibilities of compliance and enforcement squarely with the judicial branch of the government. The Supreme Court, through its provisions of implementation, allowed Eisenhower to remain steadfast in his convictions and, clearly, out of the controversy.[31] In his memoirs, United States Attorney General Herbert Brownell explained this position:

> The second *Brown* decision gave enforcement power to implement school desegregation to the Federal district courts. President Eisenhower or the Justice Department could not simply order a local school district to desegregate "or else." Enforcement had to await the submission of a plan for desegregation to the district court, the approval of the plan, the defiance of the court-approved plan, and a request from the district court to the executive branch of the federal government to enter the proceedings and exercise its vast resources for enforcement. Quite clearly the Supreme Court deliberately decided on this procedure as preferable to having the President use military force or "carpet bagger" agents directly against recalcitrant school boards or state governors.[32]

Eisenhower and his administration used this concise and narrow interpretation of the implementation mandate to guide them through several racial crises with a "hands-off" strategy.

The president's strategy for handling civil rights questions was exhibited throughout his years in the White House. On June 8, 1953, the Supreme Court invited Brownell, as attorney general and "friend of the Court," to file a brief in the rearguments of *Brown I*. Brownell and the Justice Department prepared a brief and oral presentation answering the five questions proposed by the Court and supporting desegregation.[33] On August 19, 1953, Eisenhower sent a memo to Brownell expressing his uneasiness with the brief:

> The rendering of "opinion" by the Attorney General on this kind of question would constitute an invasion of the duties, responsibilities and authority of the Supreme Court. . . . the Courts were established by the Constitution to interpret the laws, the responsibility of the Executive Department is to execute them.[34]

Eisenhower later wrote that he questioned Brownell on the brief, asking him whether he could answer the Court's questions without giving an opinion. Eisenhower was told by Brownell that as "an officer of the Court it was his duty to be prepared to state his opinions." The president accepted this. During oral argument, the Court did ask for the Justice Department's opinion. The justices were assured by the department that segregation was unconstitutional.[35]

During the summer of 1953, several southern governors wrote to Eisenhower (see Chapter 3), pleading their case against the Justice Department's brief. Brownell consulted the president on how he might respond to these requests to stay out of the school integration cases. In particular, Brownell recalled Shivers' letter asking Eisenhower to turn down the Court's invitation by reminding him that "it was a local matter." According to Brownell, "Eisenhower rejected this advice."[36]

In July the president conversed with James F. Byrnes, governor of South Carolina, on these matters and later recorded in his diary, ". . . I believe that federal law imposed upon our states in such a way as to bring about a conflict of the police power of the states and of the nation, would set back the cause of progress in race relations for a long, long time."[37] The southern governors warned Eisenhower that the states might abolish their public school systems in the wake of a school integration decision. This grew to be one of the president's greatest fears. Once again, he foresaw a disintegration of the fine line between state and federal responsibilities if the school systems had to be placed under federal protection and management. Brownell suggested that Eisenhower contact Shivers and request the Texas governor to explain to Byrnes his impression that public schools need not be abolished. These conflicts and discussions enhanced Eisenhower's determination to remain on the outskirts of the dispute.[38]

In September, Eisenhower faced a major decision with the death of Chief Justice Fred M. Vinson. Through many weeks of discussion, contemplation, and political maneuvering, the president selected Earl Warren, former governor of California, to replace Vinson. After the appointment, Eisenhower announced to the press his reasoning on the selection of Warren:

> [I] wanted a man whose reputation for integrity, honesty, middle-of-the-road philosophy, experience in Government, experience in the law, were all such as to convince the United States that here was a man who had no ends to serve except the United States, and nothing else.[39]

The public received this announcement with mixed feelings. Even the president's brother, Edgar, was unsure what the appointment of Warren would bring to the Court. Once again, Eisenhower admitted he liked the moderation Warren displayed in difficult situations. He wrote Edgar that he found Warren to be "a man of national stature . . . of unimpeachable integrity, of middle-of-the-road views, and with a splendid record."[40] Eisenhower, in public and private, hailed Warren's "middle-of-the-road" philosophies as characteristics that he believed a statesman needed to serve the nation.

The Justice Department's brief was filed in November 1953, and oral arguments were presented to the Court in December. Before the justices, Assistant Attorney General J. Lee Rankin, under the direction of Brownell, endorsed integration claiming:

> The legislative history does not conclusively establish that the Congress which proposed the Fourteenth Amendment specifically understood that it would abolish racial segregation in public schools, there is ample evidence that it did understand that the Amendment established the broad constitutional principle of full and complete equality of all persons under the law, and that it forbade all legal distinctions based on race and color.[41]

During the previous month, Eisenhower had tried to simplify his role in preparing the brief without sounding as though he was ignoring his duties as president. On November 18, during a news conference, he was asked if he planned to meet to discuss the brief with Brownell before it was filed. The president, not wanting to appear out of touch, responded, "Indeed I do. We confer regularly. And this subject comes up along with others, constantly." The media immediately accepted this statement as Eisenhower's commitment to the contents of the brief. This was not what the president wanted conveyed to the public. In less than two weeks, in a letter to Byrnes, he attempted to disassociate himself from the brief. "The questions asked of the Attorney General by the Supreme Court demanded answers that could be determined only by lawyers and historians," Eisenhower wrote, "I have been compelled to turn over to the Attorney General and his associates full responsibility in the matter. . . . it is clear that the Attorney General has to act according to his own conviction and understanding."[42] It was apparent the president feared overstepping the bounds of the executive branch under the Constitution. He also feared the misuse of power by his cabinet members. Separating the attorney general and the Justice Department from his realm of responsibility proved illogical and impossible. The public and the press accepted the executive branch as a united organization under the president of the United States. It was a farce for the president to think otherwise.

As soon as the Court affirmed its decision for school integration in May 1954, the president, acting under the duties prescribed to him as chief governing officer for the District of Columbia, called the city commissioners to a meeting and announced his decision to desegregate the district's schools immediately. He claimed he hoped to set an example of compliance and show the nation the mandate could be carried out peacefully.[43] Eisenhower's administration succeeded in several prointegration moves, including fair federal employment, the military, and the school system of the District of Columbia, but these advancements were within the guidelines of the responsibilities of the executive branch.[44]

In announcing its decision on school integration, the Supreme Court, once again, invited the United States attorney general to file a brief and present oral arguments on the implementation of the decree. The brief was carefully scrutinized by Eisenhower before its submission, and meetings were held to work out the rewording of certain phrases. In each instance, the president looked to moderation. The term "possible" was deleted and replaced with "feasible" throughout the draft of the brief. Eisenhower hoped to keep the tone of the paper moving toward gradualism and localism.[45]

The Justice Department's finished brief emphasized that integration was constitutional and implementation should be carried out using gradual measures. It implored the Court to grant sufficient time to the southern school boards to adapt, develop, and institute desegregation plans. It also stipulated that the Court should recommend supervision and implementation of the local school boards' integration programs be given to lower district courts.[46] A schedule for carrying out these programs was not included, but the brief did recommend that lower courts request the school integration program within ninety days. Brownell recalled:

> No timetable was established although we in the Department of Justice urged the Court to require that plans be submitted within 90 days. The Court said only that desegregation should be carried out with "all deliberate speed." This of course encouraged the Southern States to procrastinate.[47]

Local opposition was addressed by the Justice Department's brief. Clearly stating active opposition would not be tolerated, the brief declared:

Popular hostility, . . . is a problem that needs to be recognized and faced with understanding, but it can afford no legal justification for a failure to end school segregation. . . . There can be no "local option" on that question which has now been finally settled by the tribunal empowered under the Constitution to decide it.[48]

The conclusion, in a supplemental memorandum filed and attached to the brief on April 21, 1955, went against the position of the president. Two sentences stood out in contrast to the described designated enforcement plan:

The responsibility for achieving compliance with the Court's decision in these cases does not rest on the judiciary alone.
Every officer and agency of government, federal, state, and local, is likewise charged with the duty of enforcing the Constitution and the rights guaranteed under it.[49]

Eisenhower may have construed this entry using his own definition of "enforcement" that was limited to his interpretation of the presidency, or it may have been a memo that slipped by. But for whatever reason, this ambiguous statement remained in the brief, a possible example of the different viewpoints of those who conferred on the wording.[50]

On April 13, 1955, U.S. Solicitor General Simon E. Sobeloff presented the government's oral argument to the Court. Sobeloff reaffirmed the main points brought to the Court in the government's brief and implored the justices to take a "middle-of-the-road concept of moderation with a degree of firmness" to implement integration in the South. Using the phrase "as soon as feasible," Sobeloff reminded the Court that remanding cases to the lower courts should not instigate a stall in the process. Asked by Justice Hugo Black to clarify "feasible," Sobeloff replied, "'Feasible' means like any other question of fact—a determination after considering all relevant factors." He concluded his definition by stipulating that public opinion could not be a criteria used to weigh the social correctness of constitutional rights.[51] In presenting the oral arguments, the executive branch completed its responsibilities as amicus curiae to the Court. This was the last civil rights episode in which the president and his administration took part for almost a year.

After the Court announced its final decision on implementation in *Brown II* on May 31, the White House issued only basic compliance statements. Once again, the president chose to remain quiet, refusing to endorse the Supreme Court decision. Chief Justice Earl Warren never reconciled this indifference. In his memoirs, Warren recorded his belief that Eisenhower's subdued attitude increased the determination of the segregationists to remain steadfast:

> [Southern resistance] was aggravated by the fact that no word of support for the decision emanated from the White House. The most that came from high officials in the administration was to the effect that they could not be blamed for anything done to enforce desegregation in education because it was the Supreme Court, not the administration, that determined desegregation to be the law, and the Executive Branch of the government is required to enforce the law as interpreted by the Supreme Court.[52]

Over the next several months, incidents occurred that supported Warren's statement.

In August a Gallup Poll was released ranking citizens' criticisms concerning the president. The fourth highest complaint affirmed that Eisenhower encouraged segregation.[53] Volatile racial incidents occurred from late summer through the opening months of 1956. The executive branch made no move to investigate or intervene. During August, Emmett Till, a fourteen-year-old African American visiting Mississippi from Chicago, was brutally murdered for a minor flirtation with a white woman. Because he "wolf-whistled" at her, the case became known as the wolf-whistle murder. The murder trial of the woman's husband and a friend drew large crowds and national press. When there were no convictions, the prosecution of the case was declared a travesty by integrationists. This murder and other atrocities taking place regularly during this time spread increasing fear and racial hatred throughout the South. Also in August, an African American, leading a voter registration campaign in Lincoln County, Mississippi, was gunned down on the lawn of the courthouse. Not one witness was summoned by the authorities to testify to what they saw or heard. It was as if it never happened. In December, Rosa Parks, an African American living in Montgomery, Alabama, refused to give up her seat to white riders and move to the back of a city bus. Her subsequent arrest caused the formation of the Montgomery Bus Boycott, under the direction of Martin Luther King, Jr. Another incident took place in Alabama in February. Autherine Lucy was admitted to the University of Alabama under court order, but after rioting broke out on the campus over her enrollment, the directors of the school, charging that she was responsible for the disorder, expelled Lucy. Each of these incidents received national media attention. The public's opinions polarized, and an even deeper cleft formed in southern race relations.[54]

At a February news conference, President Eisenhower was asked if the riots at the University of Alabama and the treatment of Lucy broke federal law. He answered, ". . . you must remember, the Supreme Court decision turned this whole process of integration back to the District Courts, and [they] were specifically instructed to handle it under the conditions that apply locally as far as they can." Concerning the expulsion of Lucy, the president commented, "I would certainly hope that we could avoid any interference with anybody else as long as that state, from its governor on down, will do its best to straighten it out." Directives circulating throughout the Justice Department reaffirmed the president's moderate position, informing employees, "For the time being, investigations should not be conducted" and reminding them to "refrain from independent action." Throughout these troubled months, the president, his staff, and the Justice Department kept abreast of the mounting disturbances in the South as they continued to interpret the situations as out of their jurisdiction.[55]

In September 1955, Eisenhower suffered a heart attack. The recuperation period lasted into the new year. Although hardly incapacitated, the president sidelined many of his appointments and slowed his schedule to almost a standstill, allowing Vice-President Richard Nixon to step into the responsibilities of the presidency.[56] This illness added to the impressions of a distant attitude by the executive branch at this time.

By late December, Brownell, Nixon, and several other cabinet members emerged from the shadow of Eisenhower and began the development of a program that was to become the first civil rights legislation since Reconstruction. The program began as a way to relieve the president and the administration of public criticism on his civil rights position. The proposal evolved to include a strategy that gave the president credit for its initiation, yet Congress would pass and institute the measures. They believed it would leave the executive branch unaccountable and make the bill a bipartisan package. The civil rights bill would also swing the African American vote away from the Democrats and into the president's party, allowing Eisenhower to gain electoral ground in several northern states. By presenting the controversial bill to the fragmenting Democrats in Congress, they hoped to force a deeper wedge within that party.[57]

The proposed bill, drafted by the Justice Department, was a simple attempt to show executive concern without jeopardizing Eisenhower's hands-off posture. It proposed a presidentially appointed bipartisan commission to study infringements of civil rights. The draft affirmed a commitment to securing African Americans their right to vote. It also sought to raise the Civil Rights Section of the Criminal Division to a separate division within the Justice Department and to add an assistant attorney general to handle civil rights matters. Finally, the most debated element of the plan: Brownell wanted more authority granted to the Justice Department to file civil suits for injunctions in violations of voting and civil rights.[58]

As he regained control of his health and the duties of the presidency, Eisenhower understood the implications behind the strategy of the proposed civil rights bill. He knew acceptance of what became known as "Brownell's bill" would improve his political stature throughout the country. Therefore, on January 6, 1956, he added a straightforward reference to it in his State of the Union Address. Surprising many, Eisenhower stated:

It is disturbing that in some localities allegations persist that Negro citizens are being deprived of their right to vote and are likewise being subjected to unwarranted economic pressures. I recommend that the substance of these charges be thoroughly examined by a bipartisan commission created by the Congress. . . . We must strive to have every person judged and measured by what he is, rather than by his color, race or religion. There will soon be recommended to the Congress a program further to advance the efforts of the Government, within the area of Federal responsibility, to accomplish these objectives.[59]

In a March 9 cabinet meeting, J. Edgar Hoover, the director of the Federal Bureau of Investigation, presented a report on "Racial Tensions and Civil Rights." He concluded:

The question of civil rights is interrelated with racial prejudices; charged with highly emotional surges. The law-abiding people of the South neither approve nor condone acts of brutality and the lawless taking of human lives. On the other hand, historic traditions and customs are a part of a heritage with which they will not part without a struggle. Militant resources of both those who stand for and against segregation have been mobilized and impulsive precipitated action could unleash acts of violence. The mounting tension can be met only with under-standing and a realization of the motivating forces. Delicate situations are aggravated by some overzealous but ill-advised leaders of the NAACP and by the Communist Party, which seeks to use incidents to further the so-called class struggle.

Calm, judicious judgement, public education and real under-standing are needed to avert explosive incidents. The area of danger lies in friction between extremists on both sides ready with violence.[60]

Hoover's report had set the tone for the meeting. Those attending listened intently to the FBI director's description of the deteriorat-ing race relations in the South.

Next on the cabinet meeting agenda was Brownell's presentation of the proposed civil rights bill. Brownell laid out the proposed program, carefully explaining each section. He asserted that if the presidential appointed bipartisan commission found civil rights violations in particular areas, they could take the responsibility to find the source, the degree, the methods used in the violation, and the extent of the local community's efforts to resolve the situation. The proposed commission could then hold public hearings so that the problems might be sorted out and discussed. The final out-come would be resolutions to prevent "lawlessness." Anticipating the growing lawsuits seeking integration in education, Brownell pointed out that a new civil rights division and assistant attorney general within the Justice Department was needed to "direct the Government's legal activities." In conclusion, Brownell declared:

> I believe that the enactment of all this legislation not only will give us the means to meet, fully and intelligently, our responsi-bility for the safeguarding of Constitutional rights in this coun-try, but will demonstrate to the world at large our determina-tion to secure equal justice under law for all people.[61]

Several cabinet members and the president commented on the presentation. The president expressed his belief that the time given by the Supreme Court to implement integration "was being used up in statements of defiance rather than in constructive ac-tion." Secretary of Agriculture Ezra Taft Benson hoped Eisenhower would speak out "on the need for calmness and moderation" and thought the proposal should wait for a Republican Congress before being submitted. Brownell assured the cabinet that the program would be presented by the Justice Department and not the president, thereby easing the fear of political reprisals. After concurring on "the great danger of moving too fast," the cabinet agreed to further discussion. The president "instructed" the attorney general to return to the cabinet at a later date for a final review of the proposal before presenting it to Congress. One of the president's comments jotted down by the secretary to the cabinet, Maxwell M. Rabb, and sent to Brownell for use in the bill's revisions asserted:

> [Eisenhower] believes that Herb Brownell should put forward what he has got here, but with a statement that many Americans understandably are separated by deep emotions on this subject. These people in the South were not breaking the law for the past 60 years, but, ever since the separate but equal decision, they have been *obeying* the Constitution. . . . Now, we cannot erase the emotions of three generations just overnight. [Eisenhower] still think[s] that this is such a moderate approach—especially the emphasis on *civil* recourse rather than criminal—that it will ameliorate the situation in the South. Certainly no one could object to the proposal for the new Assistant Attorney General. People have a right to disagree with the Supreme Court decision—since the Supreme Court has disagreed with its own decision of 60 years standing—but, of course, the new decision should now be carried out.[62]

The Justice Department, with Brownell's guidance, worked diligently to revise the proposal using all the comments and opinions at hand.

Hoping for approval, Brownell resubmitted the new draft to the president. On March 24, Special Counsel Gerald Morgan issued a memo to Whitman concerning the revised bill. It claimed that Eisenhower was still concerned that the program would be construed by southern states "as an extension of Federal power." The president then stated it was the best program "under the circumstances" and told Brownell to "go ahead with it if he wished." Morgan reported that the assistant to the president, Sherman Adams, and himself left Brownell and Eisenhower alone after agreeing that the program should not be submitted until the president was "convinced." Later, Brownell emerged from the meeting and affirmed Eisenhower's "complete okay."[63]

On April 9, the civil rights proposal was submitted to Congress in letters to both houses signed by Brownell. On April 10, he made an oral presentation of the program to the House Judiciary Committee. In the letter addressed to the "Vice President, United

States Senate," the attorney general used the cautious warnings of Hoover and Eisenhower concerning the mounting turbulence in the South:

> At a time when many Americans are separated by deep emo-
> tions as to the rights of some of our citizens as guaranteed by
> the Constitution, there is a constant need for restraint, calm
> judgement and understanding. Obedience to law as interpreted
> by the courts is the way differences are and must be resolved.
> It is essential to prevent extremists from causing irreparable
> harm.[64]

This program was considered by both the House and Senate as a moderate compromise between liberals and conservatives. Representative Emanuel Celler of New York refrained from submitting a more liberal and comprehensive bill in the hope of getting Brownell's proposal through a congressional maze of politically charged committees. On July 23, through a great deal of maneuvering, the bill finally passed in the House. It was sent to the Senate too late to withstand the powers of the conservative South. The liberal senators did not have the time or clout to challenge Majority Leader Lyndon Baines Johnson and Minority Leader William Knowland. Neither of these men pushed to get the bill out of the Judiciary Committee for fear of a filibuster that would kill several other pending bills. The civil rights bill stalled and died in the committee chaired by segregationist James Eastland of Mississippi.[65]

The press and the public observed an odd alliance of the president's moderation and Congress' ineffectiveness to make any move toward aiding the civil rights movement. Once again, the inactivity of Congress placed the southern resistance movement on what they believed was legitimate ground. If the executive and legislative branches of the federal government would not endorse and support the judicial branch then why should southern segregationists.[66] When the legislation failed, the president and his staff discussed what his public reaction should be. It was agreed that Eisenhower would simply acknowledge its failure along with that of other bills that did not pass. Morrow recalled the White House atmosphere:

> There is great reluctance on the part of the staff even to talk
> about civil rights legislation. It is one of the most disturbing
> notes in the whole situation here, and I am greatly pained

when the matter comes up and there is an immediate effort to squelch all discussion or turn the talk to something else.[67]

In 1956 Eisenhower became involved in legislative manipulation in another area related to school integration. In his State of the Union Address, the president had requested Congress to complete work on a school construction bill. The executive program proposed to use federal moneys to build more schools throughout the country to aid state and local school boards in alleviating overcrowding. Representative Adam Clayton Powell, a flamboyant black Democrat from Harlem, submitted an amendment to the school bill stipulating that federal funds could not be given to states that supported segregated school systems. The amendment placed members of the Eisenhower administration in another awkward situation. It was their bill, and yet, if they supported the bill and the amendment, they would ultimately be endorsing the Supreme Court's school integration decisions. Powell was determined not to allow federal funds to be used to build segregated schools, and he also hoped to force the president into a role of support for integration. Eisenhower wanted none of this. He said very little on the amendment other than to call it "extraneous." Leaving the final decision to Congress, he stated, "If Congress wants to put the [amendment] on, and does it. I will understand why they are doing it. But I just simply say, let's get the school bill; that is what I want." Ironically, the amendment separated from the bill passed in the House. But on July 5, when attached to the school construction program, it failed by a 224-to-194 margin. Once again, by remaining uncommitted, the president forced the responsibility of support for the school integration mandates out of the White House and into the halls of Congress. This did not go unnoticed by Eisenhower's staff and advisors because by their doing so the Democratic Party continued to splinter during an election year.[68]

In March 1956, Eisenhower turned to the Reverend Billy Graham for assurances that the presidential position stood on proper and moral ground. Graham wholeheartedly agreed with the president's moderate stance. Reinforcing Eisenhower's "go slow" mentality, Graham announced a schedule of four meetings to be held throughout the South with ministers and other church clergy to discuss the "moderate" approach to integration. Eisenhower's meeting with Graham stayed centered on national race relations. The president was convinced that the churches and clergy of the South could defuse the volatile emotions over integration. He also concluded, after talking to Graham, that the progress made in race relations and civil rights had lost ground since the Court's school integration mandates.[69]

One week later, Graham wrote the president reiterating his intentions, "I will do all in my power to urge Southern ministers to call upon the people for moderation, charity, compassion and progress toward compliance with the Supreme Court decision." He encouraged Eisenhower to stay out of the turmoil during an election year:

> Immediately after the election you can take whatever steps you feel are wise and right. In the meantime, it might be well to let the Democratic Party bear the brunt of the debate. Your deeds are speaking for you. You have so wonderfully kept above the controversies that necessarily raged from time to time. I hope particularly before November you are able to stay out of this racial situation that is developing.[70]

In another letter dated June 4, Graham reasserted his recommendation for Eisenhower to remain out of the racial controversies growing in the South:

> Again, I would like to caution you about getting involved in this particular problem. At the moment, to an amazing degree, you have the confidence of white and Negro leaders. I would hate to see it jeopardized by even those in the Republican Party with an ax to grind. Your complete sincerity, honesty, fairness and religious conviction are going to carry you overwhelmingly back to the White House with a greater majority than in 1952. You don't need to yield to any pressure groups.[71]

Eisenhower deeply respected Graham, whose words weighed heavily on the president's confirmed convictions to remain outside the building fury on school integration. During the summer, as the president prepared for the upcoming Republican National Convention, he realized very clearly that to promote the side of either the integrationists or the segregationists would alienate thousands, maybe millions of voters. He was more determined than ever not to split the Republican Party in the way in which he hoped to split the Democrats. Not only did he want a solid Republican vote, he also wanted a portion of the Democratic vote.[72]

On August 21, Eisenhower flew to San Francisco to accept the nomination for president at the Republican National Convention.

At some time during the day, possibly on the plane, Eisenhower scrawled on a piece of White House stationery his assertions concerning the Supreme Court's school integration mandates. Written almost illegibly, with several words crossed out, the statement illustrated the president's interpretation of the Court's decisions. Possibly to reiterate in his own mind the strategy his administration had exemplified for four years, Eisenhower wrote:

> The most recent decision of the Supreme Court in the area of racial relations directs desegregation in publicly supported schools and designates Federal District Courts as the agencies through which compliance is to be secured with deliberate speed. . . . During whatever period of time may be required in this process the responsibility of the Executive and Legislative Branches to be limited to such support as may be properly requested of the Courts. Recognizing the validity of Supreme Court Decisions in interpreting the Constitution of the U.S. we note that its 1954 decision relating to school desegregation has created acute and far reaching problems due to ending social patterns heretofore established in some sections of the country conforming to prior decisions of the same court. The Supreme Court, aware of these difficulties took care to avoid.[73]

These thoughts trailed off in the last sentence and were left uncompleted. The jotted notes summarized Eisenhower's many public and private statements made throughout his first term as president. He seemed to be preparing for the hordes of media in San Francisco and the controversial questions that he was convinced they would ask. For the most part, Eisenhower was able to dodge any controversy at the convention.

On August 23, the president accepted the Republican nomination for a second term. In his speech, Eisenhower pointed out the accomplishments of his first term in relation to civil rights:

> Republicans have proved that it is possible for a government to have a warm, sensitive concern for everyday needs of people while steering clear of paternalistic "Big-Brother-is-watching-you" kind of interference. . . .
> What is more, the Republican Party's record on social justice rests, not on words and promises, but on accomplishment. The record shows that a wide range of quietly effective actions, conceived in understanding and good will for all, has brought about more genuine—and often voluntary—progress toward equal

justice and opportunity in the last three years than was accomplished in all the previous twenty put together. Elimination of various kinds of discrimination in the Armed Services, the District of Columbia, and among employees of government contractors provides specific examples of this progress. . . .

Now, in all existing kinds of discrimination there is much to do.[74]

Eisenhower was able to keep the civil rights issues toned down to a minimum in the Republican Party platform, skirt the issues in his acceptance speech, and still receive the united support and nomination as the party's presidential candidate.

After the convention, the president believed he had the election in his hands if he could only remain out of any type of brewing civil rights crisis in the South. He knew this would be difficult with southern school systems gearing up for the fall term, but he was determined to hold his course of action to "moderation."

What occurred in the fall of 1956, in Mansfield, Texas, put Eisenhower's "middle-of-the-road" stand on school integration and civil rights to a test that would shake it to its foundation. Every aspect of his "hands-off" strategy—his convictions and philosophies; the influence of his southern sympathies and friends; his definitions of the duties of the presidency and the separation of state and federal governments; and his interpretation of the Supreme Court's decisions in *Brown I* and *Brown II*—came into play as he was forced to deal with the unprecedented events in the small town in Texas.

5. The Mansfield School Integration Case: *Jackson v. Rawdon*

In 1955 and 1956, events occurred in Mansfield, Tarrant County, Texas, forcing the civil rights positions of national, state, and local elements to the forefront of the country's conscience. Many facets of the problems facing the United States because of the clash between integrationists and segregationists became apparent in Mansfield over a period spanning approximately eighteen months. African Americans struggling for civil rights, especially school integration and equal protection under the law, collided with officials at all levels who clung to the established traditions of the southern caste system.

Incidents in Mansfield revolved around a school integration case brought by the relatives of three African American teenagers who hoped to integrate and attend Mansfield High School. The resulting crisis exposed the explicit views of several diverse groups on civil rights in the United States during the 1950s. The significant participants in the case and crisis included: President Dwight D. Eisenhower and his administration; the judicial branch of the federal government; Texas Governor Allan Shivers and his administration; the Texas Supreme Court; the forces of the southern resistance movement and the Citizens' Council; Mansfield's local officials and the school board with their attorneys; the white segregationist residents; the moderate white minority within the town; Mansfield's African American community, its leaders, and the teenaged plaintiffs and their families; the NAACP; and the African American attorneys for the plaintiffs. Each specific group's actions, and justifications for those actions, reflected their defined positions on civil rights and race relations. Therefore, the case and crisis in Mansfield was a microcosm of the nation's struggle for and against African American civil rights and school integration during the 1950s.

Throughout the 1954–1955 school year, T. M. Moody educated

himself on the mandates of *Brown I.* Anxious to see the final decisions on implementation, Moody remained active as president of
the Mansfield Branch, Number 61, Area 9, of the NAACP.[1] Traveling to Dallas with John F. Lawson for NAACP Texas State Conference of Branches meetings, Moody surmised that African Americans were on the brink of great changes for their race and the
nation. Moody and Lawson met with the southwest regional director for the Legal Defense and Educational Fund and NAACP regional special counsel, Ulysses Simpson Tate, and the NAACP
state special counsel, W. J. Durham, at seminars called to discuss
school integration, fair housing, and fair employment. They conversed with the association's officials on how the NAACP could
aid the African American communities in Texas to take the final
step toward school desegregation. Thurgood Marshall occasionally
attended these meetings and brought an optimistic attitude to the
cautious conversations. Moody, Lawson, and other members of
Mansfield's NAACP branch spent long hours in deep deliberation
on what the changes in United States law meant for the African
American citizens of Mansfield.[2]

During this time, Moody and the subtrustees submitted several
requests to the Mansfield school board for improvements to the
black elementary school. They also requested a school bus for the
teenaged students attending James E. Guinn School and I. M. Terrell High School in Fort Worth. In spring 1955, these requests were
dismissed by the school board with no action taken. Once again,
the subtrustees felt frustrated because of the continuing negative reaction of the school board to their pleas for equalization
improvements.[3]

At one of the many NAACP regional meetings that spring,
Moody and Lawson approached Tate and other officials and asked
who, acting as an attorney, might represent the black students and
their plea for better conditions in the Mansfield school district.
Tate's choice was not a difficult one, and he suggested L. Clifford
Davis, the Fort Worth African American lawyer seasoned in school
equalization cases in Arkansas and chairman of Area 9 in the
NAACP State Conference of Branches. The Mansfield branch was
included in Area 9.[4]

In April 1955, Moody and Lawson approached Davis with their
ideas. They believed their requests were fair, straightforward, and
simple. Davis understood the dilemma Mansfield's black community faced. Many times in Arkansas, he had seen and felt the anguish of small black communities struggling for their civil rights.
He knew the risks of trying to change the southern caste system.

Davis carefully listened to their predicament. He understood they needed sincere, strong representation and accepted the job. The African Americans involved in hiring the lawyer hoped to prove to the white school board members that the subtrustees were not going to back down. They knew also that the Supreme Court was to issue the enforcement and implementation mandates soon. Moody, with his optimistic and progressive attitude, wanted to be prepared. He hoped to change the educational opportunities for the African American children for the better. He was ready and willing to lead his community into the movement for civil rights. Hiring Davis, he believed, was a step in that direction.[5]

For the time being, Moody, Lawson, and the other subtrustees limited their plans to petitions for improvements. Six specific requests were presented by Davis. Mansfield Colored School needed improvements on the school well; a lunch program; certain teaching materials; a flag and pole for the front of the school to display the United States flag; and a fence in front of the playground to prevent harm to children because the school was situated on a busy, dangerous section of West Broad Street. The final request was for a regular school bus for the older African American students to ride to their segregated Fort Worth high schools. The public Trailways bus schedule was inconvenient, and the long walk from the bus terminal to the junior high and high school was a hardship for the teens. Davis tried over the next three months, through letters and personal conversations with Superintendent R. L. Huffman, to make the needs of the black community's schoolchildren known and understood. By late June, the school board had made no move toward passing any of the requests.[6]

On May 31, the Supreme Court handed down its decisions on implementation and enforcement of school integration. In June the stipulations in *Brown II* were carefully examined at the Emergency Southwide NAACP Conference meeting in Atlanta, Georgia. Association officials from all seventeen southern and border states affected by the Court's decisions attended. Directives adopted at the conference were sent to branches and printed in the *Crisis.* These directives advised members throughout the South on how to move their local school board and system toward a compliance plan for integration. In the instructions, the NAACP defined the difficulties derived from *Brown II:*

> The decision places a challenge on the good faith of the public officials, on the militancy of Negroes and on the integrity of the federal courts. . . . we must be prepared to meet the challenge. . . .

Our branches must seek to determine in each community
whether the school board is prepared to make a prompt and reasonable start towards integration. . . . Promises unaccompanied
by concrete action are meaningless; nor can there be concern
with the attitudes of individuals towards a change in the school
system. Segregated schools are illegal [*sic*], . . . the Court . . .
does not allow time to procrastinate, stall or evade.[7]

The directive advised eight steps:

1. immediately file a petition with the local school board emphasizing the *Brown II* rulings and offering branch assistance
   in solving problems to integration;
2. periodically check on the school board's integration plans to
   assure compliance with the Court's decision;
3. emphasize over the summer and fall months, during all
   meetings and discussions within the black community, the
   importance of understanding the implementation and enforcement decrees of *Brown II* and the role of the lower federal courts in school integration;
4. inform and organize black families in the community into a
   knowledgeable group ready to be considered plaintiffs in lawsuits if school integration does not occur;
5. seek the support of liberal and moderate groups within the
   local white community, considering especially, churches,
   labor and civic organizations, and sympathetic individuals;
6. when the school board prepared a plan, request the "exact
   text" and notify the state conference and national offices for
   consultation;
7. if no plans were made by the beginning of the 1955 school
   year, "the time for a lawsuit has arrived. At this stage court
   action is essential because only in this way does the mandate
   of the Supreme Court . . . become fully operative on the
   school boards in question";
8. and the final step, the matter should be turned over to the
   NAACP Fund and handled in the courts.

A sample petition was published for the branches to use. The petition reasserted the decisions of *Brown I* and *Brown II*, reminding
the school board that the timetable for desegregation was to be "at
the earliest practicable date." Also included was a sentence on the
duties and responsibilities of the federal district courts with regard
to enforcement of school integration. The petition then called
upon the school board:

to take immediate steps to reorganize the public schools under your jurisdiction on a non-discriminatory basis. . . . you have the responsibility to reorganize . . . so that the children of public school age . . . cannot be denied admission to any school or be required to attend any school solely because of race and color. . . . the time for delay, evasion or procrastination is past. Whatever the difficulties in according our children their constitutional rights, it is clear that the school board must meet and seek a solution. . . . you are duty bound to take immediate concrete steps leading to early elimination of segregation in public schools. Please rest assured of our willingness to serve in any way we can to aid you.[8]

The local NAACP branch officials in Mansfield discussed these directives and other information sent to them from the NAACP regional and national offices. Working with Davis, the officials decided in early summer to continue to approach the school board with the several requests for improvements to the black elementary school and a bus for the high school students. "At first we were trying to get these small things," Davis recalled, "and then, when we could not get those things, [we decided] if we're going to have to fight, we're going to just fight the whole battle."[9]

By midsummer, most of the African American adults in Mansfield belonged to the local branch of the NAACP. In meetings held at Bethlehem Baptist Church, discussions revolved around the refusal of the school board to pass any motions in accordance with the subtrustees' and Davis' pleas for improvements. Discussion continued as to which path to take, especially since the black community now had the advantages of both the *Brown I* and *Brown II* decisions. Some controversy infiltrated the conversations concerning the dilemma of "how far to go?" Some contended that requesting the board to establish a black high school in Mansfield might be good enough for the time being; others wished to demand immediate and total school integration. Also a number of residents at each meeting feared for their families' well-being and hoped the status quo could be maintained. All of the adults in the black community knew that whatever move was made would certainly drive a deeper wedge in relations between the town's two races, already strained since the Supreme Court's decisions. They also understood that once the leadership of the black community and the local NAACP branch took a stand on the school issue there would be "no road back."[10]

On July 26, the Mansfield school board received a petition signed by T. M. Moody and "others" requesting the board "to take immediate steps to end segregation in the Mansfield Public School." Minutes recorded during this meeting confirmed that after a "lengthy discussion and much consideration as to the problems that would be encountered . . . [and] due to such a short notice in making the change from a dual school system to a single school system" a motion was made that "further study be made by the board and the administration." It was also moved to continue segregation at all levels in the school system throughout the 1955–1956 school year. The motions passed unanimously. A letter sent to T. M. Moody asserted the board's actions on the petition. In further action, the president of the school board, O. C. Rawdon, appointed a committee of three including Superintendent R. L. Huffman and board members O. M. Wilshire and Ira Gibson to study "segregation problems." At the same meeting, Wilshire moved "to put a bus on for colored students from Mansfield to Fort Worth." The motion passed with a stipulation that the bus "be operated only in case such is deemed justifiable, . . . and this to be determined by eligible students that are available to ride bus." Moody, the subtrustees, and many in the black community were not satisfied. For them, this was too little and too late.[11]

On August 8, the NAACP Texas State Conference of Branches in Dallas sent a memorandum to all education committees of the state branches outlining once again the NAACP strategy for school integration. Many NAACP members and officials had asked for a "plan of action." The memo answered their requests and reminded them that "Separate but Equal Has No Place." The three steps presented closely resembled the earlier eight steps drawn up by the Emergency Southwide Conference in June. The announcement concluded, "Don't wait, begin today! This ground work has to be done so that . . . legal action can proceed without delay."[12]

Late in the summer, a conference was held on a Sunday afternoon in Davis' law office in Fort Worth. Present at the meeting was Davis; T. M. Moody; John F. Lawson; J. E. Moody, T. M.'s cousin and the father of Floyd Moody, a Mansfield teenager attending I. M. Terrell High School; W. D. Jackson, the father of Nathaniel Jackson, another Mansfield teen attending high school in Fort Worth; and possibly Alfred Hicks, a resident of Mansfield. Tate may also have attended. T. M. Moody and Davis did most of the talking. After much deliberation, it was decided that Davis would attempt to enroll J. E. Moody's son, Floyd, Jackson's son, Nathaniel, and T. M. Moody's nephew, Charles, into the all-white Mansfield High School for the 1955–1956 school year.[13]

Davis set up a meeting in Mansfield with Superintendent Huffman for late August. Davis picked up the three teenaged boys,

T. M. Moody, and John F. Lawson at the church and drove them to the meeting. Floyd Moody remembered his father and W. D. Jackson also attended. He recalled "sitting around a big table" and listening very carefully to what was said.[14] Davis requested enrollment for the three students at Mansfield High School. Calmly and clearly, Huffman stated that it could not be done. He pointed out that a desegregation plan had not been approved by the school board, although a committee was working on sorting through the problems. Later Floyd Moody recalled:

> When they said, "No! They cannot enroll in this school," I was happy. Although . . . I thought about it being better to be there, but yet, I was thinking . . . if they don't want me here [Mansfield High School] I'd have all kinds of problems. If I try to go to school here, I wouldn't make the football team. I wouldn't be able to do this because of who I am and how I got in here.[15]

The meeting ended quietly. The school board met on August 22, and although the meeting with Davis and the others was not formally recognized in the minutes, "A lengthy discussion was held in regard to the segregation question." No further elaboration was included.[16]

T. M. Moody, Lawson, and the other subtrustees had closely followed the steps set down by the NAACP directives on school integration. They reviewed their position, accepting that the black community was not entirely behind them and that the white community had made only small concessions toward improving conditions for the African American students in Mansfield. In September the final decision and the strategy to see it through were fine tuned. Preparations were made to begin the process of filing a school integration lawsuit.[17]

Sometime during late summer or early fall, Davis contacted Tate in Dallas and requested his assistance in the first school integration case at the secondary level in Texas. Tate telephoned Thurgood Marshall, special counsel and director of the Fund, in New York to ask for permission to assist as regional counsel and to lend the support of the NAACP Legal Defense and Educational Fund to Davis and the Mansfield school integration case. Marshall, trusting Tate's judgment, consented and approved the use of the Fund's resources.[18]

On September 2, Davis and T. M. Moody met at Moody's home. Moody brought his sister, Jemmie Irene Moody and nephew Charles to his house for the meeting. Charles was asked by Davis for the names of the twelve students that rode the bus to James E.

Guinn and I. M. Terrell schools each day. Charles named all the teenagers and left the men on the front porch in deep discussion. Jemmie Irene and Charles remained in the house while the two men conferred outside. Charles realized the two men were discussing the possibility of a lawsuit. He understood they were attempting to integrate the white high school in Mansfield. Later in the evening, Davis told Charles Moody to plan to be at the courthouse when the hearing took place. Charles and his uncle talked later about the situation in Mansfield. Charles realized his position. His uncle wanted him to attend school in his own hometown. Legally, he knew he should be able to, but conditions within the segregated town prevented him and eleven other students from exercising their constitutional rights. Davis and T. M. Moody ended the meeting committed to the initiation of a school integration lawsuit.[19]

Both men were discouraged in the days that followed because, under the guidance of T. M. Moody, only three families actually joined in the suit. Only the parents and guardians of the original three teenaged boys, acting on behalf of the minors as friends, entered their children's names as plaintiffs in the suit. Reprisal was the main concern of the families keeping their names out of the school integration case. Those families who declined to join in the suit feared for themselves and their children. The adults worried that they would lose their jobs and rented homes and farms. They also worried for their children's physical and emotional welfare. They knew the terrible hardship they would place on their teenagers during these turbulent times if they joined the suit.[20] Many older African Americans still remembered the activities of the Ku Klux Klan in Tarrant County as late as the 1920s. For these families, the risk was too high.[21]

Davis, after conferring with T. M. Moody, Lawson, other subtrustees, the plaintiffs' parents, and NAACP members in Mansfield, decided to file a "class action suit" naming only the three students as plaintiffs, but legally representing all the African American high school students in Mansfield.[22] Floyd Moody remembered his father's words to him, "I talked to T. M., . . . it would be best for you all to go to the school down here. . . . I don't know much about that, but I trust T. M., and he thinks . . . this is the way it should be." Floyd did not talk back to his father. He recalled, "In my mind I thought, 'I don't want to go up there [to Mansfield High School]. . . . If they don't want me up there, I don't want to go.'" Floyd Moody was also disappointed that more families did not join the suit:

Even as a child, . . . I knew at that point that you had more power with people. . . . numbers may mean power, but when you splinter off two or three trying to do something it takes twice as long. If the whole community had risen to the occasion [it] probably wouldn't have been as bad as it was. . . . When you have three families cornered off and the whole white community says, "They're the only three." . . . T. M. did not hold anything against the other families. . . . this was new.[23]

As a "class action suit," the three plaintiffs requested integration of and admittance into Mansfield High School for themselves and also for all eligible African American students in Mansfield.[24]

On October 7, Davis filed the class action suit in the United States Federal District Court in Fort Worth. The complaint listed the three plaintiffs, adding "and others 'so numerous as to make it impracticable to bring all of them' into court." The defendants named in the case were the trustees of the Mansfield school board, including President O. C. Rawdon, Secretary Ira Gibson, Billy Arber, Hubert Beard, Horace Howard, O. M. Wilshire, and J. R. Lewis; the Mansfield school superintendent, R. L. Huffman; and the Mansfield Independent School District as a corporate entity. The case was titled *Nathaniel Jackson, a minor, et al. v. O. C. Rawdon, et al.*[25]

The school board called a meeting on Saturday, October 8, to discuss the lawsuit. Some board members learned only that morning of the suit, after reading the front page of the *Fort Worth Star-Telegram*. The article explained that three African American teens from Mansfield were recently denied admission into their local high school and that an integration lawsuit was filed against the Mansfield school board for its actions. The newspaper made it clear that the students were refused enrollment because of their race. The board unanimously voted to hire an attorney to represent it in the case, and R. L. Huffman and Hubert Beard were appointed to find a lawyer to represent them as defendants and to handle what they realized would be a very controversial case.[26] J. A. "Tiny" Gooch, a Dallas attorney, was contacted by Huffman and Beard. They described the situation in Mansfield and the predicament they were in as named defendants in the upcoming trial. With little delay, Gooch agreed to represent all those named as defendants in the case. A fellow attorney in his law firm, Emory Cantey, assisted in the case. Gooch had little time to spare, for the case was scheduled in Federal District Court for November 7.[27]

Davis, acting for the plaintiffs, waived the right of a three-judge panel for the hearing. District Judge Joseph E. Estes presided, acting in sole judgment over the suit. In early 1955, as a newly appointed judge, one of Estes' first duties was to admit Davis as an attorney into practice for the Northern District of Texas. Davis believed this was a "whole new shabang" for Estes and probably his first integration suit. With this in mind, Davis prepared carefully for the trial. He knew the "courts [were] willing to move carefully." He also accepted that "this type [of] litigation does not meet with great joy . . . [or] open arms." Later, speaking of the preparation for the case, Davis asserted:

> You go in [to court] with the notion that you're going to build your record so that you can get a reversal, . . . you just could not go in with the assumption that this trial court judge is going to call the cards. . . . you went to trial . . . looking at being certain that you made the record that you could get a reversal on appeal. . . . it was . . . unusual [to win] . . . because the . . . federal judges were generally older men who came up with another generation, with another train of thought, and they just were not fixing to change . . . the patterns of life.[28]

News of the school integration lawsuit traveled quickly through Mansfield's white community. Many residents were outraged. Most segregationists could not believe that the black community initiated the suit. They blamed "outside agitators," and what they believed was the "communist-backed" Supreme Court and NAACP for the troubles brewing in their small town. Many of Mansfield's white citizens were furious.[29]

On October 25, two weeks before the trial opened, Mansfield's segregationists held a meeting at the town's Memorial Hall. One hundred and twenty-five people in the Mansfield school district attended. Howard H. Beard, a Fort Worth office supply salesman and president of that city's Citizens' Council chapter, addressed the crowd. He explained the council's segregationist position stating, "Sixteen scholars and experts with notorious Communist backgrounds produced the formula for integration in the book, *American Dilemma.*" Blaming the book for the Supreme Court's school integration mandates he continued:

> If the decision is allowed to stand, our children will be guinea pigs and our days as a national race are numbered. . . . Once mixed they can never be unmixed, and this [is] the surest and

most certain way to destroy us. If we don't organize, it will be our children who will pay the price in the next two generations for our cowardice.[30]

The *Mansfield News* covered the meeting and reported, "Beard asserted that the National Association of Colored People . . . was Communist conceived and dominated and really stands for 'The National Association for the Agitation of Colored People.'" A Mansfield chapter of the Citizens' Council was established during the meeting. Bud West was elected temporary chairman, and Lon T. Hubbard was named vice-chairman. Regular yearly memberships were accepted for a two-dollar donation, or one could give five dollars for a "sustaining" membership.[31]

During the meeting, West declared that joining the new Citizens' Council chapter was a legal way to fight the school integration suit. He claimed, "We ought to get the monkey off those seven men's [school board's] back, . . . This is some kind of start as to what we intend to do. . . . the Supreme Court can't do anything if the whites refuse to integrate." Elton Jones, a Mansfield resident, was reported as telling the group, "The three plaintiffs . . . are trying to make a 'test case' of Mansfield. . . . the money to pursue the suit is put up by somebody else." Those present voted unanimously to pledge their support for the school board and to oppose school integration. Beard reiterated the Citizens' Council's stand against integration and declared integration could be stopped with "grits, guts and gunpowder." Webb Joiner, a dairy farmer and an official in the area Citizens' Council, urged the crowd not to leave the meeting and forget about what was decided and pledged. The newly formed Mansfield Citizens' Council concluded the evening with declarations of "fidelity" to the council's segregationist stand and to the recruitment of additional members.[32]

On November 3, a second Citizens' Council meeting was held in Mansfield. The program included the discussion of plans to keep Mansfield's schools segregated. Joiner announced, "The NAACP is interested in making a mulatto race . . . not [in] desegregation." He asked those present to attend the trial on November 7 and "fill every seat from front to the back in Federal District Court."[33] The newspaper also began to publish prosegregationist editorials and letters from subscribers insisting that the traditional segregated standards within the town must be maintained.[34]

On November 7, the trial convened. Davis presented the case for the three teenaged plaintiffs. His argument was straightforward.

The local school board operated under the Texas State Statutes that legalized the establishment of segregated school systems. These statutes were held unconstitutional by the United States Supreme Court in *Brown I* and *Brown II* and also by the Texas State Supreme Court on October 28, in *McKinney v. Blankenship.* Therefore, Davis contended, immediate integration of Mansfield High School and the admittance of his clients and all other students presently discriminated against was the only legal solution.[35]

Gooch presented the defense. Noting several steps taken by the school board to improve conditions, address desegregation problems, and move toward integration, Gooch asserted that the school board was making a reasonable effort to comply with the decrees of the Supreme Court. He confirmed the appointment of the board's committee to "study segregation." He asserted the school year had already started, that school funds from Mansfield had been transferred to the Fort Worth school system to support the black Mansfield students attending I. M. Terrell High School, and that a Mansfield school bus was currently transporting the students to and from Fort Worth per the request of the subtrustees. Finally, Gooch described the white community's hostility for and condemnation of school integration.[36]

School board members testified to the "local climate" in the town. Davis asked Huffman, ". . . what conditions would you have to bring about in order to carry out the court's mandate?" Huffman responded, "That would be hard to answer in a concise statement due to the fact that we have been in the two fold school system so long in Texas we just would not have time to enter into the many details that would have to be worked out in order to sell such a program in the local community." When asked to name a few details, Huffman countered, ". . . it would be the breaking down of old traditions. . . . It would be getting two different types of people ready for something new which the board deems will take time." Huffman confirmed that each member of the board spent time out in the community discussing the school integration issues and had unanimously voted to keep the school system segregated for the 1955–1956 school term. He concluded, "The court ruled we had a reasonable length of time to meet the different requirements, and we would not have time on that short notice, from May 17, 1954, until May of 1955, or between May of 1955 to September 2, 1956, to carry out the mandate of the court."[37]

Ira Gibson, board secretary and member of the committee to study segregation in the system stated, "We are going to try to desegregate as soon as we think it is practicable at all." Davis questioned his testimony: "In other words, you are going to desegregate when the tension or the reaction of your community to desegregation will be neutralized?" Gibson responded, "As much as possible."[38]

When Davis asked O. M. Wilshire, board member and also on the committee to study segregation, if the board had plans for the 1956–1957 school year, Wilshire answered that the board had no plan past the present year's program. Questioned about what were the current problems preventing desegregation, Wilshire confirmed, "Dissatisfaction among the community." Asked to elaborate on his answer, he reiterated, ". . . they are not satisfied with desegregation and are not ready to enter into it right at the present time. . . . I believe if we were given sufficient time we could work the problem out but at the present time we have no plan."[39]

Two of the plaintiffs, Floyd Moody and Nathaniel Jackson, were questioned and testified to their happiness and satisfaction with I. M. Terrell High School. They both attended vocational classes at the school that were not available at Mansfield High School. In testimony, Nathaniel Jackson explained that he had lived in the Fort Worth area before recently moving to Mansfield in August 1955. He liked the Fort Worth school but hoped to attend high school in his new town. Both plaintiffs cited as hardships the daily thirty-six-to-forty-mile round trip to Fort Worth and the inconvenience of finding transportation home after extracurricular school activities such as football.[40]

After both sides were heard, Judge Estes announced his decision, officially issued on November 21, in favor of the defendants. Recognizing that only three teenagers were named in the suit, Estes stated, "The employment of the device of a class suit here is indiscriminate if not improper where only 12 colored high school students are involved, which indicates that the other nine Negro students did not wish this action at this time." The judge believed Charles Moody had not attended the trial and took this as a show of apathy. He declared, ". . . the failure of one of the three plaintiffs to appear in court and testify raises a question as to whether he wanted to change schools now."

Sympathizing with the school board, Estes found them to be:

> struggling with breaking the tradition of generations; opening their meetings with prayer for solution; studying articles in magazines and papers; . . . appointing a committee to work on a plan for integration—making the start toward 'obeying the law' which their abilities dictated. . . . the trustees now assure the

Court that they are continuing their efforts and will work out desegregation.[41]

He believed the board showed a good-faith effort toward integration by fulfilling the plaintiffs' requests for a school bus, transferring federal school funds for the African American students to the Fort Worth school district, and establishing a committee to study integration problems.[42]

In contrast, Estes cited the plaintiffs' complaints as similar to those of many rural students traveling long distances to school. He claimed that the school year began before the Texas State Supreme Court ruled the state's statutes for segregated school systems were unconstitutional and, therefore, that a decision for integration in the middle of the year "would be unjust to the school trustees and the students alike." He continued:

It is a matter of common knowledge that the transfer of a child in the middle of a school year, . . . may bring about scholastic and emotional difficulties. This Court cannot in good conscience force this result . . . nor does it believe that the Supreme Court of the United States has made such a course adamantine.[43]

Acknowledging the decisions in *Brown I, Brown II,* and *McKinney v. Blankenship,* Estes added his belief in the use of timely caution:

It is impossible however, simply to shut our eyes to the instant need for care and justice in effectuating integration. The directions of the United States Supreme Court allow time for achieving this end. While this does not mean that a long or unreasonable time shall expire before a plan is developed and put into use, it does not necessitate the heedless and hasty use of injunction which once issued must be enforced by the officers of this Court, regardless of consequences to the students, the school authorities and the public.[44]

Summarizing, Estes stated that the school board was "making a good faith effort toward integration, and should have a reasonable length of time to solve its problems and end segregation." The suit was too much and too soon for the town of Mansfield to handle, concluded Estes. He declared, "At this time this suit is precipitate and without equitable justification. . . . I find that judgement should be entered denying the relief prayed for herein, and that this action should be dismissed without prejudice."[45] The hearing was over in a day. Davis walked away believing he had made an impressive record for appeal. Many in the black community saw the decision against the plaintiffs as the normal pattern of life in the South. Others were deeply disappointed and discouraged. T. M. Moody and NAACP branch members realized the initial court case was only a stepping-stone. They were determined to continue the struggle for integration.[46]

The school board and Gooch hoped the reprieve would give them time to find legal alternatives to integration. Meeting on November 8, the school board voted unanimously to end a policy of allowing T. M. Moody to tap the water well at the black elementary school for his personal use. Moody had permission in a written contract dated September 19, 1950, to lay a pipe from his property to the well. Huffman notified Moody by registered mail to remove the pipe and prepare to pay his past due water bill for the provided service. The letter also stated that, under the terms of the contract between Moody and the board, the water arrangement was to be terminated sixty days from January 7, 1956. No mention of the school integration case or its outcome was recorded in the board meeting minutes.[47]

The local newspaper reported reactions to the court's decision within the community. The *Mansfield News* watched cautiously for an appeal. On November 10, an article appeared proclaiming "Segregation Appeal Not Filed Thursday." In the same edition, a segregationist was quoted using the Bible to support his opposition to integration. One week later, the newspaper reported the first sign that the tension among the town's segregationists might be slightly relaxing. An article announced the cancellation of a Citizens' Council meeting and explained the council's scheduled meeting conflicted with a Boy Scout cake auction.[48]

Throughout the following year, the local newspaper continued to publish prosegregation editorials and letters. The authors used similar arguments in their zeal to maintain a dual school system including: the Supreme Court overstepped its legal bounds and cannot make laws; the Supreme Court was infiltrated by communists; parents must do everything in their power, even defy the courts, to protect their families from integration; the Bible taught segregation; state's rights must be maintained over the encroachment of the federal government; the school system in Mansfield was being forced to be a "guinea pig" for the state and nation in the NAACP's fight for integration; separate but equal was satisfactory to both races; and the NAACP was a northern agitator, supported by the Communist Party, brainwashing the local black community. The continual publication of these statements kept many of the town's white residents adamantly determined to maintain the traditional segregated school system.[49]

In the early months of 1956, Mansfield's segregationists appeared to split into two distinct groups. A majority of them continued to oppose integration by all legal means available. Many in this group maintained their membership with the Citizens' Council, although the group's chapter was not quite as active as it had first professed it would be. This group discussed segregation often and at length. Determined to keep the schools segregated, they stayed well informed of the issues and events around the town. Their commitment to segregation did not lessen, but it also did not fester.[50]

Those who grew increasingly hostile and threatening proved to be small in number but loud in voice. These segregationists splintered from the original group and became the more "radical" and menacing. Their main difference was the negative emotionalism they espoused.[51] One of the leaders of this group was interviewed and asked whether white residents would abide by the Supreme Court's decision to integrate the schools. The man replied, "No self-respecting white man would abide by the Communist-dominated court decision. They will use force, violence, anything and everything they can to keep their children from becoming mixed with the niggers." Asked, "Are white children afraid of being physically assaulted?" He stated, "Little girls are afraid to go out at night, afraid niggers'll rape them. If they went to school with them, they'd be sure to." Also questioned on the involvement of "outsiders" agitating for integration, the radical segregationist answered, "The [expletive] NAACP forced these colored folks down here to do this. They bought 'em off. They lied to 'em. They cheated 'em." Many Mansfield residents believed the outspoken opinionated attitudes of the radical segregationists made race relations worse within the town. Through the early months of 1956, the radical group's opinions and tactics were mocked and ridiculed.[52]

On November 10, 1955, Tate wrote to Marshall reiterating a phone conversation concerning the Mansfield school case. Tate wrote, "As I told you on the phone, we tried the Mansfield case Monday in the District Court at Fort Worth and lost it but we made an excellent record for appeal." After mentioning several cases, Tate concluded, "I will send you the material that you requested about our plan for the future in a few days."[53] Later, on

December 6, Tate once again wrote Marshall concerning these plans. He explained the legal actions taking place in southwestern cities and stated there were school integration lawsuits pending in Dallas and Mansfield. Tate confirmed, "We are developing plans for at least five suits in East Texas." The NAACP officials were not discouraged by Judge Estes' ruling. A forthcoming appeal was encouraged and expected.[54]

On February 11, 1956, the Legal Committee of the NAACP Texas State Conference of Branches held a special meeting. Their purpose was to draw up a "legal action program" for 1956, and submit it to the Special Executive Committee for approval. Under the headings "Areas of Activity . . . in Public Education" the committee noted, "It is recommended, . . . that during the year 1956, each branch of the Texas State Conference of NAACP will take the elimination of racial segregation from the public schools in its area as its activity of primary importance." The report concluded:

> With respect to racial segregation, particularly in our schools, no branch of NAACP in Texas is authorized to indulge in or commit itself to any COMPROMISE. Our NAACP is jealous of its reputation in this area. We fought for more than fifty years and won without compromise. We cannot betray that tradition now. We have no right to bargain with respect to the rights of others. Let us not assume to do so.[55]

Tate, Davis, T. M. Moody, and other members of Mansfield's NAACP branch took these recommendations seriously. After discussion and consultation, they agreed to move forward with an appeal.[56]

In early spring 1956, Davis filed an appeal with the United States Fifth Circuit Court of Appeals. The Fifth Circuit encompassed six southern states, including Texas, and the Panama Canal Zone. The hearing was set for June 7, in New Orleans, exactly eight months after the original case was filed. *Jackson v. Rawdon* was heard by a panel of three circuit judges. Chief Judge John Chappell Hutcheson Jr. and Circuit Judges Rives and Brown. Hutcheson was born in 1879, in Houston, Texas. He was appointed to the Fifth Circuit Court by President Herbert Hoover in January 1931. Living through the years since the *Plessy* decision, Hutcheson brought insight and experience to the court in civil rights cases.[57]

Lawyers on both sides and Mansfield school officials traveled to New Orleans to present their arguments. Davis represented the appellants, and once again, Gooch argued for the school board and all others named as defendants. Davis presented a direct appeal to the court for reversal of the earlier decision insisting, ". . . the board has not brought itself within the protection of the 'prompt and reasonable start' requirements of the Supreme Court." He confirmed that the plaintiffs were still being denied their constitutional rights. He asserted that personal opinion and community sentiment or readiness were not valid factors in determining the constitutional rights of others under already existing Supreme Court decrees. Gooch adamantly supported the original decision by Estes. He claimed the ruling was "right" and "within the sound discretion of the district judge." Both attorneys clearly and precisely stated their cases, but ultimately Davis, using the mandates of *Brown I, Brown II,* and *McKinney v. Blankenship,* delivered a clear message to the Mansfield Independent School District that could not be refuted. The United States Supreme Court and the Texas Supreme Court, in their school integration decrees, upheld and supported the African American teenagers' constitutional rights to attend Mansfield High School.[58]

On June 28, Chief Judge Hutcheson issued the opinion of the court. After reviewing and summarizing testimony from the first trial, Hutcheson declared:

> We think it clear that, upon the plainest principles governing cases of this kind, the decision appealed from was wrong in refusing to declare the constitutional rights of plaintiffs to have the school board, acting promptly, and completely uninfluenced by private and public opinion as to the desirability of desegregation in the community, proceed with deliberate speed consistent with administration to abolish segregation in Mansfield's only high school and to put into effect desegregation there.[59]

The opinion pointed out that if the district court had ordered a plan of implementation, possibly even including a "deferment" of desegregation for a later time, the district judge "may well have been within his discretion." The district court, according to Hutcheson, failed to issue a declaration establishing the legal responsibilities of the school board to uphold the students' constitutional rights. He stated:

> The issuance of such a declaration of rights with retention of the case would have given the court the means of effectually dispelling the misapprehension of the school authorities as to the nature of their new and profound obligations and com-

pelling their prompt performance of them. This misapprehension appears from the undisputed evidence of superintendent and board members which plainly shows that the board had not given serious consideration to its paramount duty not to delay but to proceed with integration in respect to the sole high school in Mansfield, but quite to the contrary, had taken definite action to continue segregation there throughout the coming school year.[60]

Once again referring to board members' testimony in the original case transcripts, Hutcheson pointed out that the school board, ". . . declined to fix or even give serious consideration to the time when it [segregation] would cease, and the only reason it gave for not instituting it at once in the case of the plaintiffs and the Mansfield High School was its concession to public opinion." In conclusion, Hutcheson announced:

The judgement is, therefore, REVERSED and the cause is REMANDED with instructions for further and not inconsistent proceedings, including instructions to the district court that it declare: that plaintiffs have the right to admission to, and to attend, the Mansfield High School on the same basis as members of the white race; that the refusal of the defendants to admit plaintiffs thereto on account of their race or color is unlawful; that it order the defendants forever restrained from refusing admission thereto to any of the plaintiffs shown to be qualified in all respects for admission; and that it retain jurisdiction of the cause for further orders at the foot of the decree to promptly, fully, and effectively carry out this mandate.[61]

The Mansfield school board and the superintendent discussed the possibilities of an appeal to the Supreme Court with their attorney. They met throughout the following weeks with Gooch so that every alternative could be understood and given consideration. Some of these meetings lasted long into the night. In April 1956, Ira Gibson and Horace Howard finished their terms on the school board and did not seek reelection. Two new members, Melvin M. Meeks and Harry D. Blissard, were elected to fill the openings. O. C. Rawdon sought reelection and received the highest number of votes. During the spring and summer months, the school board minutes were recorded by the new secretary, Billy J. Arber. Discussions on school integration were noted briefly and without detail. On July 6, Arber's minutes concluded, "After a lengthy discussion in regard to the recent court decision and plans for the coming term, the board adjourned."[62] Meeks recalled these discussions:

> When this took place . . . we started discussing it. We didn't think we ought to be integrated. . . . that was the normal feeling of that day. That's everybody's feeling. We sat up there til' two o'clock in the morning . . . talking about this [integration]. Discussing it. What we're gonna do. . . . we got Tiny Gooch. . . . He didn't charge us a thing. He took the case for nothing. . . . Gooch said, "Looks like we're gonna have to integrate. . . . I'll tell you we'll go back to the Fifth Circuit Court. . . . We'll go back to the Supreme Court. . . . All the way around again." That really didn't make sense. You had a little school district against the Supreme Court. . . . That wouldn't have done much good.[63]

In July, Tate issued his bimonthly report as regional counsel of the Legal Defense and Educational Fund. A large part of it summarized the events surrounding the Mansfield school integration case. Explaining the reversal on appeal, Tate wrote, "We feel that this decision will go a long way in this area towards settling the question of when, and how, admissions shall be made. It entirely eliminates the question of time and puts the admission of Negroes on the same basis as the admission of white pupils." Tate stated, "[I] did yeoman's service in perfecting the appeal and writing the brief." Tate's optimism was shared by Davis and many of the African American residents in Mansfield.[64]

On August 17, the Fifth Circuit Court of Appeal's reversal officially arrived and was processed at the Federal District Court in Fort Worth. Judge Estes received the decree and spent ten days reviewing the instructions and preparing new orders for the defendants in compliance with the circuit court's reversal.[65] On Saturday, August 25, Estes called the attorneys for both sides into his chambers and went over the new order he was about to issue. Repeating the Fifth Circuit Court's reversal, Estes read the order:

> It is ADJUDGED and DECREED that the minor plaintiffs, Nathaniel Jackson, Charles Moody, and Floyd Stevenson Moody, and all other negro minors of the same class as the named minor plaintiffs, have the right to admission to, and to attend the Mansfield High School on the same basis as members of the white race, and that the refusal of the defendants to admit plaintiffs thereto on account of their race or color is unlawful.[66]

Naming all the defendants in the case, Estes proclaimed they were "forever restrained from refusing admission to Mansfield High School to any of the plaintiffs shown to be qualified in all respects for admission." He also charged the plaintiffs for court costs in the appeal and for the issuance of his orders.[67] Before the meeting ended, Estes told the lawyers he would not issue the order until Monday, August 27. Gooch announced his intention to seek a legal avenue to delay the order. After the session, Tate prepared an NAACP news release. A note to editors at the bottom of the release described the meeting with Estes and requested, "PLEASE do NOT release before Monday noon to any radio or other News Media."[68] Both sides hoped to get through the weekend without the decree being made public. Those involved in the case knew that Mansfield's white residents were anxiously waiting to see whether integration was to be forced on their community.

Throughout the summer, area segregationists became increasingly more vocal. The radical group gained in number and respectability. The wait-and-see position faded to a more active, determined attitude. Discussions throughout the white community revolved around the question, "What are we going to do now?" When the conversation turned to "eventual integration," tempers flared.[69]

In the July Texas Democratic Primary, Mansfield's Democrats overwhelmingly voted in favor of all three prosegregation questions on the referendum (see Chapter 3). On the question of stronger laws against integration, residents voted 407 to 31 for the measure. The second question, stronger laws against racial intermarriage, brought 404 votes for and 26 against. Mansfield's residents voted in favor of the final question on state's rights and the use of interposition 400 to 26. Clearly, these voters believed segregation should be maintained in Mansfield.[70]

By August both races in Mansfield found the anxiety over integration extremely high. The *Fort Worth Star-Telegram* ran a series of articles by C. L. Richhart concerning the racial tension in Mansfield over the school integration case. Richhart wrote, "This otherwise peaceful farming community is running an emotional temperature matching the mid-summer heat." In the article, J. L. Curry, owner of a drive-in restaurant that refused to serve African Americans, stated the views of many segregationists in the town on desegregating the high school, "It just won't work and it makes me mad because more people here haven't done anything about it. It's a plain case of pressure from the Communists, that's what this desegregation idea amounts to, they want to make trouble."

Another businessman who asked to remain anonymous proposed a "community-wide boycott of Negroes." He claimed, "I think the Negroes that have lived here a long time and want to get along peaceably will see that the trouble-makers are silenced."[71]

J. E. Moody, father of Floyd Moody, was told by Horace Williams, owner of the land and home Moody rented, that he would have to move off the land and out of the house if he pursued the integration of the high school and tried to get Floyd to attend in the fall. Williams told Moody that he was worried the house might be burned down if the Moody family stayed. When asked what he thought of Williams' reasoning for the move, J. E. Moody stated, "I think that's just a bunch of bull."[72]

Later in August, events occurred in Mansfield that forewarned the residents of both races of an impending crisis. On the nights of August 22 and 23, crosses were burned in the black section of town. It was not believed to be organized Klan activity, but no one who saw the crosses took the warning lightly. African American families in Mansfield knew the struggle for civil rights and school integration did not end with the court order to immediately integrate. For them the real struggle had only begun.[73]

6. A Collision Course:
The Crisis at Mansfield High School

The Federal District Court's order for the Mansfield Independent School District to immediately integrate the high school was released on Monday, August 27, 1956. This decree was the first in Texas history to order a local school board and school district to integrate a secondary school in accordance with the Supreme Court mandates of *Brown I* and *Brown II*.[1] No one in Mansfield predicted the events that evolved over the next ten days. The town erupted into a controversy that caught national media attention. Officials at the top of federal and state governments became entangled in the turmoil. The crisis in Mansfield came to represent an epitome of the southern struggle between those for civil rights and school integration and those inflexibly opposed to change. The phenomenon in Mansfield throughout the coming days foretold what many communities across the South would experience in the movement to integrate town high schools entrenched in the southern traditions of segregation. The Mansfield High School crisis became a prologue for what unfolded at Central High School in Little Rock a year later.

Over the next several days, T. M. Moody received a number of threatening phone calls and was told to "get out of town." The callers warned that his well-being, family, and home were in grave danger if he did not stop pushing for integration. T. M. Moody reported the calls to the local police and the sheriff's department, but was told very little could be done unless something actually happened. On Thursday, August 30, Tarrant County Sheriff Harlon Wright was asked several times why he was in Mansfield with four deputies. At one point, he told a reporter, "I'm here with deputies because an old man who lived in the Mansfield colored section for 50 years tells me that he received telephone threats giving him 20 minutes to leave his house before it is bombed." During this time, several African American men armed themselves and began guarding T. M. Moody's home in shifts throughout the following days and nights. One night in particular, rumors prevailed throughout the black community that white men planned to "get rid" of T. M. Moody. A contingency of Mansfield's African American men laid with loaded guns on the ground in the field in front of Moody's home guarding the area. The black men planned to protect Moody's home with their weapons and their lives if necessary. It was a long and strained night. Tension filled the air as the silence in the field grew heavier by the minute.[2]

On Tuesday, August 28, at nine o'clock in the morning, Mansfield school board trustees met with Gooch in his office in Fort Worth to discuss the court order and decide on a plan of action. Interviewed Monday night, Gooch stated he planned to present three paths the board could take, including to comply with the integration order immediately, to ask for a stay or delay of the order, or to appeal to the United States Supreme Court. Gooch was not sure an appeal would be accepted and encouraged the group to file a plea for a one-year delay of the court order. The stay of order plea had two bases. First, the school board did not have enough time to change its "curricula" for integration to take place. And second, all the African American high school students and their school funds had been officially transferred to the Fort Worth schools. These funds, amounting to $75.00 per student, were accepted by the Fort Worth school district in June 1956 for the coming school year. If Judge Estes refused a "stay of enforcement," then the attorney planned to ask for permission to appeal to the Supreme Court. If both requests were denied, the board agreed to comply with the order rather than face contempt of court charges. Gooch announced the consensus of the board's decisions at a meeting Tuesday night.[3]

On August 27 and 28, there were conflicting rumors concerning how many African American students planned to attend Mansfield High School under the latest court order. Charles Moody's mother, Jemmie Irene Moody, told reporters that a meeting had been recently held in the black community to discuss enrollment and that all but one of the teenagers planned to enroll at the local high school. Other reports stated all but one of the African American students intended to continue to take the bus to I. M. Terrell High School in Fort Worth.[4]

Sometime during the night of August 28, an effigy was hung at the intersection of Broad and Main Streets. Dangling from a wire stretching from a building across the street to a pole, the figure was packed with straw and dressed in men's work clothes. The hands and head were painted black, and the body was covered with splotches of red paint. Painted signs hung from the effigy threatening, "THIS WOULD BE A TERRIBLE WAY TO DIE" and "THIS NEGRO TRIED TO ENTER A WHITE SCHOOL." A person driving through town reported the effigy to the sheriff's department, and late Wednesday deputy sheriffs removed it. Sheriff Wright interviewed several residents to find out where the effigy originated; he recorded in his report that most white residents believed it to be a "practical joke." He told reporters he was not too worried about the effigy because he believed those who put it up were "just trying to scare somebody." He pointed out that he would become concerned if there were reports of Negroes being accosted in their homes. While Wright was in Mansfield, he checked into rumors that African Americans had bought all the guns and ammunition in town. Wright reported the rumor to be totally unfounded. Mansfield Police Chief H. E. Cannon confirmed he was "uneasy" over the effigy and the racial tension building in Mansfield. He told reporters he thought the hanging was "a lot more serious than pranksters. . . . I wouldn't be surprised by almost anything happening in Mansfield within the next few days." Cannon later left town for the Labor Day weekend. Judge David McGee of the Criminal District Court, Number 2, ordered a grand jury investigation into the incident.[5]

On Wednesday morning, August 29, Gooch filed a petition in the United States District Court in Dallas for a stay of enforcement of the ordered school integration until after the current school year. Estes scheduled a hearing on the plea for Thursday at 9:30 A.M.[6]

Throughout the day, several impromptu meetings were held among members of Mansfield's chapter of the Citizens' Council. One in particular took place in the local pool hall. It was decided among those in attendance, including a group of "radical segregationists," to meet on the grounds of the high school at 7:00 A.M. and stand together against any African American students attempting to enroll on the first day of registration. News traveled quickly through the town, and by evening many white residents decided to go to the high school the next morning, either to join the segregationists in their plan to prevent integration or to see what might unfold.[7]

Registration for all Mansfield's students was to begin on Thursday, August 30. Children from within the town limits were to enroll from 9:00 A.M. until noon at the three schools: Mansfield High School, Erma Nash Elementary School, and Mansfield Colored School. On Friday, August 31, children from outside the town limits were to be brought by bus to the schools to register during the same hours. The schools were to close for the Labor Day weekend and reopen for a final day of registration on Tuesday, September 4, the first day of school.[8]

In the early hours of Thursday, August 30, another effigy, similar to the one on Main Street, was hoisted up the high school flagpole, which stood several feet in front of the building. It hung from the top of the flagpole as if it had been lynched. Before 8:00 A.M., a crowd of white residents gathered outside Mansfield High School on the field between the front of the building and East Broad Street. This crowd gradually grew to between two and four hundred people depending on the hour of day. Most were from within the Mansfield school district boundaries, but others came from outlying towns curious to see what might occur. Cars parked up and down East Broad Street for several blocks.[9]

The group, more men than women, was a mixture of people and opinions. The radical, outspoken segregationists, believing it was their duty to keep the high school segregated, declared their commitment to prevent the black children from enrolling. Others strongly believed in segregation and were there to show their support, but they were also eager to see what might happen. A majority of those present believed in states' rights and were convinced the federal government had overstepped its authority. Blaming the federal court system for their predicament, these people felt the Supreme Court was at fault for the trouble in Mansfield.[10] Kenneth Pressley explained this attitude

> The federal government was gonna take a little sleepy community . . . and make an example out of it for the rest of the state or maybe the nation. . . . I don't think . . . it had anything to do with color. I think it had to do with the people on each side, one pushing too hard and the other resisting change. . . . it just all came together when it looked like the federal government was gonna make them do something that they hadn't all agreed they wanted to do. . . . I don't think it was black versus white. I think it was the federal government versus little Mansfield.[11]

The crowd remained for hours, leaning against trees and cars, discussing scenarios of what might occur if the African American students showed up. At some point before noon, Willard Pressley and his cousin, J. T. Pressley, tried to shimmy up the flagpole and remove the effigy, but it was too difficult and the effigy remained in place. A reporter asked Willie Pigg, the high school principal, about removing the effigy from the flagpole. He replied, "I didn't put it up there and I'm not going to take it down." A white teenaged girl in the crowd declared, "If God had wanted us to go to school together He wouldn't have made them black and us white." People milled around, carrying signs stating, "Negro stay Away," "NIGGER STAY OUT," "WE DON'T WANT NIGGERS, THIS IS A WHITE SCHOOL," "A DEAD NIGGER IS THE BEST NIGGER," "COON EARS $1.00 A DOZEN," "$2.00 a dozen for nigger ears," and "Dead coons are the best coons."[12]

The town's only constable, Tom Beard, asked Sheriff Wright to come to the school to see the situation for himself. Wright arrived and told several in a group that they should not attempt to "take the law into their own hands." There was an exchange of words between Wright and a few of the leaders of the radical segregationists. A Mansfield segregationist, identified by several newspapers as Owen Metcalf, shouted that if Wright attempted to give the black students an armed escort into the school to register there would be a confrontation. Someone shouted to Wright, "We are gonna have to get guns ourselves." The sheriff answered that charges would be filed on anyone found carrying a weapon. Another man yelled to Wright, "You'd better clean out the jail. You're gonna have alot of us down there." Wright countered, "We've got plenty of room." Willie Pigg recalled that many of the men brought guns with them, but very few carried loaded weapons or ammunition. Several had firearms in their vehicles.[13]

During the morning hours, the "radical segregationists" sent a contingency from their group to businesses on Main Street. They told the owners to close their shops for at least two hours and join the crowd in a show of support. Many complied, but a few were hesitant. They were then pressured with economic reprisals if they did not do as the group wished.[14]

Before the crowd dispersed in the afternoon, word was passed along for everyone concerned to arrive at the school grounds by 7:00 A.M. on Friday, August 31, the day that children from outside the town limits were to register. This would include most of the African American students. Many white residents expected something to happen on Friday as the buses pulled up to the high school.[15]

On Thursday morning at the same time the crowd gathered on the lawn at the school, Gooch presented his plea for a stay of enforcement to Estes in Dallas. Rawdon and Huffman represented the defendants. Tate and Davis attended on behalf of the plaintiffs and argued against the motion. Tate argued that the school board was making a "circus" of the case. He told the judge he believed the defendants were seeking publicity for their cause. Pointing to

the reporters in the courtroom, Gooch retorted, "These newspa-
permen will verify that I've not sought publicity, but you can't stay
away from reporters." In turn, Estes denied the plea, "without prejudice to the defendants' rights to apply for an appeal to the circuit
court or any justice of the U. S. Supreme Court." In conclusion,
Estes declared to the defendants and Gooch, "By taking an attitude
of prayerful obedience to the law, the school will stand as a proud
monument to the patriotism of the people of this land." Gooch left
the hearing and called Circuit Court Judge John R. Brown in Houston for an appointment on Friday morning. He planned to approach Brown with an application for the right to file a writ to
supersede and stay the order of the district court to integrate immediately.[16]

By evening several more events developed. A number of white
people were still congregated at the high school and on the main
streets of town. This was atypical because in the evening the
streets were usually quiet and almost empty. Tarrant County District Attorney Howard Fender and the grand jury issued a firm
warning to the Mansfield community. In his statement, Fender insisted that the county's law enforcement agencies would not accept violence or mob rule. He stated, "Both this office and the
grand jury would like to issue a stern warning to all parties that
violence is not the proper way to achieve a solution to our problem
and will not be tolerated by the law enforcement agencies of this
county."[17]

On Thursday night, Mansfield city commissioners called a special meeting at City Hall. Mayor W. A. Halbert and four commissioners attended. Minutes recorded during the meeting do not
mention any of the events at the high school, but it was assumed
that these men discussed in detail what was happening in their
town. Soon after this meeting, Halbert left town for the Labor Day
weekend.[18]

Davis was informed of Thursday's demonstration and warned
the African American students to "stay away" until their safety
could be guaranteed. During the evening, Davis sent a telegram to
Governor Allan Shivers requesting additional law enforcement
officers be sent to Mansfield to aid in keeping peace. He hoped
they would maintain "law and order" on Friday, when the registration of the African American teenagers was to take place at
Mansfield High School. In the telegram, sent after hours, and
therefore dated August 31, Davis, with the help of Tate, wrote:

A valid order from a United States Court has been entered directing admission of Negro students to the High School at

Mansfield, Texas. I understand the Board will enroll them in good faith and the students want to enroll.

This morning a mob of 300 men gathered at the school to prevent their enrollment. The sheriff of this county has been diligent, but advises me his force is inadequate to control a mob of such proportion. Violence is almost certain to occur when these students attempt to enroll on Friday unless additional law enforcement officers are dispatched to this area.

These Negro students are exercising a constitutional right and the full strength of law enforcement agencies of the state should protect them if law and order is to prevail in our great state.

I call upon you as Governor to cause to be dispatched additional law enforcement officers to Mansfield to assure that law and order will be maintained and that these students will be protected in their right to attend Mansfield High School. I respectfully request answer will contact you tomorrow if necessary.[19]

The same text was sent in a telegram to Colonel Homer Garrison, director of the Texas Department of Public Safety. After the telegrams were sent, Davis telephoned Garrison to reiterate his plea. Garrison told Davis that officers could not be sent unless the county sheriff requested assistance. Davis also called Shivers' office and was told the governor was out of town and would not return until Friday.[20]

Late on August 30, Sheriff Wright was asked by reporters for his opinion of Davis' telegrams. He simply replied, ". . . if we need additional help, we can get it quickly." Wright spoke to Texas Ranger Captain Bob Crowder, commander of the Dallas area Rangers. Crowder told Wright the Rangers were "available if needed."[21]

Early Friday morning, August 31, people once again gathered on the high school grounds. In a short time, between three and four hundred stood in small groups and contemplated their actions should any African American students arrive to register. Local, state, and national media arrived to cover the day's events. Radio, television, and newspaper reporters at the school numbered approximately one hundred. Pressley was at the high school on Friday and described the scene, "Most of the people I was talking to and walking around with [thought] it was amusing. It was kind a like going to the circus. . . . They were just talking and visiting and didn't want something shoved down their throats." Young children handed out free sodas to the throngs of people and newsreporters. As the crowd mingled, a third effigy hung from an outdoor light on the peak of the roof above the bricked archway framing the front door of the high school. The blackened effigy dressed in work clothes was strung up by the neck. It was the size of a man and dangled in the air as young white teens walked under it through the front door to register. The effigy on the flagpole remained from the day before. No one made an effort to replace it with the United States flag. A car parked at the side of the school grounds had racial slurs in white paint on it.[22]

Huffman was the first school official to arrive at the high school. Quickly walking toward the building, he called to several in the crowd, "Now you guys know I'm with you, but I've got this mandate hanging over my head." It was recorded that at that point he pulled his pointed finger across his throat. He refused to remove the effigies and told reporters to take them down if they wanted to. A few men approached Huffman and told him they had checked all the entrances where African American students might sneak into the building unnoticed. Huffman reminded them of two doors in the back, "Now remember, I'm not telling you what to do, but I'm just telling you about those doors."[23]

W. Lee "Pappy" O'Daniel, former Texas governor and currently an independent candidate for reelection, appeared on the school grounds to present his opinion on the situation. Attracting a crowd of fifty residents and newspeople, O'Daniel showed his beliefs on segregation by stating, "When I'm Governor, we're not going to pay any attention to those nine old men in the Supreme Court." His campaign workers passed around petitions seeking signatures to get O'Daniel's name on the November ballot.[24]

During the morning, Fort Worth Assistant District Attorney Grady Hight was escorted from the school grounds after a confrontation with a group of outraged men. County Sheriff's Patrol Captain Bob Morton removed Hight from the crowd for his own safety, hoping to end a fist fight. At approximately 10:00 A.M., Hight talked to five or six men, including Owen Metcalf and J. L. Curry, two men that many in the crowd claimed were segregationist leaders. When asked what he was doing in Mansfield, Hight claimed he came to see whether anyone needed prosecuting. Harsh words were exchanged between several radical segregationists and Hight. Several different versions of the incident were recorded by the press. Pressley recalled Hight and the men exchanging expletives. The angry group closed in around him pushing and shoving. Pressley remembered, ". . . he almost got jumped on, in fact he got hit a time or two . . . the sheriff had to get him out of here." The deputy walked with Hight to his car, he got in the car with two other assistant district attorneys, and the three drove away. After the altercation, one of the radical leaders of the group that confronted Hight remarked to a reporter, "Anyone with a silk shirt and fancy pants who comes down here and tells a man in overalls what to do, he is looking for trouble." Another newsman asked Owen Metcalf if he were a leader of the segregationists. He quipped, "Lord, no. There ain't nobody leading this. This is just a damn mob." [25]

Television photographer Maurice Levy attempted to take pictures of the Hight confrontation, but part of the radical group turned on him. When Gordon Yoder, another television photographer, tried to take a picture of the skirmish with Levy, he was pushed and shoved. He attempted to lay his camera on the ground to protect it, but as he did his amplifier was knocked by the crowd, dropped, and broken. Levy and Yoder were called "outsiders" and told to "get out of town." Yoder was reported to have yelled back at the crowd as he jumped into his car, "I am getting out of here . . . I'm outnumbered and know when I'm licked." Both "outsiders" were Texans from the Dallas–Fort Worth area. [26]

A number of men in the crowd became angrier as the day wore on. Pushing matches and verbal assaults took place within small groups. One radical segregationist told Irwin Frank, an Associated Press reporter, "It's the outsiders stirring up this trouble. It's the NAACP getting those little Nigger kids to register." Frank was also told to "get out" of town. He left, but on his way out of town a red and white car forced his car off the road. Men jumped out and confronted Frank about his intentions. They said, "We wanted to make sure you weren't some instigator from out of state." [27]

Many of the people outside the high school were unhappy with the publicity the loud radical segregationists attracted. They were also concerned at the level of anger and bitterness this group showed to the press. Meeks recalled two radicals he met at the height of the demonstrations, "They were so mad! Something built up inside of [them]. I'd known them all my life. They didn't look like the people I knew. . . . Their faces was so blood red . . . it was just like the skin was turned inside out . . . horrible looking." [28]

Sometime during the morning, Tate drove to Mansfield to see for himself what was happening at the high school. He later reported:

The area for a block was jammed and crowded with cars and people who moved purposefully about. It was a crowd that was apparently there for a vague and uncertain reason. Women and children mingled freely in the crowd. They appeared to be there just out of morbid curiosity. Newsmen of all sorts were there. There were cameras, sound recording trucks and the like. I

spoke to no one but moved freely about without attracting any
attention. I will admit that I did not have a sign on my back
with my name inscribed on it. I wore blue jeans and a T-shirt.
No one paid the slightest attention to me. I got out of it without incident, with a sinking feeling that America may be coming to the cross-roads that divide democracy from fascism.[29]

During the morning of August 31, a press memorandum was released from Shivers' office in Austin acknowledging the telegram
from Davis. Giving his opinion of the crisis, Shivers stated:

Law and order must be maintained in Mansfield, as in the rest
of Texas.

Neither the Governor's Office nor the Department of Public
Safety has received any request from the Tarrant County sheriff
for assistance. When and if such a request is made, it will be
honored.

I am certainly not inclined to move state officers into Mansfield at the call of a lawyer affiliated with the National Association for Advancement of Colored People, whose premature
and unwise efforts have created this unfortunate situation at
Mansfield.[30]

Later in the day, a second memorandum was released from Shivers' office announcing a three-step plan for dealing with the Mansfield crisis. Outlining his program Shivers proclaimed:

1. Under the general powers of the Governor to enforce the
   laws and see that order is kept in Texas, I have instructed
   Colonel Garrison to send Texas Rangers to Mansfield to cooperate with local authorities in preserving peace.
2. I have talked by telephone with R. L. Huffman, superintendent . . . and have wired O. C. Rawdon, . . . urging that the
   Board go ahead and transfer out of the district any scholas-
   tics, white or colored, whose attendance or attempts to attend Mansfield High School would reasonably be calculated
   to incite violence. These transfers should be for the general
   welfare, to preserve peace and orderly conduct, and not for
   any other reason. This action would be in line with the U.S.
   Supreme Court decision in the Lucy Case in Alabama.
3. I have asked Colonel Garrison to instruct his men to arrest
   anyone, white or colored, whose actions are such as to represent a threat to the peace at Mansfield.[31]

In the memo, Shivers reprimanded the plaintiffs' lawyers, declaring, "Contrary to the contentions of the NAACP lawyers, the legal recourse of the Mansfield School District has NOT [*sic*] been exhausted." The governor reminded the lawyers that an appeal to the Supreme Court was still an option and added, "Personally I hope that the U.S. Supreme Court will be given an opportunity to view the effect of its desegregation decision on a typical law-abiding Texas community." To justify the steps taken, Shivers reiterated his position, "I am taking this action not in a spirit of defiance of federal authority but as the only course I can conscientiously pursue in upholding my constitutional responsibility for maintaining law and order in Texas." Shivers then took the threat of contempt into his own hands, announcing that, should the school board be charged with contempt of the federal court order, he would suggest that he be charged with contempt not the local members of the Mansfield school board. He then closed the statement with a clarifying paragraph supporting and legitimatizing the assemblage of the white citizens at the high school. Shivers concluded:

> It is not my intention to permit the use of state officers or troops to shoot down or intimidate Texas citizens who are making orderly protest against a situation instigated and agitated by the National Organization for the Advancement of Colored People. At the same time we will protect persons of all races who are not themselves contributing to the breach of peace. If this course is not satisfactory under the circumstances to the federal government, I respectfully suggest further that the Supreme Court, which is responsible for the order, be given the task of enforcing it.[32]

This statement revealed exactly the position Shivers intended to take throughout the Mansfield crisis. During the following days, Shivers did not waver or back down on any of the provisions instituted in the memo. He had a purpose and reason behind each step stated in the memo. The governor's actions ensured that segregation was maintained in Mansfield. Texas Rangers were sent to Mansfield to keep peace and not to offer aid or escort African American students to enrollment at the high school. The latter duties were conspicuously left out of their orders.[33]

The second step in the memo used the precedent set by the regents at the University of Alabama against Autherine Lucy. Board members had the governor's permission to "transfer out" of the district any African American students arriving at the high school for registration if their presence provoked violence from the white crowd. The board could easily claim, as the University of Alabama regents did with Autherine Lucy, that the students were "inciting" a riot. Shivers gave the board a prosegregation solution.[34] Placing states' rights over federal authority, Shivers stated his provisions were necessary to keep peace and order within the state. He placed his constitutional responsibility to maintain order above the Supreme Court's mandates in *Brown I* and *Brown II*. By announcing his instructions to Garrison to arrest anyone whose actions represented a threat to peace, Shivers authorized the Rangers to arrest African Americans who arrived at the high school, because radical segregationists would have surely stirred a percentage of the crowd into verbal and, more than likely, physical protest.[35]

By offering himself if contempt charges were filed, Shivers united himself with the white crowd as "a good ol' boy." Therefore, he quickly became a martyr and hero to the white residents and school board in Mansfield. Shivers legitimatized the crowd's commitment to preventing the African American teenagers from registering and integrating the high school. In a letter of appreciation to the governor concerning his handling of the Mansfield crisis, an employee of the *Dallas Morning News* wrote, "I thought your statement issued when you sent Rangers to Mansfield the other day was a classic. I'm sure a lot of troubled school officials breathed easier on learning your approach to the troublesome problem." Shivers fueled the emotion and confidence of the segregationists.[36]

Mansfield's segregationists now had the governor of Texas dedicated to their position. Surely, they believed, segregation was a noble and sincere cause. Pressley described this attitude:

> Governor Shivers was feeling, as Governor of Texas, that this was his state, and . . . "the federal government [is] not going to tell me what to do in my state." Just like we as a small community were feeling, "well this is our town, the federal government's not gonna tell us what to do in our little ol' town. Let us do it the way we want to do it."[37]

A reporter questioned several radical segregationists at the high school on states' rights. One man stated, "We ain't going to go to school with niggers until we have to." Another in the group added, "They will be a long time making us do it." A man who joined the conversation insisted Texas was admitted to the United States on a states' rights platform and "it is still in the Texas Constitution that Negroes can't go to school with whites." A conversation ensued among the men over the involvement of "filthy politics" and "communism" in the efforts to integrate the school. The first speaker ended the exchange declaring, "What's filthy politics but communism." [38]

Late Friday morning, August 31, Crowder of the Texas Rangers sent Sergeant Jay Banks and Ranger Ernest Daniel to Mansfield with orders to "protect against violence." When the two men arrived, they found a dwindling crowd as the day continued and stayed only two to three hours. A back-up plan was devised in case any incidents occurred over the weekend and more Rangers were needed. [39]

The same morning, Gooch met with three Fifth Circuit Court of Appeals judges, Joseph Hutcheson, John Brown, and Benjamin Cameron, in Houston, seeking a stay of order. The plea was turned down. Gooch once again approached the school board for instructions. The school board met on Friday in Gooch's law office and unanimously voted to pursue every legal recourse available to postpone integration for one year. The school board meeting minutes were sparsely written and contained nothing on this decision. It was also decided that school board members should remain out of the controversy at the high school as much as possible. Gooch, following school board instructions, prepared to present the stay of order to a Supreme Court justice for review. He hoped the justice would grant a postponement of the order, pending an appeal to the highest Court. [40]

Sometime during the morning, the school board received Shivers' telegram reiterating the contents of his press releases. The governor closed the wire, "Please call on me for any additional help you think my office can render." [41]

Davis attempted to register Charles Moody, Floyd Moody, and Nathaniel Jackson by telegram. Addressed to Huffman, the telegram requested enrollment of the three students into Mansfield High School. Davis wrote, "The presence of an assembled mob of more than two hundred white persons and other immediate threats of harm such as the hanging of a Negro in effigy restrain and prohibit the petitioners from appearing in person. Constructive tender of the persons is hereby made by this communication." Huffman and the school board denied the request. The superintendent stated students could not register by "proxy." When a reporter asked Huffman if the students could enroll after the official school closing at noon, he replied, "The President's daughter herself could not register after noon." Asked if the board was in contempt of the court order, Huffman pointed out that no child had been turned away from registration.[42]

On Friday afternoon, Lawyer Stroud, the school bus driver for the African American students, reported to several newspeople that he had picked up five students from the black section of town and, following his established route, drove them to I. M. Terrell High School for registration. He was told the other black students were "sick or something." Upon arrival, the students were told by I. M. Terrell officials to return the following Tuesday for enrollment. Two of the plaintiffs, Floyd Moody and Charles Moody, were reported as part of the five in attendance by Fort Worth school authorities.[43]

During this time, newspeople interviewed both Charles and Floyd Moody. Floyd remembered being surrounded by reporters after getting off the bus at I. M. Terrell High School. He also recalled people from the media staking out his home and the fields around his house hoping to get an interview. A confusing story emerged in at least five newspapers after one interview. Some of the articles quoted Floyd Moody responding to a reporter's inquiry: "Mister, I don't wanna go to school in Mansfield. I'd rather go to school among my own people in Fort Worth. But I'll go to the Mansfield school if the NAACP makes me." Other newspapers claimed Charles Moody made this statement.[44] It became quite controversial. After hearing of the purported statement, an outraged citizen sent Shivers a telegram confirming what many segregationists believed:

> When a nigger student states that he would rather go to Ft Worth I M Terrell Nigger School because it is a better school in every manner and with his own race and would do so unless forced by the NAACP to go to the Mansfield School therefore it is time for you to direct the Attorney General to act. This should be justification for the jailing of all NAACP officials and to throw out the whole organization from the state of Texas for attempting to create riots. I think this commands immediate action.[45]

On September 15, the *Dallas Express*, an African American newspaper, ran a front-page article with a picture of Floyd Moody, declaring the young teen denied making the statement. The story confirmed that Floyd Moody would attend Mansfield High School when it was safe for him to go, but until then, he would continue to attend I. M. Terrell High School. Floyd Moody recalled on several occasions reporters hounding him with questions, but he does not recall making the controversial statement. He believed the story and quote were taken out of context and purposely misconstrued for sensationalism.[46]

By late afternoon on August 31, Mansfield's streets were quiet. Businesses remained open as usual throughout the day. The small shops along Main Street sold items to both whites and blacks without incident. The only outward signs of what had taken place earlier at the high school were the effigies swinging in the breeze on the school grounds and the heavier flow of traffic, sightseers driving through the town out of curiosity. Black residents walked down Main Street unhampered by whites.[47]

During the same day, Davis telegraphed to United States Attorney General Herbert Brownell and the Justice Department seeking help from the federal government. He explained the court order to integrate and asked for assistance stating, ". . . an assembled mob of more than two hundred angry and unruly white citizens stand ready to prevent [the African American students] admission by violence and lawlessness." After explaining the lack of coordinated law enforcement efforts in the county to control the mob, Davis concluded:

> We therefore, feel compelled to call upon you, as Attorney General of the United States, to use the facilities of your office to officiently [*sic*] protect the persons and rights of the Negro children concerned. There is but one public high school in Mansfield, Texas, and if petitioners are denied the right to attend that school, they shall have been denied their civil rights to receive a public education in the public schools of the State. Your help is urgently solicited.[48]

The Justice Department officially announced Davis' telegram was "under study."[49]

The Justice Department did not announce that Herbert Brownell had just returned from the Seventy-Ninth Annual American Bar Association Meeting held in Dallas. On August 25, Brownell flew directly from the Republican National Convention in San Francisco to Dallas. On August 26 and 28, he addressed the convention. He then stayed in Dallas until August 29 or 30. Shivers also attended this meeting and presented a speech on August 27. In his emotional oration, the governor stated, "The state should not be a mere housekeeping agency for the federal government." A panel discussion titled "Interposition: What Is It?" was scheduled for the same day.[50] Brownell described the convention and once again dispelled rumors that he and Shivers met to discuss politics, civil rights, or school integration:

> I went to Dallas to address the National Conference of Bar Presidents in August 1956 but did not meet Governor Shivers and, as far as I can remember, didn't see Texas Attorney General John Ben Shepperd and certainly did not discuss desegregation if we shook hands. I never discussed with Shivers or anyone else the possibility that DDE might dump Nixon or put Shivers on the national ticket.[51]

President Eisenhower held a news conference on August 31, in Washington, D.C. Asked by a reporter to comment on the Republican platform with regard to civil rights and school integration, the president replied:

> I think that no plank could satisfy everybody exactly. It couldn't possibly be done. . . . Here is a problem, . . . charged with emotionalism, . . . I believe we've got to have goodwill and understanding for all. We are not going to settle this thing finally by great show of force and arbitrary action.[52]

Late Friday evening, Shivers received a telegram from State Representative Joe Pool of Dallas requesting that the governor begin procedures to call a special session of the Texas Legislature. "Your statement that the NAACP instigated and agitated the Mansfield crisis has resulted in a flood of calls from Dallas County constituents demanding a special session to outlaw the NAACP," Pool wrote. "The leaders of the NAACP don't care how many Negroes get killed or injured just so they get martyrs get [sic] their southern integration scheme." He urged the special session for the purpose of outlawing the NAACP to "protect our public institutions from its insidious influence." Concluding, Pool called attention to the July Democratic Primary Ballot vote on segregation, intermarriage, and interposition. He believed a special session could put the proposed mandates into effect.[53]

The weekend brought a calm to Mansfield. On the surface, both black and white people went about their normal routines, but the anxiety of the last two days remained in their hearts and minds.

Residents of both races talked among themselves, attempting to predict the outcome of the case. The town was not the same as it had been only a week before. Some believed it would never be the same again.[54]

Traffic throughout the weekend was heavier than usual. Cars carrying sightseers cruised up and down Main Street and East Broad Street, stopping in front of the high school to gawk at the effigies. Newsreporters hung out in the local drug store, pool hall, and cafe. They hoped to catch some conversation hinting of what segregationists had planned for the following week. Storekeepers wished that they had stocked more souvenirs of Mansfield because curiosity seekers kept asking for them. Stores remained opened through Labor Day.[55]

African Americans gathered at their usual spot, the southwest corner of Main Street, and chatted in low tones, wondering where all the animosity in the town came from. They understood the court order was a victory for their children, but no one in the black community predicted the consequences of that decision. Several African American men stood in the alley behind the buildings on the west side of Main Street. Their wives and other family members were running errands while the men waited and discussed the situation. The men truly worried about the welfare of the students of their community. They believed it impossible to send the teenagers into the crowd on the high school grounds to register.[56]

On Saturday, September 1, Owen Metcalf was interviewed at his home. "I just can't see why they're trying to cram this down our throats," he told a reporter. "It's just a guinea pig deal. If they get in here they'll get in everywhere." Metcalf predicted there would be another protest at the high school on Tuesday, the first day of school. Tom Beard, the local constable, told reporters he believed all the African American teenagers "have definitely decided to attend Fort Worth schools. They don't want any part of this and I don't blame them. Continuing, Beard explained that Mansfield's white residents were very happy with Shivers' stand, and several had told him that "they wouldn't have voted for Shivers before, but they sure would now." Everyone felt the tension in town, but for the next two days all remained quiet.[57]

On Saturday, September 1, Gooch and Cantey prepared a petition to a justice on the United States Supreme Court to postpone the enforcement of the court order for one year pending an appeal to the Court. They also began to formulate a direct appeal to the Supreme Court to review the *Jackson v. Rawdon* case. This procedure is legally known as a writ of certiorari. In the early afternoon,

Gooch telephoned United Sates Supreme Court Justice Sherman Minton in Washington, D.C., asking him to accept the petition for delay. In an interview, Cantey confirmed, "He can stay the execution of the judgment until the Supreme Court can pass on an appeal. Of course it will be entirely up to his discretion." Describing the package sent to Washington, the lawyer explained that a copy of the *Fort Worth Star-Telegram* article on the Mansfield crisis was included with the petition and appeal request, ". . . we hope that it will convince them that we're having trouble down here in Texas." Gooch and Cantey knew that an appeal could not be accepted for consideration until at least October 1, when the Court reconvened. An appeal request must be accepted by at least four justices for a Court hearing to be scheduled. They believed the petition to stay the lower court's order for integration therefore would quell the crisis and give the Court time to review the case. On Sunday, Minton received the petition but chose not to handle it. In the telephone conversation with Gooch, Minton explained that upon receipt of the petition he would pass the entire package to Justice Hugo Black. Black presided over the Fifth Circuit Court of Appeals and the case was under his jurisdiction, not Minton's. Black received the petition on Tuesday, September 4.[58]

Over the weekend, Davis was interviewed for the *Fort Worth Star-Telegram*. He candidly told newsmen, "I'm just about blank. I must wait until I get some more thoughts about the matter. We haven't had this situation before in any of our other cases. We're just going to wait and see." In contrast, he was also quoted in the *Dallas Morning News*, "We have plans under way but can't reveal them now . . . but we're going to do something." Asked if the plans included filing contempt charges, Davis replied that it was under consideration.[59]

Sometime Saturday, J. Evetts Haley of Canyon, an unsuccessful segregationist candidate for governor, visited the town. He spoke to a group of citizens, suggesting the Texas State Legislature could review the school case and crisis in Mansfield and enact new laws on interposition. Webb Joiner of Arlington, an official in the Citizens' Council, joined Haley and invited everyone to a Citizens' Council meeting on September 6 to discuss interposition at length. Haley claimed segregation to be a state right and condemned the Supreme Court's mandates on integration. He congratulated the Mansfield segregationists for their efforts.[60]

By Monday evening, several meetings were held to organize a third demonstration for Tuesday. J. L. Curry told reporters, "We'll be there with bells on. We don't think any Negroes will show up to go to school but we'll be there anyhow."[61]

On Tuesday morning, September 4, Captain Crowder dispatched six Texas Rangers to the high school grounds. Three more Rangers acted undercover, infiltrating the area as curious bystanders. Arriving at 7:15 A.M., their presence was kept as quiet as possible. As the mob of white residents grew to approximately two hundred, several of the original six Rangers blended into the crowd. Tuesday's press accounts claimed six Rangers were present. The three undercover agents were never explained to the press. A report by Sergeant E. Jay Banks to Homer Garrison on October 8, 1956, explained Crowder's plan and the true number of Rangers present. Banks wrote, "Defensive and offensive equipment for controlling the mob was made ready for instant use, and Captain Crowder gave orders for strategic stationing of men and equipment in the school area."[62] Captain Crowder was one of the six Rangers identified by the press at the school, along with E. Jay Banks, Lewis Rigler, Ernest Daniel, George Roach, and B. C. Currin. County Sheriff Wright joined the Rangers along with his men, George Brakefield, Bob Morton, and Bud Alexander. Two or three Dallas County Sheriff's Department officers were posted at the Tarrant County–Dallas County line on alert if needed. The crowd seemed more subdued Tuesday morning, and Crowder commented to newsmen, "We are not expecting any trouble. I do not think any Negroes will try to enroll."[63]

Huffman and Crowder discussed the situation and agreed to uphold Shivers' recommendations of the previous Friday. If any African American students attempted to enroll at the high school, they would be transferred out of the district to Fort Worth. Mansfield's white teenagers began arriving for the first day of school at 8:00 A.M. Classes began at 8:30. Huffman greeted students at the door. Rangers stood close by and observed. The effigies still hung from the flagpole and the light near the roof directly above the front door. Someone brought a small monkey to school with a round sign tied to its neck reading, "I want to play football at Mansfield High School." It was in reference to the two African American plaintiffs who hoped to play football that fall.[64]

At 9:30 A.M., Reverend D. W. Clark, rector of Saint Vincent's Episcopal Church in Fort Worth entered the crowd to tell people that he came as a Christian to do everything he could to end the controversy. He told the crowd that their assemblage was against "God's law and the law of the land." He stated, "There are Christians in the community who need leadership. They are acting like barbarians. . . . I would particularly like to cut down these effigies. . . . That is blasphemy." Several in the crowd closed in on Clark and shouted and jeered that he had no business being there. One group of men were outraged over his accusations. Sergeant E. Jay Banks pushed through the crowd and protectively escorted Clark to his car. After the rector left, J. L. Curry told several men, "He had about as much business being down here as Grady Hight did." Metcalf added, "Down here we go to church on Sunday. He had no business telling us we should love them like brothers."[65]

About the same time that the Reverend Clark came to Mansfield, a man who believed he was Jesus Christ reincarnated arrived. His real name was William L. Lightfoot Jr. of Dallas, and he was the founder of the United Service-Aid Plan. The plan was "Aimed to end Segregation problems, Misunderstanding, Hatred and Unhappiness among all Peoples Regardless of Age, Race, Creed, Class, Color, or Education." Lightfoot, using the name Jesus Christ, wrote Huffman on September 1 to announce his plan to come to Mansfield on September 4. In the letter, he stated:

> To my great sorrow I read in the papers and saw over T-V [*sic*] the sad plight of the Negro students and their parents who are being bullied and denied their Constitutional Rights to go to a public school near their home like any other citizens in Mansfield, Texas. The Devil is having a Holiday but the Holiday ended at midnight, August 31st. . . .
>
> I am personally coming to Mansfield this Tuesday, Sept. 4th, to personally escort . . . Negro children in and around Mansfield who desire and are entitled to go to school in the Mansfield's public schools. I expect them to be able to register according to the Law with no ifs, ans, [*sic*] or buts about it!
>
> Please tell the people of Mansfield that if there is any trouble or violence in connection with my presence or efforts to keep peace in this case, I shall let loose the Wraft [*sic*] of My Father in Heaven upon every last one of the trouble makers.
>
> I shall come in Peace and I expect to leave in Peace.[66]

Copies of the letter were sent special delivery to J. Edgar Hoover, Eisenhower, Brownell, Shivers, Shepperd, Davis, Hight, Fifth Circuit Court Judge John R. Brown and others. Lightfoot signed all his correspondence "Jesus Christ."[67]

Arriving in Mansfield, Lightfoot went to the local post office and convinced the postmaster to give him a U.S. flag to replace the effigy at the school. He then went to the high school and asked Huffman to help him take down the effigy. Huffman refused. He also sought help from the crowd, but they turned him away. He then went to the fire department and local businesses for a ladder. They also declined to help.[68] According to White House Records, at 10:28 A.M. on Tuesday, September 4, "Jesus Christ" called from Mansfield asking to speak to the president. The call was declined and immediately turned over to an Agent O'Driscoll, either of the Secret Service or the Federal Bureau of Investigation.[69] Returning to the post office for help, Lightfoot claimed that the postmaster "took the American Flag away from me by force . . . with the weak and spineless excuse that he lived in Mansfield and was afraid of what the citizens would do to him.[70] Apparently after this took place, Lightfoot left town disgusted, but without further incident. Later in the day, it was reported the flagpole effigy was removed in order that the U.S. flag might fly over the school grounds on Wednesday, the second day of classes. However, the effigy on the building hung in place for several more days.[71]

Late in the morning on September 4, J. L. Curry brought a petition to the school grounds and claimed it was a true document signed by the African American students and their parents. It supposedly confirmed they had no intention of enrolling in Mansfield High School. He insisted a man from the black section of town wrote the petition which stated:

> We the high school students of the Mansfield Negro School, do hereby wish to inform you that in spite of the favorable decision handed down by the federal court of the State of Louisiana and the City of New Orleans, which gives us the privilege of registering in the high school (white) of Mansfield, we do here and now give our word to the person bearing this letter that we will by no means and under no circumstances apply for registration in the white high school in Mansfield for the term of 1956–1957.
>
> We have all planned to attend school in Fort Worth the entire term unless provision is made at the colored school in Mansfield.[72]

Curry read the petition to reporters announcing he had the school board's permission to do so, but he refused to allow newspeople to examine the signatures. He claimed that the African American man circulated the petition and forwarded the completed form to a white citizen of the community to be presented to the school board. Davis was asked about the possibility that the document was authentic. He told reporters the wording in the petition made it very unlikely to have originated in the black community. Jemmie Irene Moody, mother of Charles Moody, told a reporter she did not remember signing any such paper.[73]

On September 4, Justice Black announced his decision on the petition to stay the court order to integrate. He simply wrote in large letters across the request papers, "Denied." Refusing to postpone the order to integrate, Black sent a clear message to Mansfield's school board. Black upheld the lower court order to integrate the high school immediately. The board's last effort was a direct appeal to the Supreme Court.[74]

On Wednesday morning, September 5, all the African American students traveled by bus to James E. Guinn School and I. M. Terrell High School to register for the 1956–1957 term. Davis announced to the press that the students would remain in the Fort Worth schools until the crowds subsided and it was safe for the children to go to Mansfield High School. "If they can't go down there in peace, there's no alternative," said Davis. Again, later in the evening, Davis disclosed to newspeople the endeavor to enroll the African American students in Mansfield High School was to be abandoned for the present time. Davis stated, "We could not take them in there while that mob is standing there to do violence. There will perhaps be some further legal proceedings in an effort to ease the situation and make it safe for the enrollment of Negro students."[75]

On September 5, many white residents returned to work or stayed home rather than mill around the high school. Only a handful remained on the school grounds that morning. One deputy sheriff and a few Texas Rangers stood in front of the building watching white students file in for the second day of classes. All of the African American teenagers continued to ride the bus to James E. Guinn and I. M. Terrell Schools. The crisis was over. The Mansfield newspaper printed pictures of the crowd with a caption that stated, "The human wall around the school grounds protected it against the deteriorating outside factors."[76]

When President Eisenhower held his weekly press conference on September 5 in Washington, the Mansfield case and crisis were brought up in questioning. Eisenhower clearly displayed his positions on civil rights, school integration, and states' rights. A reporter inquired:

There have been several instances of violence or near violence on the segregation issue as the fall school term begins. In some cases Negro children are risking physical injury to attend school. Do you think there is anything that can be said or done on a national level to help local communities meet this problem without violence?[77]

The president responded:

> Well, in each case I think the local governments have moved
> promptly to stop the violence. And let us remember this: Under
> the law, the Federal government cannot—on the ordinary nor-
> mal case of keeping order and preventing rioting—cannot move
> into a State until the State is not able to handle the matter.
>
> Now in the Texas case there was—the attorney for the stu-
> dents did report this violence and ask help, which apparently
> was the result of unreadiness to obey a Federal court order.
> Then, before anyone could move, the Texas authorities had
> moved and order was restored. So the question became
> unimportant.[78]

Immediately after the president's answer, Sarah McClendon, a
reporter representing the *El Paso Times,* asked Eisenhower if he
had discussed Governor Shivers' statement concerning Mansfield
with anyone in the Justice Department? She explained to the president: "Governor Allan Shivers sent Rangers to defy the Court order, reassigning out Negro pupils, and sent a public statement . . . 'I
defy the Federal government. You tell the Federal courts if they
want to come after anyone, to come after me and cite me in this
matter.' " Eisenhower replied he had not "discussed it." Continuing, he asserted:

> Because you are quoting both an order I haven't read and a state-
> ment that I haven't seen. Now I have—we actually sent for the
> District court order to know what it says. I don't know what it
> says. And remember that the Supreme Court placed in the
> hands of the District judges the primary responsibility for insur-
> ing that progress in every sector was made here. Now just ex-
> actly what Governor Shivers said, I don't know. This is the first
> I have heard of it.[79]

Eisenhower remained as far removed from the Mansfield situation as he could, skirting the issue every time it was brought up.
He continued to espouse the role of the lower courts in implementing and enforcing integration. Because Shivers restored peace,
Eisenhower did not attempt to interfere even though it meant
African Americans were denied their constitutional rights and protection under the law. A *Time* magazine reporter asked the president whether he wished to speak to young Americans through
the press regarding the school integration problems. Eisenhower

delivered one of his sermons on the difficulty in changing the hearts of men. Once again, he warned that "extremists on both sides" must change and recognize the equality of men. "The South is full of people of goodwill, but they are not the ones we now hear," declared the president. "We hear the people that are adamant and are so filled with prejudice that they can't keep still—they even resort to violence; and the same way on the other side of the thing, the people who want to have the whole matter settled today."[80]

Questioned once again on an endorsement of the Supreme Court's school integration mandates, the president stated it did not matter what he thought because it was now law under the Constitution as the Supreme Court interpreted it, and he would uphold the law to the best of his abilities. Later, Eisenhower explained that he did not know how long Shivers meant to "transfer" the African Americans out of the school district and whether it was for their safety that the governor took this step. Justifying his position of noninvolvement, Eisenhower stated:

> When Police power is exercised habitually . . . by the Federal Government, we are in a bad way. So until States show their inability or their refusal to grapple with the question properly . . . we'd better be very careful about moving in and exercising police power.[81]

Eisenhower asked Brownell to look into the case and crisis in Mansfield. Brownell recalled the posture of the executive branch on its responsibilities in Mansfield's desegregation crisis:

> Eisenhower was questioned about Mansfield . . . and immediately referred the matter to me. I had seen the press reports of the Mansfield matter so was ready to give a prompt answer to the President. . . .
> To the best of my knowledge there was no communication between Governor Shivers or his staff, and the White House or the Department of Justice.
> In Mansfield, no plan of desegregation was filed . . . and there was no request from the local District Court for us to intervene. There was therefore no Court-ordered plan to desegregate and obviously no violation of a Court order and no rioting that got beyond the capability of local authorities.
> We therefore advised President Eisenhower that we did not have requisite Federal jurisdiction to enter the Mansfield case. . . .

We were well aware that if we made a test case of *Brown II* at Mansfield or elsewhere on shaky legal grounds, and lost, we would have set back the cause for a long time, and would have strengthened the position taken by the White Citizens Councils throughout the South. Instead, we took the test case in Arkansas [in 1957] where all jurisdictional premises were met.[82]

Members of the administration, using their interpretation of the Supreme Court's decision in *Brown II,* justified staying out of the controversy in Mansfield. Because of Eisenhower's support of states' rights and federal separation of powers, he stood back and watched as African American teenagers were denied their constitutional rights. President Eisenhower and the Federal District Court did not challenge Shivers' use of interposition in Mansfield. To keep peace and order in Texas, the governor prevented the implementation of the federal court-ordered school integration. This was a perfect example of states' rights impeding federal authority. The president and the federal court system allowed it to happen, and the segregationists celebrated.[83]

McClendon's question to Eisenhower on Shivers' defiance of the court order became a political issue in the days following the September 5 news conference. On September 6, Shivers held his own news conference in Austin. He claimed his actions in Mansfield were successful because the crisis was over. Citing the restoration of order and peace at the high school, the governor announced the success of his policy of sending Rangers in to "insure absence of violence and the protection of law-abiding citizens." A reporter told Shivers about McClendon's misquote at the president's news conference. Shivers retorted, "I have not taken any action in defiance of anyone. I acted to prevent trouble and not . . . cause further trouble. So long as I am Governor, I will act to uphold the law and dignity of people in lawful pursuits." The governor then blamed the problems in Mansfield on "paid agitators," referring to the NAACP. He retorted, "Without paid agitators we would not have trouble. . . . And it is unfortunate that in the National Association for the Colored People [sic] some white people are the worst offenders—some prominent in the so-called Liberal Democratic circles in Texas." This was a reference to Ralph W. Yarborough and other less conservative Democrats. In conclusion, Shivers blasted the NAACP once more, "The agitators ought to be put in jail, but unfortunately they are sitting back in plush offices."[84]

On September 6, Davis filed a notice in Federal District Court in Fort Worth. The notice scheduled a meeting on September 17 in district court for three members of the Mansfield school board to

give oral depositions under oath concerning the unsuccessful implementation of the court order to integrate the high school. Specifically, Davis wanted a statement from the board members on
their failure to enroll any African American students into Mansfield High School.[85]

The next day, September 7, John Morsell, NAACP public relations official, released a statement on the policy of the association
with regard to Mansfield:

> In Mansfield, Texas, the course of action pursued at state and
> local levels was in effect a refusal to comply with the desegrega-
> tion order of the U. S. Circuit Court. Such further legal action
> as may be needed to secure admission of the Negro students to
> the Mansfield High School will be taken.
>   . . . In Mansfield, a cheap and temporary peace was purchased
> by surrendering to those who threatened violent overthrow of
> the law. Recent world history contains a number of deadly par-
> allels to this kind of appeasement.[86]

Roy Wilkins, executive secretary of the NAACP, reiterated this
view a few days later, saying that when a court order had been
issued, as in Mansfield, "Governor Shivers did not measure up to
the demands of his office."[87] Governor Shivers' manipulations in
Texas succeeded in widening the gap between the already polarized sides on the southern school integration controversy.

After Eisenhower's September 5 news conference, Thurgood
Marshall spoke out against Shivers' actions in the Mansfield crisis. Marshall believed Shivers' maneuvering with the Texas Rangers and the school board were "wrong" and "above all law." He
maintained that the president misunderstood the implications of
Shivers' statements and orders in the incidents surrounding the
crisis. Shivers' method of "transfer" was "completely opposite"
from the directives of the Supreme Court on school integration.
Referring to Texas Attorney General John Ben Shepperd, Marshall declared, "Governor Shivers is being advised by an attorney
who thinks that the governor is above all law and that the federal courts have no means of proceeding against his action. That is
wrong."[88]

Shepperd was furious over Marshall's comments, and the next
day released a statement in his official capacity of Texas attorney
general. Calling Marshall's words a "verbal attack" and "outra-
geously vicious," Shepperd countered, "[It is] just another con-
certed scheme by the NAACP to stir up hatred among the people

of Texas who have lived side by side in peace for years." Questioning Marshall's professional integrity, Shepperd challenged:

Marshall's statement was not only a misstatement of the true facts but of the law as well. He knows the Supreme Court has not passed on the power of the school districts to make transfers. Many states have called special sessions of their legislatures to pass laws regarding transfers, but Texas already had a strong one in this regard. If he thinks the action of the Governor of Texas in trying to maintain law and order and establish peace among the citizens was in contempt of Federal Court, he should cite him before that Court—and I defy him to do so.[89]

In conclusion, the Texas attorney general declared, "The NAACP and other outside interests whose objectives are to stir up trouble should keep out of Texas matters for the people of Texas are quite capable of working out their own problems."[90] Shepperd failed to realize that several thousand law-abiding African American native Texans belonged to the NAACP. These citizens were not "outside agitators." The events in Mansfield, surrounding the school integration case and the crisis, originated in the black section of town in the homes and church of Mansfield's African American Texans.

On September 6, Eisenhower was sent two letters dissecting his remarks of September 5. Both requested him to reconsider his expression "extremists on both sides." Each explained to the president the misconception of referring to African Americans peacefully acquiring their constitutional rights through the court system as "extremists." The letters pointed out the fallacy of comparing the African Americans' civil rights movement with the segregationists' massive resistance movement.

Thurgood Marshall wrote the first letter, opening with a paragraph on the importance of presidential leadership and guidance. Marshall hoped the president would "take an unequivocal stand against mob action wherever it occurs and regardless of the participants." He explained that many citizens were upset with the president's statements of September 5 concerning integration and civil rights. After quoting Eisenhower's answers at the press conference, Marshall professed his fear that many of the president's words not only gave credibility to the resistance movement but also abandoned "Americans who seek only their lawful rights in a lawful manner, often after unbelievably long periods of waiting." Describing the escalating actions of the crowds in school integration incidents, including Mansfield, Marshall wrote, "Please bear in mind that at this stage it is not a question of Negro citizens versus white citizens, but it is a question of unlawful violent opposition against the orders of duly constituted federal courts." Referring to Eisenhower's phrase "extremists on both sides," Marshall continued:

These are the only "two [sides]" involved. Surely, you do not mean to equate lawless mobs with federal courts as "extremists." Certainly the dozen Negro children involved in each instance trying to get an adequate education in a lawful manner could not be classified as "extremists."

... I fear that you are comparing the lawless mobs with those of us who are trying under most difficult conditions to obtain the rights which have been enjoyed by all other Americans for these many years. If so, we respectfully suggest that the use of this language in this context is most unfortunate. There is nothing [to] ... justify the use of such phrases in commenting upon ... Mansfield, Texas. To do so ... tends to alleviate the full responsibility of the lawless mob by giving the impression that there is someone else or some group of people who are equally guilty of bringing about the lawless situation. Otherwise, the real guilty parties would be the framers of the Declaration of Independence and the Constitution of the United States.[91]

Marshall closed the letter "respectfully," suggesting that the president reevaluate his statements and "speak out in forthright terms," denouncing anyone interfering with the federal judicial process.[92]

A second letter to Eisenhower, sent on the same day, was written by Norman Thomas, a syndicated columnist and a six-time Socialist Party candidate for president. Thomas wrote about his concerns for the "Negro students" in Mansfield:

It would appear that Gov. Shivers' idea of order is to use his police power to do what the mob wants; namely, bar Negro students from any school. Surely, it is not an "extreme" demand that our colored fellow citizens make when they request some better example of enforcement of the law than that.

I confess that I was a little disquieted about your reference to "extremists on both sides." Unfortunately, that expression is too often understood as apportioning guilt about equally between the aggressive segregationists and the advocates of obedience to the order of the Court.[93]

Thomas also asked the president to rethink his manner of speech on the civil rights issues. He hoped the president would consider acknowledging the peaceful and lawful movement for civil rights demonstrated by African Americans, emphasizing the "restraint of a race whose dignity and patience in the face of persecution is worthy of all praise."[94]

By the September 11 presidential press conference, it seemed as though Eisenhower reconsidered his phrasing of answers on civil rights. His statements were construed by reporters as "less cautious" and more direct. Still, the "middle-of-the-road" attitude remained. Asked for a "formula" for the federal government to intervene in school integration disputes, the president replied with a simplified version of the established executive branch's responsibilities if a lower court requested aid. Eisenhower explained, "[The] Court must decide whether it believes . . . someone is in contempt of that Court. . . . [Then] it is customary for the Court to call in the Justice Department to assist in bringing the evidence and thrashing the case out." Referring to the involvement of states, Eisenhower's answer proved more direct than in the past. He professed:

> The States . . . would exercise first of all their responsibility and authority in carrying out police functions to preserve law and order . . . and certainly a concurrent responsibility . . . to help to see that that State has—the orders of a District Court are carried out.

This was not what he stated in his previous press conference. With regard to the Mansfield school integration case, a reporter inquired if the president had seen the court order. He confirmed that he had seen it and that Brownell wrote across the bottom of it the same policy on federal intervention that the president disclosed earlier to the press. Further reaching questions on this policy seemed to confuse Eisenhower. He gave sketchy and faulty legal answers when pressed. Clearly the president did not thoroughly understand the legal ramifications of the responsibilities of the executive branch of the federal government, especially with regard to *Brown II.*[95]

On September 17, Davis and Tate took oral depositions from Rawdon, Huffman, and Willie L. Brown, principal of Mansfield Colored School. They hoped this would help them in "further proceedings" in the Mansfield school integration case. The hearing

was held with a district court reporter present to record the testimony of the three men under oath. Huffman and Rawdon insisted
Mansfield was not ready for desegregation. Rawdon claimed the
white community did not want to integrate the school and neither
did the school board. He explained that the board voted to integrate on August 28 and comply with the order, only if all other legal recourse failed. Brown described a petition he sent to all the
African American parents in Mansfield to support a proposal to
elevate the Mansfield Colored School to "high school status." He
reported that all but two families signed the petition and the
African American families wished to continue to send their children to the high schools in Fort Worth if the "colored" school
could not be upgraded.[96]

On September 25, Gooch, Cantey, and R. K. Hanger, lawyers for
the Mansfield school board, appealed directly to the United States
Supreme Court to overturn the lower courts' decisions to integrate
Mansfield High School. The lawyers contended that the lower
courts, in ordering an immediate move to desegregate, did not consider the local problems and varied programs of implementing
school integration.[97] On December 3, the Supreme Court denied
hearing the appeal. The Court chose not to accept the official writ
of certiorari. For the Mansfield school board, it was the end of the
process. The court order for immediate integration of the high
school remained.[98]

The denied appeal should have placed the plaintiffs in a strong
position for filing contempt charges against the defendants, but
they never did. Davis recalled the African American families of
Mansfield were fearful and apprehensive about furthering their
cause for school integration. He believed the white community's
actions shocked the plaintiffs and their families into discontinuing
the struggle. The African American parents chose not to subject
their teenaged children to the hatred and animosity exemplified by
the radical segregationists within the crowd at the high school.
Through the fall, events occurring in Texas intensified the commitment of the African American families in Mansfield to "let
it rest."[99]

7. A Significant Aftermath: The Mansfield School Integration Case and Crisis

In the fall of 1956, many of Mansfield's African Americans were deeply saddened and bewildered by the crisis at the high school that resulted from their hard-won integration court order. They believed their efforts to integrate had failed dismally. What they did not comprehend at the time was the success of their courage and integrity. Many people in the town, state, and nation quietly applauded their calm fortitude and peaceful behavior throughout their ordeal. In the face of threats, cross burnings, hanging effigies, racial slurs on signs, and the crowds on the school grounds, especially the outspoken radical segregationists, the African American residents went about their daily routines with dignity.

The inception and execution of the Mansfield school integration case was a pathway to equality. The African Americans involved in the case initiated a slow breakdown of the suppressive southern caste system in their town. The state and the nation watched. The segregationists were determined to resist change and force the town's African Americans back into their traditional roles. The security, safety, and strength of the close-knit African American community within Mansfield were challenged by threats and displays of violence from radical white segregationists. On the surface, the segregationists succeeded, but emotionally and psychologically the African Americans in Mansfield never returned to "second-class status." The Mansfield case created a pathway forward for the younger generation of African Americans to slowly forge ahead in their search for equality. Change came haltingly, but there was no turning back.

Mansfield's African American residents remained fearful of repercussions from the white radical segregationists for years after the crisis at the high school. Throughout the coming months, events occurred in the town and state, and across the country, reinforcing their concerns. The momentum of the southern resistance movement increased with each new racially motivated incident in the South. At the national level, President Eisenhower continued to maintain a low profile on civil rights issues, stepping in only when no other alternative existed. In 1956 and 1957, every branch of the Texas state government joined in efforts to quell school integration within the state. In Mansfield the black community's anxiety created by their own case and crisis, and magnified by the increasing racial suppression in Texas, initiated a begrudged commitment by the older African American residents to return, at least on the surface, to the safety of the status quo.

Mansfield was not the only town in Texas battling over school integration. Less than a week after the Mansfield crisis, white students at Texarkana Junior College in Texarkana, Texas, held their own anti-integration demonstration, turning away two African Americans attempting to enroll under a federal court order. W. H. Stillwell, president of the college, announced to the demonstrators, "If integration results in lowering educational standards, it is not only your right but your duty to resist it." Governor Shivers sent Texas Rangers to the campus with orders similar to those he used in Mansfield. The black students asked the Rangers for help, but Sergeant Jay Banks, one of the Rangers also sent to Mansfield, reiterated the governor's instructions, "Our orders are to maintain order and to keep down violence. We are to take no part in the integration dispute and we are not going to escort anyone in or out of the college."[1]

Ulysses Simpson Tate was the attorney for the Texarkana plaintiffs. Seeking assistance from President Eisenhower, Tate sent a telegram to the White House describing the situation in Texas. He wrote:

A state of general disorder prevails to intimidate and threaten the Negro population of the community. Texas Rangers are present at the scene but acting under orders from the governor they refuse to provide safe conduct for the Negro students to and from classes. Although Negro students now attend more than half of the thirty three junior colleges in the state. . . . [Shivers] has sent Rangers but with the orders to protect the will of the mob. . . . these Negro students and their families are without protection in their persons and in their rights at the county and state level. . . . Unless . . . help is provided by your office a state of anarchy will exist as to these Negro students and they will be at the mercy of a maddened mob and without protection of either their persons or their civil rights at the county, the state and the federal levels.[2]

On September 17, Eisenhower answered in a brief letter in which he restated his abhorrence to violence and disorder:

The use of violence is directly opposed to the traditional American way of settling differences of opinions through peaceful and law-abiding means. I have repeatedly expressed my prayerful hope that we will not allow anger and bitterness on either side of this critical problem to defeat its solution.[3]

The president concluded by informing Tate that the United States attorney general, Herbert Brownell, had been asked to "look into the matters you have described." No assistance ever came from the White House. After several tension-filled days, the junior college remained segregated. The first African American enrolled in the school in 1963.[4]

On September 18, Governor Shivers officially announced he would once again cross party lines and support President Eisenhower for reelection. Shivers released a statement the same day explaining his decision. In part it stated, "I believe he has proved himself to be a bigger and better man, by any and all the political, moral and spiritual standards by which we judge men, than his opponent of 1952 and 1956. . . . The answer for me is still Dwight David Eisenhower." Shivers actively supported the president, and in November, Eisenhower carried Texas and the nation to be reelected for a second term.[5]

At the national level, three towns stood out because of school integration incidents. Sturgis and Clay, Kentucky, and Clinton, Tennessee, experienced mob action against federal court orders to integrate. The governors of both states, Frank Clement of Tennessee and A. B. Chandler of Kentucky, called in their state's National Guard to uphold the court orders to integrate the three school systems. Chandler explained his actions, "Mobs led by bad tempered men were taking over. You can't let mobs enforce the law. The rights of people were at stake." Clement, in a radio address broadcasted across the state, explained he could not "sit back as governor and allow a lawless element to take over a town and county in Tennessee." Using National Guardsmen instead of Texas Rangers, Chandler and Clement used the same state powers, upheld the same responsibilities to keep law and order, and kept peace within their states in the same way that Shivers had done in Texas, with one exception. Shivers maintained segregation; Clement and Chandler enforced integration.[6]

On September 19, President Eisenhower campaigned on radio and television. Beginning a review of his administration's accomplishments, he stated, "Peace, like all virtues, begins at home." Later turning to civil rights, the president repeated his position:

> Peace in our society involves . . . understanding and tolerance among all creeds and races. . . .
>
> We have applied, . . . a clear philosophy to the whole conduct of the government. We have rejected all concept of a nation divided into sections, groups or factions. We have insisted that, in the American design, each group in our nation may have special problems, but none has special rights. Each has peculiar needs, but none has peculiar privileges. And the supreme concern, equal for all, is the justice, the opportunity, and the unity shared by 168 million Americans.
>
> We have shown this concern by working to secure, wherever the authority of the Federal Government extends, equality of rights and opportunity for all men regardless of race or color.[7]

Eisenhower and his administration carefully maneuvered through the school integration struggles in the fall of 1956. With the election only two months away, Eisenhower was determined to maintain his "middle-of-the-road" philosophy. He believed his commitment to moderation prevented the alienation of voters, both black and white. His speeches throughout the coming year were homilies laced with praise for civil rights and racial equality, but there was little indication during the campaign that the president was willing to back his words with action.[8]

It was events in Little Rock, Arkansas, in 1957, rather than those in Mansfield a year earlier, that forced the executive branch to act in the area of civil rights. For four years, Eisenhower and his administrators proclaimed what conditions had to be present for the executive branch to intervene in school integration cases. The criteria for intervention was met at Little Rock's Central High School largely because of the actions of Federal Judge Ronald N. Davies and the Little Rock mayor, Woodrow Wilson Mann.[9]

African American families in Little Rock successfully obtained a federal court order to integrate Central High School. In the fall of 1957, the school board agreed to uphold the order and to proceed with integration. On the pretext of preventing violence, Governor Orval Faubus sent the Arkansas National Guard to the high school. But as it soon became clear, his goal was to maintain segregation. Faubus' orders mimicked Shivers' orders of a year earlier to the Rangers in Mansfield. For several months before the confrontation at Central High School, Faubus contemplated his role as the governor in the integration dilemma. In late spring 1957, Little Rock's Citizens' Council president and defeated school board candidate, Robert E. Brown, wrote an open letter to Faubus outlining the Faubus-Shivers similarities. He suggested that Faubus could take the same path the Texas governor took in Mansfield. "As sovereign head of the state," Brown explained, ". . . you are immune to federal court orders." Brown's letter was used in hundreds of circulars and advertisements across the state promoting state law over federal law. Throughout the summer, Faubus attempted to remain aloof and uninvolved. In July he told the press, "Everyone knows no state law supersedes a federal law, . . . If anyone expects me to try to use them to supersede federal laws they are wrong." [10]

In September, when Faubus went against his earlier words and sent the National Guard in as a state police force, the president and Brownell arranged several meetings and exchanged numerous telegrams and phone calls with Faubus to discuss the situation in Little Rock. It became obvious during the impasse in September that the governor was not following through on agreements negotiated with Eisenhower and Brownell. [11]

Governor Shivers visited Eisenhower and Brownell in the midst of the strained conversations with Faubus at the president's vacation home in Newport, Rhode Island. Shivers later recalled discussing integration and Little Rock with the president:

> It [integration] was something that all of us knew was going to come. It was a question of degree, how fast, in what measure it came. I don't think any of us really realized that it was going to . . . become the great burning issue, violence and non-violence, that it has become. During the Little Rock controversy, I went up to, I think Newport and visited with Eisenhower and with Brownell, trying to keep them from sending troops in there, trying to get them to send US Marshals, if they were going to do anything. They had to do something. And they said, "Governor Faubus has absolutely lied to us about it," and I'm inclined to think that's true. [12]

Ironically, only one year after the Mansfield crisis, Shivers was advising Eisenhower and Brownell on how to handle Faubus. Interviewed years later, Shivers was asked how the president reacted to the Texas governor's suggestions. Shivers stated, ". . . he was leaving it to Brownell and the others [to handle]. He didn't know the legal ramifications. . . . he wasn't going to let a governor of a state run over the President of the United States. I don't blame him for that." [13]

Brownell advised the president that the executive branch could not ignore the requests for intervention. Neither Faubus nor Eisenhower predicted the commitment of Judge Davies to see the court order through implementation. Davies called upon the Justice Department to investigate Faubus and other segregationists in Little Rock on possible obstruction of justice charges. Later, the judge asked the Department of Justice to file injunction proceedings against those preventing integration, including Faubus. Under court order, the governor removed the guardsmen from the high school and left the volatile situation in the hands of the local police. Enraged mobs gathered at the school and refused to let the young African American teenagers enter the building. Mayor Mann sought help from the president, asking him to call in federal troops to maintain order. Eisenhower, by his own interpretation, could not back away. On September 24, 1957, the president federalized the Arkansas National Guard and returned 9,936 men to Little Rock and the high school to enforce integration. On the same day, he ordered 1,000 paratroopers from the U.S. Army's 101st Airborne Division into Little Rock to escort the African American students to their classes. [14]

The president issued a Proclamation of Obstruction of Justice ordering anyone preventing the implementation of the school integration order to immediately refrain from their unlawful activities. Citing in part, Chapter 15, Title 10, Sections 332–334 of the United States Code, Eisenhower asserted his authority to send federal troops into areas where obstruction of justice prevented laws from being carried out. On November 7, Brownell wrote the president a long letter that carefully outlined the legality of presidential authority in the use of federal troops to quell civil disturbances. Reviewing the statutes empowering the president to order troops into a state, Brownell explained, ". . . a series of statutes of broad sweep enable the President to deal effectively with civil disturbances within a State when compelling circumstances are present." Referring to Title 10, Section 332, he wrote:

> The President is vested with . . . authority as to the militia and
> Armed Forces when, in his judgement, unlawful obstructions,
> combinations, or assemblages, or rebellion against the authority
> of the United States makes it impracticable to enforce the
> laws of the United States in any State by the ordinary course
> of judicial proceedings. [15]

Continuing, Brownell explained the importance of Section 333, similar to Section 332:

> [It] gives the President like powers to suppress in a State any insurrection, domestic violence, unlawful combination, or conspiracy which so hinders the execution of the laws of the State and of the United States that any class of its people is deprived of a right, privilege, immunity, or protection named in the Constitution and secured by law, and the constituted authorities of the State are unable, fail, or refuse to protect the right, privilege, or immunity, or to give that protection, or which opposes or obstructs the execution of the laws of the United States or impedes the course of justice under those laws. Congress declared in this statute that when the execution of the laws is so hindered, without State protection, the State shall be considered to have denied the equal protection of the laws secured by the Constitution.[16]

Emphasizing Sections 332 and 333, the attorney general explained to Eisenhower that Section 334 required a formal proclamation be made before either of the previous statutes could be "invoked." The president was reassured that all criteria for the use of federal troops in Little Rock were implemented correctly.[17]

In conclusion, Brownell confirmed that the executive branch's use of federal authority and that the action taken in Little Rock was the only proper solution. Brownell closed:

> When an unruly mob arrogates to itself the power to nullify a constitutionally-secured right, a statutory prescription, and a court order, it may reasonably be assumed that the danger of a fast-moving, destructive volcanic force is immediately present. Success of the unlawful assemblage in Little Rock inevitably would have led to mob rule, and a probable breakdown of law and order in an ever-increasing area. When a local and State Government is unable or unwilling to meet such a threat, the Federal Government is not impotent.[18]

The president and the attorney general chose to institute these statutes to justify their use of federal troops in Little Rock, but one year earlier, in the crisis in Mansfield, they had interpreted the law and the authority of the executive branch quite differently. In 1956 they had treated the three statutes as if they had not existed.

In the midst of the Little Rock crisis, Eisenhower signed the Civil

Rights Bill of 1957. This was a revised and politically "softer" version of Brownell's unsuccessful 1956 Civil Rights Bill. Texas Senator Lyndon B. Johnson and Speaker of the House Sam Rayburn negotiated the bill through the House and Senate, even withstanding a filibuster of slightly over twenty-four hours by Senator Strom Thurmond. The bill was described as a watered-down version of the original. The 1957 act created a Civil Rights Commission, a separate Civil Rights Division within the Justice Department, and measures to ensure African American voting rights. Section III, however, was rewritten and amended several times. The Justice Department was not allowed to initiate injunctions against civil rights offenders. In addition, jury trials were limited to voting rights violations, and in these cases only the judge could call for a jury. Although during deliberations, Eisenhower stated with disgust, "I cannot understand how eighteen Southern Senators can bamboozle the entire Senate," his lack of support, guidance, and clear endorsement strengthened the southern Democrats' determination to push for jury trials. The bill, when finally accepted, became the first civil rights legislation since Reconstruction.[19]

In the year following the Mansfield crisis, the resistance movement in Texas took control of the state at every level, solidifying the commitment to keep Texas segregated by all legal means deemed necessary. The Texas State Democratic Executive Committee met on September 10. The sixty-two committee members stood and cheered Shivers' actions in the Mansfield crisis. A resolution praising his orders passed without discussion or dissent. The committee then proceeded to pass a second resolution unanimously to place the three referendum statements against integration, from the July primary ballot, in the Texas Democratic Party platform. Both resolutions were presented to the platform committee before being sent to the full convention for a final vote. The resolutions passed the convention and were added to the party platform. They also endorsed a request to the governor to call a special session of the state legislature to enact the three prosegregation statements into law.[20]

The resolution praising Shivers asserted that Mansfield had been selected by the NAACP to promote the "destruction of the southern way of life and Texas traditions." Blaming the NAACP for the state's racial problems, the resolution declared, ". . . at the instigation of the NAACP, the people of these United States have seen exhibitions of rule by force comparable only to the treatment of the South during the tragic Reconstruction Era." It described Shivers as a governor of "indomitable courage" and a man of "wisdom without bombast." In 1956 the controlling political party in Texas easily and readily supported segregation practices throughout the state, denying black Texans their constitutional civil rights under the law of the land.[21]

The members of the governor's Texas Advisory Committee on Segregation in the Public Schools, established in July 1955, released their completed report, dated September 1, 1956, on September 24. The Legal and Legislative Sub-Committee, operating within the advisory committee, met throughout the previous year to compile the report. The result of the research and discussions was the development of a program, adopted by a vote of thirteen to five, to legally circumvent the Supreme Court decisions in *Brown I* and *Brown II*, except where school integration was accepted by popular election, and then only under specific circumstances. The plan, if accepted and implemented, would not only stop the process of school integration in districts ready to accept it but would return newly integrated school districts to dual systems.[22]

The subcommittee's report claimed the Supreme Court's integration mandates were "clearly wrong and judicially unsound." The Court's decisions, the subcommittee stated, represented "a deliberate and willful departure from or violence to the United States Constitution." In a section titled "The Court's Scientific Authorities," the report disapproved of the justices' use of Gunnar Myrdal et al.'s *American Dilemma* and professed:

> This, then is the decision which has been used as the wedge which will force integration of not only our schools, but also our transportation system, our recreation system, and every other facet of our lives. . . . we reiterate our firm conviction that if this decision is left unchallenged in our law books, the beginning of the end of our liberty is upon us.[23]

The report addressed the state's current status on school integration, the "will of the people," in Texas, including a summary of the July Democratic Primary Ballot referendums on segregation and the definition and implementation of interposition. Quoting from five school integration cases that they believed were significant to the Texas education system, including *Jackson v. Rawdon*, the subcommittee surmised that the decisions in these cases were "quite clear as to what the States are and are not required to do." Taking into consideration all the information the report outlined, the subcommittee proceeded to introduce twenty proposals they believed the State legislature should pass into law. Presenting the recommendations, the authors stated:

> This subcommittee finds itself confronted with a dilemma. The federal courts, correct or not, have ruled in favor of integration, but the people of the State of Texas have made their wishes in regard to segregation quite clear. We believe that the recommendations herein submitted reconcile the two as far as is possible.[24]

The members of the subcommittee believed their proposals could easily bypass the straightforward language of the court system. The recommendations contained evasive tactics. Any student would be exempted under certain conditions from attending an integrated school. The state would pay tuition for students from integrated districts wishing to transfer to a state-funded nonsectarian private school. The only way a school board could abolish a dual system of education would be by popular vote of the residents of the school district, and in cases of lawsuits or racial disputes the local school boards would not be held accountable because a special joint legislative committee would be appointed to handle the responsibility.[25]

The report concluded with a final call for the Texas State Legislature to support an amendment to the United States Constitution redefining the Ninth and Tenth Amendments. It would limit the powers of the federal government over state and local governments. The resistance to change and the disdain for integration were now found at the highest levels of state government and by a majority of the appointed members of the governor's advisory committee.[26]

The governor turned over the twenty recommendations to Attorney General Shepperd to be transformed into bills. Shivers planned to submit them for consideration at the opening of the next legislative session in January 1957. The recommendations, if passed into law, would resegregate already integrated school districts. Those still segregated would remain so under the protection of several of the new laws created to circumvent the federal and state courts' school integration mandates. The dual system of education in Texas would be reestablished and securely entrenched under the newly passed provisions.[27]

During 1956 several state governments across the South waged a legal battle to outlaw the NAACP. Tactics used to alienate the

NAACP from southern African Americans included propaganda linking the association with communism, various subversive "un-American" activities, and the illegal use of funds. States charged the association with misuse of corporate privileges within the state, evading corporate and franchise taxes in accordance with state law, and barratry, the solicitation of plaintiffs.[28]

In September 1956, Texas, joining other southern states, launched an extensive investigation into the management and organization of the NAACP within the state. The Mansfield school integration case and crisis became a part of the inquest, and L. Clifford Davis, the attorney for the plaintiffs, was investigated on possible barratry charges. On September 13, Davis Grant, first assistant to the state attorney general, wrote to J. A. Gooch to explain that he and another assistant state attorney, Horace Wimberly, intended to be present when Davis took depositions from the school board members in Mansfield on September 17. It was his opinion, Grant stated, "that Davis and other NAACP attorneys were probably soliciting business." Grant told Gooch that general counsel for the State Bar of Texas, John R. Grace, pursued Grant to investigate for barratry. Grant wrote, ". . . he would like for us to explore the possibility of developing evidence that this is true." On the same day, another assistant state attorney, Elbert Morrow, arrived at Tate's offices in Dallas and spent hours photographing NAACP and the Fund's records.[29]

On September 14, an unidentified investigator from the Attorney General's Office arrived in Mansfield and spent two days interviewing residents about their knowledge of Davis' activities. During his stay, the investigator interviewed only one African American, the owner of the barbecue stand where blacks and whites ate in separate areas. On the other hand, the three-and-one-half-page report contained statements from several white residents, including Constable Tom Beard, Willie Pigg, O. C. Rawdon, and R. L. Huffman. The information given was filled with "hearsay" and rumors. No concrete evidence was presented in the report proving barratry against Davis.[30]

On September 18, 1956, Attorney General Shepperd announced a state investigation into all branches of the NAACP in Texas. He informed the NAACP officers that under his authority, vested him by the state of Texas, representatives from the state would be sent to their offices and should be given access to all records upon request. He was investigating five possible violations of the association under Texas law. These included: acting as a business corporation in Texas without a permit; failing to file a franchise tax report;

failing to pay franchise tax to the state including penalties for evasion; participating in political activity prohibited by corporations
within Texas; and determining what other laws were in violation
by the corporation. Thus began a comprehensive "witch hunt"
into over one hundred branches of the NAACP in the state.[31]

District Judge Otis T. Dunagan of Tyler granted a temporary re-
straining order against the NAACP in Texas on September 21, effectively putting the association "out of business" in the state.
The charges brought before Judge Dunagan by Shepperd claimed:
the NAACP was a corporation based in New York and, therefore,
was foreign to the state and operating without a permit; it consistently violated barratry laws, soliciting business and plaintiffs in
school integration cases that brought "racial prejudice, picketing,
riots, and other unlawful acts" upon the citizens of Texas; it
profited from its business in the state and was required to pay
taxes as a corporate entity; and the association practiced law ille-
gally and outside the bounds of a corporation within Texas. In the
petition to the court, Shepperd wrote, "For over 100 years the
white and colored races in said state have lived together peacefully
and in harmony without strife or litigation and that, were it not for
the activities of the defendants [the NAACP], they would now and
in the future continue to do so." A hearing on a temporary injunction against the NAACP was scheduled for September 28.[32]

Thurgood Marshall believed Shivers and Shepperd were attempting to "cover up" for the negative national publicity they received
after the Mansfield and Texarkana school integration incidents.
Shepperd was hoping to fill Price Daniel's United States Senate
seat when Daniel became governor. Marshall dismissed Shivers as
a "lame duck."[33]

Preceding the trial in Tyler, a Court of Inquiry was held in
Kennedale, Texas, on September 26 and 27. Assistant Attorney
General Bill King subpoenaed several key African American participants in the Mansfield school integration case to testify before
justice of the peace, B. T. Webb. King was authorized by the state to
question the black residents of Mansfield on the case and the activities of Davis and Tate, including possible barratry violations by
both men. The findings were to be used against the NAACP in
Shepperd's upcoming lawsuit.[34]

On the first day, T. M. Moody and John F. Lawson were called in
to testify.[35] On the second day, deputy sheriffs met the Mansfield
school bus at I. M. Terrell High School and escorted Floyd and
Charles Moody to the Kennedale Fire Department, where the
Court of Inquiry was held. Under oath J. E., Floyd, and Charles

Moody answered questions concerning the manner and sequence in which Davis was retained by the black community in Mansfield to represent them in the school integration lawsuit.[36]

J. E. Moody seemed cautious and vague in answering the attorney's questions. He was asked if he discussed the previous day's inquiry with T. M. Moody. He acknowledged that he had. He was asked if he had ever solicited or signed any document requesting Davis to represent his son, Floyd Moody, in the school integration case. He answered, "I did not," but in further testimony, he admitted to meeting with Davis, T. M. Moody, John F. Lawson, and several others in Davis' law offices to discuss the situation in Mansfield. He clearly stated several times that he let T. M. Moody and John F. Lawson do the talking and make the decisions. J. E. Moody discussed the suit and the possibility of sending his son to Mansfield High School. He also admitted that a new black high school was what he originally thought was needed in Mansfield. He explained how he signed a petition requesting the school board to open the white high school to the black students. In seventeen pages of testimony, J. E. Moody gave the impression he was skirting the issues. It was unclear whether he truly allowed T. M. Moody and Davis to take over and file the suit for him, or if he were intimidated by the proceedings, and, prompted by T. M. Moody, carefully avoided lengthy, in-depth answers.[37]

The teenagers, Floyd and Charles Moody, gave depositions recounting what they knew of the lawsuit, how many times they had met with Davis, and their recollection of efforts to integrate the white high school in Mansfield. Both were asked if they ever signed any papers requesting Davis to represent them in a school integration case. Both boys answered they had not. During the inquiry, the attorney asked many of the same questions several times. At times the two teens seemed scared, confused, and coerced. Floyd Moody carefully described the 1955 meeting at the high school with Superintendent Huffman. Charles Moody explained the events surrounding the meeting at T. M. Moody's home in September 1955, where final decisions were made on filing the school integration lawsuit. These testimonies were placed on record but were never used as evidence in a court of law.[38]

The state attorney general also ordered an investigation into the role Tate played in the Mansfield school integration case. When attorneys with Shepperd met to formulate a brief against the NAACP, they discussed Tate's part in several school integration cases in Texas. In notes taken at the meeting, Tate's innocence on barratry in the Mansfield case was clarified. In longhand on yellow legal paper, a notation described Tate's entrance into the Mansfield case to assist Davis. The abbreviated message stated, "NAACP + Fund D/n [did not] participate until L. C. Davis asked that they enter—Tate + Davis agreed that Tate would act as Reg. [regular] counsel for NAACP—D/n ask Davis to solicit Pl's [plaintiffs]— H/n [has not] solicited Pl's in Mansfield." Clearly, according to this note, Tate had followed proper procedures and was not guilty of barratry.[39]

On September 28, race relations in Texas reached a new level of tension when the trial brought by the state of Texas against the NAACP convened in Tyler. Testimony and arguments were heard for seventeen days in a packed courtroom. Eleven of the seventeen days were used by the state to present 472 exhibits supposedly proving the NAACP's unlawful practices within Texas. Numerous exhibits pertained directly to the Mansfield school integration case. Several canceled checks were admitted as evidence. These checks were drawn from the Southwest Regional Conference of Branches account and made payable to Davis and Tate for services rendered and expenses incurred while representing the plaintiffs in the Mansfield case. Other testimony given by Thurgood Marshall and Tate indicated that the proper client-attorney procedure was established in the Mansfield case. Tate testified he met with the plaintiff's parents in Davis' office in Fort Worth to discuss the school integration case. He explained he did not talk to the teen-aged plaintiffs. It was not legally necessary for Tate to meet with the young boys because they were underaged and their parents initiated the lawsuit acting in their behalf. In redirected examination, W. J. Durham, representing the NAACP, asked Tate, ". . . how did you get into the Mansfield case?" Tate explained, "Clifford L. Davis [*sic*], who practices law in Fort Worth invited me into that case." Durham then inquired, "Then you talked with the parents of those children before you filed suit?" Tate answered, "That's right."[40]

In the NAACP's closing statement, Marshall delivered a blow to segregationists. He told the court:

> The intent [of the suit] is to keep status quo. This is not a status quo situation, it's the opposite of the status quo. . . . The people in these organizations in Texas are not people who willingly violate the laws. . . . we have done nothing worse than getting Texas people to obey the law of the land. . . . Once the Supreme Court decides the law in a particular case, regardless of what it is, the Supreme Court can't go from county to county

to enforce it. Negroes' faith in American life is supported by the belief they can get justice in the courts.[41]

Judge Otis Dunagan took only four hours to determine his decision and grant a temporary injunction against the NAACP in Texas. The NAACP was restrained from activities within the state, including collection of contributions and filing lawsuits. Later, on May 8, 1957, Dunagan issued a permanent injunction against the NAACP. This injunction lessened certain stipulations of the temporary injunction. The NAACP was allowed to direct educational and charitable programs, but Dunagan ordered them to refrain from any legal activity. The association was also mandated to pay Texas franchise tax. For several years, the NAACP and the Fund remained estranged from open operations in Texas until federal courts reversed the decision as unconstitutional.[42]

Interviewed in his chambers in late October 1956, Judge Dunagan explained, "Don't think this is a suit against the nigger people. . . . Actually it isn't. It's true it [the NAACP] is an organization for the nigger people, but after all, three fourths of its directors are white people. Later, Dunagan, referring to "the Nigrahs," stated, "I ain't got nothing against the nigger people." On November 14, the Texas Attorney General's Office sent a letter, including the writ of temporary injunction, to T. M. Moody that closed down Mansfield's NAACP Branch 61, Area 9.[43]

In January 1957, the Fifty-Fifth Texas State Legislature opened a new session with Governor Shivers' farewell address. Shivers briefly introduced the Legal and Legislative Sub-Committee of the Advisory Committee on Segregation in the Public Schools' numerous proposals to promote segregation practices throughout the state. He reminded the legislators of the results of the State Democratic Primary referendums accepted by a majority of Texas voters in July. Describing the report, the governor stated he believed it took "into account . . . the legal and moral aspects of the integration-segregation struggle." Shivers told the legislators:

In connection with the public schools, I feel I should mention the controversial but inevitable problem of *segregation*. I hope and believe that this Legislature will approach that sensitive problem, at the proper time, with a minimum of emotion and a maximum of common sense.

It is an important problem, and we cannot solve it merely by hoping that it will "just go away."

Personally, I have no better solutions and no different

convictions than those I have expressed on many occasions.
I still think that the nine members of a local school board are
better qualified to run a local school than the nine Supreme
Court members in Washington.[44]

Shivers left office confident that his segregationist tendencies
would be carried on by the new governor, Price Daniel, and his
administration.[45]

Shivers did not consider that, although Daniel signed the Southern Manifesto as a United States senator from Texas, he did not
want the controversy of the southern resistance movement cloud-
ing his first days in office. By political maneuvering, Daniel moved
the segregation proposals to the end of the 120-day session. Each
prosegregation bill was meant, in some fashion, to circumvent the
Supreme Court's mandates in *Brown I* and *Brown II*. Twelve bills
and two resolutions were eventually introduced. One of the resolutions, supporting the use of interposition in Texas, failed in the
House with a vote of 85 to 52. In the second resolution, the legislature formally opposed "the effort of the Federal Government to assert an unlawful dominion over her citizens." Requesting a constitutional amendment, the legislature called for a greater distinction
between states' rights and federal encroachment. Included in the
bills were measures to ban members of the NAACP from state employment; to suppress state funds from integrated school districts;
to place pupils within a district in particular schools, designating
seventeen criteria the school boards might use to shift students
from one school to another and camouflaging the race issue with
psychological, emotional, and mental stipulations; to support private segregated schools with state funding; to require integrationists to register with the state; and to prevent local school
boards from integrating their schools unless the registered voters
of the district approved the move in an election.[46]

In the House, eight bills passed by a two-thirds majority and
traveled to the senate. In the last days of the session, five of the
bills reached the senate floor. With great determination, two senators, Henry B. Gonzales of San Antonio and Abraham Kazen of
Laredo, launched a thirty-six-hour filibuster to defeat the bills. Because of their efforts, only two of the five passed. The two new
laws, signed by the governor, provided Texans the legal means, under state statutes to circumvent the Supreme Court's school integration mandates. The first law, required an initial petition signed
by 20 percent of a school district's voters and a subsequent election
to accept integration into their school system. Any district already

integrated could be returned to a dual system with the proper procedure of a petition and a majority vote for segregation. The second
law dealt with pupil placement and transfer within a district, and
without if negotiated with another district, under the discretion of
the local school board. The new statute listed all seventeen standards, discussed in House and senate committees, for legally placing or transferring a student from one school to another. Included
in the seventeen were:

> The adequacy of the pupil's academic preparation . . . the psy-
> chological qualification of a pupil for the type of teaching and
> associations involved; the effect of admission of the pupil upon
> the academic progress of other students in a particular school . . .
> the possibility or threat of friction or disorder among pupils or
> others; the possibility of breaches of the peace or ill will or eco-
> nomic retaliation within the community; the home environ-
> ment of the pupil; . . . the morals, conduct, health and personal
> standards of the pupil; the request or consent of parents or
> guardians.[47]

The law stipulated that no students could be forced to attend an
integrated school against their will. Under the guidelines of the
statute, an appeal against a school board's decision could be filed in
the state's district courts. Although these laws were counter to the
school integration decisions of the Supreme Court, Governor
Daniel signed them before the end of the year.[48]

Later in the year, Daniel called a special session of the state legislature, and three more prosegregation bills were passed and
signed by the governor in December 1957. The first law was passed
in response to the crisis in Little Rock. The legislators legalized
the closure of any public school within the state by the school
board or the governor when violence could not be prevented without military troops being sent in by federal authority to maintain
order in or around the school. In addition, the second law allowed
the Texas attorney general to assist in any proceeding in the federal court system to defend the constitutional grounds for any
state law in Texas. The final law struck directly at the NAACP and
their school integration efforts. It stated that any organization "engaged in activities designed to hinder, harass, and interfere with
the powers and duties of . . . Texas to control and operate its public
schools" was required to register, at the request of a county judge,
membership lists, information on its officers, business locations,
purpose of the association, and relationship to any national ties.

The organization's records official was required to turn this information over to the state immediately upon request.[49]

Three resolutions were also passed during the special session. The first was a direct request to the president to "desist and refrain" from ordering federal troops into Texas and "interfering with the constitutional right of the State of Texas to provide, operate and discipline the public schools of Texas." The second recommended a constitutional amendment clarifying the limits of federal authority. And finally, the third sought the establishment of more stringent requirements, by the Congress, for appointment to the United States Supreme Court. By 1958, because of the determined efforts of the Texas executive and legislative branches, school integration in Texas came to an almost complete stop.[50]

Between August 1957 and May 1962, only ten school districts integrated in Texas. None of these were in East Texas. The laws were rarely challenged in these years because the NAACP was held under tight restrictions by the Texas executive and judicial branches. The state legislature reinforced this commitment.[51]

After the Mansfield integration crisis, John Howard Griffin, an author and resident of Mansfield, contemplated writing an article about the school case and the incidents that had occurred over the previous year. He was approached by representatives from the Anti-Defamation League with a project proposal soon after the crisis at the high school. They hoped to publish a pamphlet on Mansfield that would be included with other "field reports on desegregation." Griffin accepted their offer and joined Theodore Freedman, another author linked to B'nai B'rith, to write the piece. Griffin spent long hours interviewing people in Mansfield who were tied to the case and crisis. He carefully protected the identity of those interviewed by using letters of the alphabet instead of their names. For example, one of the radical segregationists was referred to as Mr. F., a letter that did not coincide with the man's initial. Griffin received several indirect threats during the time he researched the project. He believed the interviewees were candid, but many, both black and white, remained tense and fearful of speaking out against the radical segregationists. Griffin attempted to discuss the town's situation with many of the residents he met. He recorded his observations:

> The steam has died down in all except the small group of fanatics. I find great resentment, and after the interviews, I attempt to explain the situation to each interviewee. The findings become obvious and there are many embarrassed and red-faced people here, some who think that what we lost is far greater

than what we gained. . . . The fanatics, losing none of their ardor, gradually lost prestige. It began to play out. Still, no one spoke up. The preachers had been repudiated. The feeling of triumph was still strong.[52]

During September 1956, Griffin wrote in his journal that his family was concerned about the negative attitude of several people in Mansfield over Griffin's research and interviews. The author shared their worries. In his journal, he devised an escape plan from his house if those he feared came after him. He speculated about leaving his tape recorder on in the house to record any threats or violence should they occur. No one came for him, and these plans were never utilized. Griffin based his final report on interviews, newspaper articles, and his own opinions. Under "Personal Impressions," the author wrote a final insightful observation, "Most people think it will take a long time to overcome the great damage done these crisis-weeks in this community."[53]

Maggie Briscoe exemplified the feelings of many of the African American families in Mansfield after the crisis. Thoughtfully, she contended:

The negro race have had it very very hard and some of us it has made real real bitter, but I guess because the Lord saved me, I just didn't let it make me bitter. I just kept praying, cause my mommy used to tell us all the time, and my daddy was a preacher, and he would read the scriptures and he'd always say, "Pray . . . love your enemy . . . pray for those that despitefully use you." We were just brought up like that.[54]

These families turned inward to each other, to their small neighborhood, and to their church for support and security. T. M. Moody remained a leader in the tight-knit community, but because of the constraints on the NAACP and the fear of reprisals, no further legal measures to integrate were initiated. Late in 1956, J. E. Moody lost his home and sharecropping position on land outside Mansfield. Anticipating this action, J. E. bought a small lot in the black section of town, moved his family, and got a new job in town. Floyd Moody was very pleased to "get off" the farm. Life returned to the "normal routine," and although the African American residents remained anxious, their inner spirit remained committed to civil rights and racial equality.[55]

The fall of 1956 was a critical time for Davis. He was involved to a certain degree in four significant civil rights litigations in Texas. In addition to the Mansfield school integration case, Davis was working on a housing integration crisis in the Riverside section of Fort Worth and an alleged voter fraud scandal in a Fort Worth election precinct. He was also well aware he was being investigated by Shepperd on barratry violations and for evidence in the suit against the NAACP. During the month, a deputy sheriff, a Texas Ranger, and a state trooper arrived at his law office in Fort Worth with a search warrant to photograph and investigate his records. This lawful intrusion never amounted to charges. Davis remained in Fort Worth and continued the legal struggle for racial equality.[56]

In the following years, T. M. Moody, John F. Lawson, and other past "subtrustees" did not try to integrate Mansfield High School. The school remained segregated for nine more years. Not until 1965 were African American teenagers allowed to attend classes in their own hometown. Title VI of the Civil Rights Act of 1964 stipulated federal funding could not be allocated to school systems practicing discrimination. The following year, the Elementary and Secondary Education Act of 1965 was passed offering increased federal funding to public schools operating under the integrated guidelines in Title VI. These monetary incentives finally pushed Mansfield's school board to integrate.[57]

On January 26, 1965, the Mansfield school board voted to sign the Assurance of Compliance Form H. E. W. 441 and to release to the public a statement to that fact. They chose to publish the following announcement in the *Mansfield News Mirror:* "We the School Trustees of the Mansfield Independent School District declare that we have filed the Court Order dated August 21, 1956 Civil Action No. 3152, with The Texas Education Agency, and so state that we will comply with it and Title VI of the Civil Rights Act of 1964." Pigg recalled later, "They wouldn't have integrated then, [but] . . . the federal government told them we're gonna shut-off the federal money. . . . They could not've operated here then. . . . It was a struggle to operate."[58]

In September 1965, Willie Pigg, now Mansfield's school superintendent, opened the doors of the high school and enrolled the community's African American students. Nine of these students joined the football team, and several others signed up for the school band. "Times have changed," Pigg told a reporter. "Nine years ago, integration was new to everybody. They weren't ready for it. The attitude has now changed." Pigg guided the black students on a tour of their new school. Thirty African American teens registered the first year. There were no reported racially motivated incidents inside or outside of the school.[59]

In the fall of 1956, without Mansfield's African American adults fully realizing it, the seed of the civil rights movement was planted and sown for their children to reap benefits from. Their efforts raised the consciousness of Texas and the nation to the growing movement for equal justice in all aspects of life in the United States for all citizens. Their children grew to lead freer, less restricted lives. Eventually, the barriers of segregation fell one by one. New opportunities in education, employment, housing, social status, and acceptance paved new paths toward equality.

The older generation of African Americans in Mansfield remained cautious and wary of racial advancements, accepting them more slowly than did their children. But the children succeeded in expanding their goals and visions further than their parents ever dreamed possible. Many of the new generation did not take their parents' efforts for granted. A respect for what the older generation experienced emerged as the younger ones grew to maturity. Many, such as Floyd Moody Sr. and L. Clifford Davis carried on the struggle for racial equality and respect in their own ways: one in a church, the other in a courtroom. The words of Thurgood Marshall exemplified their attitude toward the movement for civil rights. When asked what he thought of how far African Americans had come in the last forty years with regard to acquiring their constitutional rights and equal protection under the law, Marshall replied, "Stop talking about how far we've come and start talking about how close we are." [60]

Many of Mansfield's residents, both black and white, recalling the case and crisis from the perspective of 1992 said, "It was no big deal." They believed what happened in their "little ol' town" was insignificant within the broad spectrum of the civil rights movement. Not until recently did they begin to realize their place in the history of the United States struggle for racial equality. What the older generation began in the 1950s, the second and third generations carry on. Their quest for equality touched the hearts and minds of U.S. citizens from the small homes of the African Americans on West Broad Street in Mansfield, to the Governor's Mansion in Austin, to the White House in the nation's capital.

The traditional caste system of the South did not fall easily. Enablers to the segregationists' cause were found at all levels of state and federal government. The unending struggle for racial equality proved long and difficult, but African Americans in Mansfield and across the United States put faith in the inspirational words of integrationists such as Walter White. During the 1950s, White wrote of the future, ". . . in true brotherhood race and skin color have no pertinence. . . . One by one the long-assaulted barriers crumble,

Notes

1. Pathway to Equality: The Determination to Change

1. *Plessy v. Ferguson*, United States Supreme Court, 163 U.S. 537 (1896) (hereafter referred to as *Plessy v. Ferguson* and *Plessy*); see also Albert P. Blaustein and Robert L. Zangrando, eds., *Civil Rights and the American Negro: A Documentary History* (New York: Trident Press, 1968), 294–311; Albert P. Blaustein and Clarence Clyde Ferguson Jr., *Desegregation and the Law: The Meaning and Effect of the School Segregation Cases* (New Brunswick: Rutgers University Press, 1957), 98–99, 118; Harry S. Ashmore, *The Negro and the Schools* (Chapel Hill: University of North Carolina Press, 1954), 48–50; Richard Kluger, *Simple Justice: The History of Brown v. Board of Education and Black America's Struggle for Equality* (New York: Alfred A. Knopf, 1975), 12–14, 294; Norman C. Amaker, "The 1950s: Racial Equality and the Law," *Current History* 56–57 (1969): 276–277.

2. Walter White, *A Man Called White* (New York: Arno Press, 1969), 344; see also Roy Wilkins, "Desegregation: North and South," *Current History* 32–33 (May 1957): 284; Harry S. Ashmore, *An Epitaph for Dixie* (New York: W. W. Norton, 1957), 56–57. For a description of the southern caste system and segregation, see Sarah Patton Boyle, *The Desegregated Heart: A Virginian's Stand in the Time of Transition* (New York: William Morrow, 1962), part 1, chapters 1–19.

3. Unidentified African American scholar quoted in Robert Penn Warren, *Segregation: The Inner Conflict in the South* (New York: Random House, 1956), 41.

4. Ashmore, *The Negro and the Schools*, 48–50; Kluger, 294; Wilkins, "Desegregation North and South," 287; Thomas R. Brooks, *Walls Come Tumbling Down: A History of the Civil Rights Movement, 1940–1970* (Englewood Cliffs, New Jersey: Prentice-Hall, 1974), 89–90; Robert A. Leflar, "Law of the Land," in *With All Deliberate Speed: Segregation — Desegregation in Southern Schools*, ed. Don Shoemaker (New York: Harper and Brothers, 1957), 2–3; Robert F. Burk, *The Eisenhower Administration and Black Civil Rights* (Knoxville: University of Tennessee Press, 1984), 133.

5. Harry Golden, *Only in America* (New York: World Publishing, 1958), 138.

6. Boyle, 48–51; Golden, 146–148; Chester C. Travelstead, "Southern Attitudes toward Racial Integration," in *The Countdown on Segregated Education*, ed. William W. Brinkman and Stanley Lehrer (New York: Society for the Advancement of Education, 1960), 48–50; Gunnar Myrdal, Richard Sterner, and Arnold Rose, *An American Dilemma: The Negro Problem and Modern Democracy* (New York: Harper and Brothers, 1944), I:xli–xlix; for a condensation of Myrdal, Sterner, and Rose's volumes, see Arnold Rose, *The Negro in America* (New York: Harper and Brothers, 1948), chapter 1; Harvard Sitkoff, *The Struggle for Black Equality, 1954–1980* (New York: Hill and Wang, 1981), 16–17. Walter White, *How Far the Promised Land?* (New York: Viking Press, 1955), 195; Numan V. Bartley, *The Rise of Massive Resistance: Race and Politics in the South during the 1950's* (Baton Rouge: Louisiana State University Press, 1969), 3–4, 14–15.

7. Myrdal et al., xix; Rose, xvii.

8. Short-phrase quotes used in context in Myrdal et al., 91–93, xliii–xlvii; condensed in Rose, 10–11; see also Kluger, 256; White, *How Far the Promised Land?* 26–28; foreword by Ralph J. Bunche in White, *How Far the Promised Land?* ix–xii; Boyle, part 1, chapters 16–19; an example of several racial studies conducted in the United States under the direction of the Fund for the Advancement of Education is listed in Ashmore, *The Negro and the Schools*, 216–217; also fourteen years of studies conducted by the National Opinion Research Center are discussed in Herbert H. Hyman and Paul B. Sheatsley, "Attitudes toward Desegregation," *Scientific American* 195 (December 1956): 35–39.

9. For a discussion of topography and migration patterns in East Texas including an emphasis on the impact of the "ninety-eighth meridian," see Walter Prescott Webb, *The Great Plains* (Lincoln: University of Nebraska Press, 1931), chapter 5; see also Ashmore, *Epitaph for Dixie*, 133; Lerone Bennett, "The South and the Negro: Rev. Martin Luther King Jr., Alabama Desegregationist, Challenges Talmadge," *Ebony* 12 (April 1957): 77; Robert Lasch, "Along the Border," in Shoemaker, 56–70.

10. Mansfield Historical Society, *Historic Mansfield, Texas* (Mansfield: Mansfield Historical Society, 1992), pamphlet; Mansfield Chamber of Commerce, "Welcome to Mansfield" (no date), handout; John Howard Griffin and Theodore Freedman, *Mansfield, Texas: A Report of the Crisis Situation Resulting from Efforts to Desegregate the School System* (New York: Anti-Defamation League of B'nai B'rith, 1957), 3; see also Harry K. Wright, *Civil Rights U.S.A.: Public Schools Southern States, 1963 Texas* (Washington, D.C.: United States Civil Rights Commission, Government Printing Office, 1964), 7; maps provided for the author's use by the *Mansfield News Mirror* and the City of Mansfield Planning and Zoning Offices.

11. Mansfield Historical Society, pamphlet; Maggie Briscoe interview by Robyn Duff Ladino (hereafter referred to as RDL), Mansfield, Texas, October 5, 1992 (Briscoe has lived in Mansfield for over fifty years and was

raising her family in the 1950s); see also Ashmore, *Epitaph for Dixie,* 133–134.

12. Mansfield Historical Society, pamphlet; Briscoe to RDL, October 5, 1992.

13. Ibid. For twentieth-century southern migration patterns, see Jack Greenberg, *Race Relations and American Law* (New York: Columbia University Press, 1959), 8; White, *A Man Called White,* 305; Ashmore, *The Negro and the Schools,* 52–56; C. Vann Woodward, *The Strange Career of Jim Crow* (New York: Oxford University Press, 1955), 128–129.

14. Briscoe to RDL, October 5, 1992; Floyd Moody Sr. interview by RDL, Fort Worth, Texas, October 6, 1992 (Moody is a minister who, during the 1950s, grew up in Mansfield and became one of the plaintiffs in the Mansfield school integration case; see Chapter 5. He is cited as Floyd Moody Sr. because he has a son named after him, but in the text he is referred to as Floyd Moody because his son was not born until after the Mansfield school integration case and crisis occurred); L. Clifford Davis interview by RDL, Fort Worth, October 6, 1992 (Davis was a district judge in Fort Worth and is an active member of the NAACP. In the 1950s, Davis was the lawyer for the plaintiffs in the Mansfield school integration case; see Chapter 5).

15. Ibid., description of community is a consensus opinion of those interviewed.

16. Ibid. For a brief description and discussion of several of the Mansfield businesses mentioned, see "Investigation Report Possible Barratry Activities of Clifford Davis," State of Texas v. NAACP Files, Investigation of Texas Branches, 1956, Folder 8, Box 3N158, Barker Texas History Center, University of Texas, Austin (hereafter referred to as BTHC). This report is also found in the Attorney General's Records, Folder location 302–347, Box 199/17-4, Texas State Archives, Austin, Texas (hereafter referred to as TSA); two of the eating establishments are also mentioned in Griffin and Freedman, 3–4. For pictures and text of particular segregation practices in Mansfield, see *Fort Worth Star-Telegram,* August 7, 1956. This article is also found in Richard M. Morehead Papers, Folder News Clippings—Mansfield, Box 3F282, BTHC.

17. Floyd Moody Sr. to RDL, October 6, 1992.

18. The racial attitudes of Mansfield's white residents in the late 1940s and early 1950s are taken from a consensus of interviews: Kenneth Pressley interview by RDL, Mansfield, Texas, October 5, 1992 (Pressley is a Mansfield businessman and was a young adult in Mansfield in the 1950s); Willie Pigg interview by RDL, Mansfield, Texas, October 6, 1992 (Pigg is a retired school superintendent and was the principal of Mansfield High School in the 1950s); and M. M. Meeks interview by RDL, Mansfield, Texas, October 6, 1992 (Meeks is a retired resident of Mansfield and was a school board trustee in Mansfield in the 1950s). The African American residents' racial attitudes for the described era are taken from a consensus of interviews: Briscoe to RDL, October 5, 1992; Floyd Moody Sr. to RDL,

October 6, 1992; Davis to RDL, October 6, 1992; John F. Lawson telephone interview by RDL, January 5, 1993 (Lawson was a resident of Mansfield in the 1950s and an active member of the African American community and the local branch of the NAACP); short quotes from Briscoe to RDL, October 5, 1992, and Floyd Moody Sr. to RDL, October 6, 1992.

19. *Mansfield News*, August 16, 1956.

20. Davis to RDL, October 6, 1992; Davis telephone interview by RDL, December 17, 1992.

21. Davis to RDL, October 6, 1992; Briscoe to RDL, October 5, 1992; Floyd Moody Sr. to RDL, October 6, 1992; Lawson to RDL, January 5, 1993.

22. Ibid.; Willie Steward telephone interview by RDL, December 8, 1992 (Steward has been a resident of Mansfield for more than fifty years); see also Tom Dodge, "Black Like Me Now," *Dallas Observer*, September 6, 1990, 13; George Fuermann, *Reluctant Empire* (New York: Doubleday, 1957), 204.

23. Floyd Moody Sr. to RDL, October 6, 1992.

24. Ibid.; Briscoe to RDL, October 5, 1992; Davis to RDL, October 6, 1992.

25. Ibid.; see also Griffin and Freedman, 4; Wright, 7; T. M. Moody is formally recognized as president of the Mansfield branch of the NAACP, in "1955–1956 Texas State Conferences of Branches: NAACP Officers and Branch Roster," State of Texas v. NAACP Files, Folder 4, 1955–1956 and Undated, Box 3N161, BTHC.

26. Floyd Moody Sr. to RDL, October 6, 1992; Briscoe to RDL, October 5, 1992; Davis to RDL, October 6, 1992; Lawson to RDL, January 5, 1993; see also Griffin and Freedman, 4; Wright, 7; Fuermann, 203.

27. Ibid.

28. Davis to RDL, October 6, 1992; Floyd Moody Sr. to RDL, October 6, 1992; Briscoe to RDL, October 5, 1992; Pigg to RDL, October 6, 1992; Lawson to RDL, January 5, 1993; Griffin and Freedman, 4; Wright 7; Fuermann, 203; Mansfield Independent School District, Mansfield, Texas (hereafter referred to as MISD), School Board Meeting Minutes, August 29, 1950; June 15, 1951; April 7, 1952; June 29, 1954.

29. Davis to RDL, October 6, 1992; Floyd Moody Sr. to RDL, October 6, 1992; Lawson to RDL, January 5, 1993; Griffin and Freedman, 4; Wright, 7; *Mansfield News*, August 28, 1953; see also MISD, School Board Meeting Minutes dated 1950–1954, for numerous improvements approved for the white schools in Mansfield.

30. *Mansfield News*, August 28, 1953.

31. *Oliver Brown et al. v. Board of Education of Topeka, Shawnee County, Kansas, et al.*, United States Supreme Court, May 17, 1954, 347 U.S. 483, 74 S.Ct. 686, 98 L.Ed. 873, this designation encompasses four school segregation cases decided on the given date; *Spottswood Thomas Bolling et al. v. C. Melvin Sharpe et al.*, United States Supreme Court, May 17, 1954, 347 U.S. 497, 74 S.Ct. 693, 98 L.Ed. 884, accompanied the four state school segregation cases, but originated in the District of Co-

lumbia. The five cases were combined for the 1955 implementation decision and documented as United States Supreme Court, May 31, 1955, 349 U.S. 294, 75 S.Ct. 753, 99 L.Ed. 653 (hereafter referred to as *Brown v. Board of Education* or *Brown I* and *Brown II* for the May 17, 1954, and May 31, 1955, Court opinions, respectively, except where clarified in Chapter 2). For the Supreme Court opinions, see *Race Relations Law Reporter* 1 (December 1956): 5–12.

32. Davis to RDL, October 6, 1992; Lawson, January 5, 1993; see also Woodward, 154; Thurgood Marshall and Roy Wilkins, "Interpretation of Supreme Court Decision and the NAACP Program," *Crisis* 62 (June–July 1955): 329–333; "Directives to the Branches Adopted by Emergency Southwide NAACP Conference," *Crisis* 62 (June–July 1955): 339–340, 380.

33. Letter from Mansfield School Board to T. M. Moody, August 18, 1954, NAACP Records, Mansfield File, Library of Congress, Washington, D.C. (hereafter referred to as NAACP Records, Library of Congress), received upon request.

34. Ibid.; see also MISD, School Board Meeting Minutes, August 17, 1954.

35. Davis to RDL, October 6, 1992; Floyd Moody Sr. to RDL, October 6, 1992; Lawson to RDL, January 5, 1993.

2. The Dismantlement of "Separate but Equal"

1. Minnie Finch, *The NAACP: Its Fight for Justice* (Metuchen, New Jersey: Scarecrow Press, 1981), 115; White, *A Man Called White*, 344; Alfred H. Kelly, "The School Desegregation Case," in *Quarrels That Shaped the Constitution*, ed. John Arthur Garraty (New York: Harper and Row, 1964), 248; Brooks, *Walls Come Tumbling Down*, 89–90.

2. President Harry Truman, in Finch, 117. For a description of the meeting and Truman's speech, see White, *A Man Called White*, 347–348; see also Kluger, *Simple Justice*, 250–251; Brooks, 60–61.

3. Woodward, *Strange Career of Jim Crow*, 130–131; Stephen L. Wasby et al., *Desegregation from Brown to Alexander: An Exploration of Supreme Court Strategies* (Carbondale: Southern Illinois University Press, 1977), 58; see also A. Philip Randolph, in Brooks, 70–71.

4. Finch, 116–117; for a description of the development of this committee, see White, *A Man Called White*, 330–333; see also Kluger, 252–253; Brooks, 61; Benjamin Muse, *Ten Years of Prelude: The Story of Integration since the Supreme Court's 1954 Decision* (New York: Viking Press, 1964), 3–4.

5. Woodward, 136–137; Finch, 115–116; Brooks, 73.

6. For a discussion of specific incidents in southern race relations and the difficulties faced by African Americans after World War II, see White, *A Man Called White*, chapters 38, 39; Finch, 116, 118; Brooks, 54–58.

7. For a discussion of problems African Americans experienced seeking fair employment and housing after World War II, see White, *A Man Called White*, chapter 37; see also Finch, 118–119.

8. Finch, 118–119; see also Chapter 1, n. 13.

9. National Association for the Advancement of Colored People (hereafter referred to as NAACP). NAACP objectives quoted in Finch, 19, see also 120, 122–123; White, *A Man Called White,* 344; Kelly, "The School Desegregation Case," 250; Sitkoff, *Struggle for Black Equality,* 7–8.

10. Finch, 122–123; Kelly, "The School Desegregation Case," 250–251.

11. The NAACP Legal Defense and Educational Fund (hereafter referred to as the Fund); Davis to RDL, October 6, 1992, and December 17, 1992; Kelly, "The School Desegregation Case," 251–253; Finch, 127; Kluger, 221–224, 273–274.

12. Thurgood Marshall, in Kluger, 221.

13. Herbert Hill, in Kluger, 223.

14. Finch, 127; Kelly, "The School Desegregation Case," 252; Muse, 78–79.

15. Kelly, "The School Desegregation Case," 251–253; Finch, 122–123; Kluger, 257–258; Muse, 78–79.

16. Kelly, "The School Desegregation Case," 253–254; Finch, 127–128; Sitkoff, 19–20.

17. *Sipuel v. Oklahoma State Regents,* 332 U.S. 631, rev'g 180 P. 2d. 135 (Okla.) (hereafter referred to as *Sipuel v. Oklahoma);* see also Herbert Hill and Jack Greenberg, *Citizen's Guide to Desegregation: A Study of Social and Legal Change in American Life* (Westport, Connecticut: Greenwood Press, 1955), 66–67; Finch, 128–130; Kluger, 258–260.

18. *Gaines v. Canada,* 305 U.S. 337 (1937); *Sipuel v. Oklahoma;* case proceedings also quoted in Roger L. Goldman, *Thurgood Marshall: Justice for All* (New York: Carroll and Graf, 1992), 84–85; Kluger, 259; Finch, 128; Kelly, "The School Desegregation Case," 254–255; Norman C. Amaker, "The 1950s: Racial Equality and the Law," *Current History* 56–57 (1969): 278.

19. *Sipuel v. Oklahoma;* Hill and Greenberg, 66–67; Amaker, "The 1950s," 278; Finch, 128–130; Kluger, 259–260; Goldman, 86.

20. *Sweatt v. Painter,* 339 U.S. 629, rev'g 210 S.W. 2d 442, (1950) (hereafter referred to as *Sweatt v. Painter* and *Sweatt);* for an excellent description of the case and trials, see Michael L. Gillette, "Heman Marion Sweatt: Civil Rights Plaintiff," in *Black Leaders: Texans for Their Times,* ed., Alwyn Barr and Robert A. Calvert (Austin: Texas State Historical Association, 1985), 156–188; G. Theodore Mitau, *Decade of Decision: The Supreme Court and the Constitutional Revolution, 1954–1964* (New York: Charles Scribner's Sons, 1967), 57; Hill and Greenberg, 67–71; Kluger, 260–266; Amaker, "The 1950s," 278; Kelly, "The School Desegregation Case," 255–256; Finch, 130–132; Goldman, 87–89.

21. Ibid.

22. Kluger, 262.

23. *Sweatt v. Painter;* Finch, 132; Wasby et al., 58; Kelly, "The School Desegregation Case," 255; Kluger, 262–266; Goldman, 88–89.

24. *McLaurin v. Oklahoma,* 339 U.S. 637, rev'g 87 F. Supp. 528, (1950) (hereafter referred to as *McLaurin v. Oklahoma* and *McLaurin);* Finch,

132–133; Hill and Greenberg, 72–73; Kelly, "The School Desegregation Case," 256; Kluger, 266–269; Goldman, 90–91.

25. *McLaurin v. Oklahoma;* see also Hill and Greenberg, 73; Kluger, 268.

26. *Henderson v. United States,* 339 U.S. 816, (1950) (hereafter referred to as *Henderson v. United States* and *Henderson);* Kluger, 277–278; Finch, 135–136; Hill and Greenberg, 73–75.

27. Ibid.

28. *Plessy v. Ferguson;* Hill and Greenberg, 73–74; Finch, 134–136; Kelly, "The School Desegregation Case," 256.

29. *Sweatt v. Painter;* brief quoted, in Finch, 133; and Kluger, 275–276, see 282; see also Richard Bardolph, ed., *The Civil Rights Record: Black Americans and the Law, 1849–1970* (New York: Thomas Y. Crowell, 1970), 273; Hill and Greenberg, 73–76.

30. *McLaurin v. Oklahoma;* Finch, 134; Kluger, 283; Hill and Greenberg, 76–77.

31. *Henderson v. United States;* Finch, 135–136.

32. *Plessy v. Ferguson; Sweatt v. Painter; McLaurin v. Oklahoma; Henderson v. United States;* Finch, 134–136; Kluger, 280–284; Hill and Greenberg, 75–77.

33. *Sweatt v. Painter;* see also Blaustein and Zangrando, 282; Finch, 136.

34. Hill and Greenberg, 76–77; Kluger, 284; Gillette, "Heman Sweatt," 79; Bartley, 5–7.

35. Marshall quoted, in Finch, 137–138; Kluger, 293–294; see also Muse, 7.

36. Ibid.; Sitkoff, 20; Goldman, 93.

37. Goldman, 93–96; Sitkoff, 20.

38. *Brown v. Board of Education.* For a discussion and concise history of the five individual cases that became *Brown v. Board of Education,* see Finch, chapters 16–18; and also Hill and Greenberg, chapter 7; see also Kelly, "The School Desegregation Case," 257–258; Ashmore, *The Negro and the Schools,* 98–102; Sitkoff, 20; Muse, 8–11; Woodward, 145–146. For a concise overview of *Brown v. Board of Education,* see Liva Baker, "With All Deliberate Speed," *American Heritage* 24 (February 1973): 42–48.

39. *Plessy v. Ferguson;* United States Constitution, Fourteenth Amendment.

40. United States Constitution, Fourteenth Amendment.

41. Marshall, in Goldman, 98; see also Bardolph, 276; Finch, 172.

42. Goldman, 96; Hill and Greenberg, 109; Kluger, 558–561; Finch, 171.

43. Goldman, 98–99; Hill and Greenberg, 109.

44. Goldman, 99; Finch, 172; Kelly, "The School Desegregation Case," 259; Hill and Greenberg, 110; Kluger, 572.

45. Goldman, 99; Finch, 173–175; Kelly, "The School Desegregation Case," 259–260; Ashmore, *The Negro and the Schools,* 102; Hill and Greenberg, 110–111.

46. Goldman, 100–101; Finch, 175–177; Kelly, "The School Desegregation Case," 260–261; Hill and Greenberg, 111–112. For a discussion of the tactics and strategies used by the NAACP and the people involved in the preparation of their reargument brief in 1953, see Kluger, chapter 24, in particular, 637–646.

47. Brief quoted, in Kluger, 645–646; Goldman, 103; Finch, 176–177; Hill and Greenberg, 112–113.

48. Hill and Greenberg, 115; Kluger, 647; Finch, 177–179.

49. Marshall, in Hill and Greenberg, 115–116; Finch, 179, 181.

50. *Brown v. Board of Education; Race Relations Law Reporter* 1 (February 1956): 5–10; see also Finch, 182–184; Bardolph 277–278; Goldman, 105–106; Ashmore, *The Negro and the Schools,* 107; Kluger, 700–708.

51. Ibid.

52. Kelly, "The School Desegregation Case," 267–268; Finch, 187.

53. *Brown v. Board of Education; Race Relations Law Reporter* 1 (February 1956): 11–12; Blaustein and Zangrando, 444–447; Finch, 189–190; Kluger 744–745.

54. *Brown v. Board of Education; Race Relations Law Reporter* 1 (February 1956): 11–12; J. Harvie Wilkinson III, *From Brown to Bakke: The Supreme Court and School Integration, 1954–1978* (New York: Oxford University Press, 1979), 80–81; Harrell R. Rodgers Jr. and Charles S. Bullock III, "School Desegregation: A Policy Analysis," *Journal of Black Studies* (June 1972): 413–414; Jack Walter Peltason, *Fifty-Eight Lonely Men: Southern Federal Judges and School Desegregation* (New York: Harcourt, Brace and World, 1961), 17–19; Finch, 192; Kluger, 745; Woodward, 152–154; Goldman, 110–112; Amaker, "The 1950s," 279; Sitkoff, 23–24 (italics added).

55. Thurgood Marshall and Roy Wilkins, "Interpretation of Supreme Court Decision and the NAACP Program," *Crisis* 62 (June–July 1955): 329–330.

56. Marshall, in Goldman, 111.

57. *Brown v. Board of Education;* Marshall and Wilkins, "Interpretation of Supreme Court," 333; see also Marshall, in Goldman, 112; Finch, 192; Kluger, 745–747.

58. Kluger, 746–747, 749; Finch, 192; Hill and Greenberg, chapter 13.

59. Davis to RDL, October 6, 1992, and December 17, 1992.

60. Ibid.

61. *Matthews v. Launius,* United States District Court, Western District, Arkansas, October 4, 1955, 134 F. Supp. 684; see also *Race Relations Law Reporter* 1 (February 1956): 45–48.

62. Ibid.

63. Ibid.

64. Davis to RDL, October 6, 1992, and December 17, 1992; Lawson to RDL, January 5, 1993.

65. Davis to RDL, October 6, 1992, and December 17, 1992.

66. Ibid.; see also "Texas State Conference of Branches," State of Texas v. NAACP Records, Folder 4, 1955–1956 and Undated, Box 3N161, BTHC.

67. Quote by Davis to RDL, October 6, 1992; Lawson to RDL, January 5, 1993. Lawson recalled NAACP meetings and conferences held in Dallas that were very similar to what Davis described. Discussions took place; questions were answered; and strategies were developed in reference to school desegregation.

68. "Testimony of Thurgood Marshall," October 18, 1956, State of Texas v. NAACP Records, Folder: Case Proceedings, 1956–1957 and Undated, Box 3N153, BTHC; see also Letter, U. Simpson Tate to Thurgood Marshall, November 10, 1955, Attorney General's Records, Folder 302-347, Box 199/17-4, TSA.

69. Davis to RDL, October 6, 1992.

70. Ibid.

71. Ibid.

3. The Creed of Segregation and States' Rights in the South with an Emphasis on Texas

1. Thomas R. Waring, "The Southern Case: Against Desegregation," *Harper's Magazine* 212–213 (January 1956): 39–45; David Goldfield, *Black, White, and Southern: Race Relations and Southern Culture, 1940 to the Present* (Baton Rouge: Louisiana State University Press, 1990), 75–78; W. D. Workman Jr., "The Deep South," in *With All Deliberate Speed: Segregation—Desegregation in Southern Schools*, ed. Don Shoemaker (New York: Harper, 1957), 88–90; Sam J. Ervin Jr., "The Case of Segregation," United States Senate, *Congressional Record* 102 (March 22, 1956): 5349–5350; James Jackson Kilpatrick, *The Southern Case for School Segregation* (New York: Crowell-Collier, 1962), 7–9; for a descriptive overview of the South in the 1950s, see Neil R. McMillen, *The Citizens' Council: Organized Resistance to the Second Reconstruction, 1954–1964* (Urbana: University of Illinois Press, 1971), chapter 1.

2. James Jackson Kilpatrick, *The Sovereign States: Notes of a Citizen of Virginia* (Chicago: Henry Regnery, 1957), 258.

3. Kilpatrick, *The Southern Case*, 20–21. For an example of others using the phrase "a state of mind" in reference to the South, see Blaustein and Ferguson, *Desegregation and the Law*, 211.

4. Guy B. Johnson, "Freedom, Equality, and Segregation," in *Integration versus Segregation*, ed. Hubert H. Humphrey (New York: Thomas Y. Crowell, 1964), 100.

5. J. Edgar Hoover to Maxwell M. Rabb (secretary to the cabinet), Letter and Report, March 9, 1956, *Racial Tension and Civil Rights*, Dwight David Eisenhower Papers as President of the United States, 1953–1961 (hereafter referred to as DDE Papers), Ann Whitman File, Cabinet Series, Box 6, Dwight David Eisenhower Library, Abilene, Kansas (hereafter referred to as DDE Library); James McBride Dabbs, *The Southern Heritage* (New York: Alfred A. Knopf, 1958), 68–131; Kilpatrick, *The Southern Case*, 13–101; Workman, 89–91; Allan Morrison, "The South and the Negro: Senator Herman Talmadge, Georgia Segregationist, Defends

'Southern Way,'" *Ebony* 12 (April 1957): 76+; Ashmore, *Epitaph for Dixie*, 45– 46; Ashmore, *The Negro and the Schools*, chapter 12; Waring, "The Southern Case," 39–43; Muse, *Ten Years of Prelude*, 38–41; Johnson, "Freedom, Equality and Segregation," 101; William Peters, *The Southern Temper* (New York: Doubleday, 1959), 206–209.

6. Poll results in R. Ray McCain, "Reactions to the United States Supreme Court Decision of 1954," *Georgia Historical Quarterly* 52 (December 1968): 373.

7. J. Edgar Hoover to Maxwell M. Rabb, Letter and Report, *Racial Tension and Civil Rights*, March 9, 1956, DDE Papers, Ann Whitman File, Cabinet Series, Box 6, DDE Library.

8. Bartley, 85; McMillen, 17–18; Brady, in Goldfield, 76; John Bartlow Martin, *The Deep South Says "Never"* (New York: Ballentine Books, 1957), 17.

9. Bartley, 85; McMillen, 17–20.

10. Patterson in Martin, 2; see also Francis M. Wilhoit, *The Politics of Massive Resistance* (New York: George Braziller, 1973), 111, n. 12.

11. Ibid.

12. Harold C. Fleming, "Resistance Movements and Racial Desegregation," *Annals of the American Academy* 304 (1956): 46–50; Frederick B. Routh and Paul Anthony, "Southern Resistance Forces," *Phylon* 18 (1957): 50–58; Bartley, 83–85; Woodward, 152–154; for an in-depth history of the White Citizens' Council see McMillen, *The Citizens' Council*; quote, in *Texas Citizens' Council of Greater Houston*, pamphlet (Texas Citizens' Council of Greater Houston, no date), Lyndon Baines Johnson Papers (hereafter referred to as LBJ Papers), United States Senate Files, 1949–1961, 1956 General Files—Civil Rights, Box 567, Lyndon Baines Johnson Library, University of Texas, Austin (hereafter referred to as LBJ Library). A map of the southern states designating the number of White Citizens' Councils in each state in J. Edgar Hoover to Maxwell M. Rabb, Letter and Report, *Racial Tension and Civil Rights*, March 9, 1956, DDE Papers, Ann Whitman File, Cabinet Series, Box 6, DDE Library.

13. Peters, 146–147.

14. Ibid., 154; Woodward, 156.

15. Talmadge, in Morrison, "The South and the Negro," 77.

16. Routh and Anthony, "Southern Resistance Forces," 51; see also Herman Edelsberg and David A. Brody, *Civil Rights in the 84th Congress, 1955–1956*, October 29, 1956, LBJ Papers, United States Senate Files, 1949–1961, Office Files of George Reedy, 1956–1957, Reedy: Convention 1956 Folder, Box 418, LBJ Library.

17. Routh and Anthony, "Southern Resistance Forces," 51.

18. *Texas Citizens' Council of Greater Houston*, pamphlet, LBJ Papers, United States Senate Files, 1949–1961, 1956 General Files—Civil Rights, Box 567, LBJ Library.

19. Ibid.

20. Fleming, "Resistance Movements," 47; see also Edelsberg and Brody, *Civil Rights in the 84th Congress*, October 29, 1956, LBJ Papers, United

States Senate Files, 1949–1961, Office Files of George Reedy, 1956–1957, Reedy: Convention 1956 Folder, Box 418, LBJ Library.

21. Goldfield, 79–80; Routh and Anthony, "Southern Resistance Forces," 51–52; *Texas Citizens' Council of Greater Houston*, pamphlet, LBJ Papers, United States Senate Files, 1949–1961, 1956 General Files—Civil Rights Folder, Box 567, LBJ Library.

22. Muse, 28–29.

23. Kilpatrick, *The Sovereign States*, 305.

24. J. Edgar Hoover to Maxwell M. Rabb, Letter and Report, *Racial Tension and Civil Rights*, March 9, 1956, DDE Papers, Ann Whitman File, Cabinet Series, Box 6, DDE Library. For a discussion of the southern press, see Peters, chapter 7.

25. Fleming, "Resistance Movements," 47–48, unidentified Citizens' Council member quoted on 48; see also Martin, 15; Routh and Anthony, "Southern Resistance Forces," 52; Adam Clayton Powell, "What's Happening in School Integration?" House of Representatives, *Congressional Record* 103 (May 16, 1957): 7116.

26. United States Constitution, Tenth Amendment; Robert Brisbane, "Interposition: Theory and Fact," *Phylon* 17 (1956): 12–16; Reed Sarratt, *The Ordeal of Desegregation: The First Decade* (New York: Harper and Row, 1966), 38–39; Blaustein and Ferguson, 243–247; Wilhoit, 62–66; Report on Interposition (no author, title or date), LBJ Papers, United States Senate Files, 1949–1961, Office Files of George Reedy, 1956–1957, Reedy: Convention 1956, Box 418, LBJ Library.

27. Ibid.

28. Ibid.; Jefferson, quoted in Brisbane, "Interposition: Theory and Fact," 13.

29. Ibid.

30. Sarratt, 38.

31. Blaustein and Zangrando, 447–448, "Southern Manifesto" reprinted on 451–453; Bardolph, 381–383; Fuermann, 197; Goldfield, 84–85; Sitkoff, 26; R. Alton Lee, *Dwight David Eisenhower: Soldier and Statesman* (New York: Nelson-Hall, 1981), 258; Manning Marable, *Race, Reform, and Rebellion: The Second Reconstruction in Black America, 1945–1982* (Jackson: University Press of Mississippi, 1984), 45; Herbert S. Parmet, *Eisenhower and the American Crusades* (New York: Macmillan, 1972), 440; Edelsberg and Brody, *Civil Rights in the 84th Congress*, LBJ Papers, United States Senate Files, 1949–1961, Office Files of George Reedy, 1956–1957, Reedy: Convention 1956 Folder, Box 418, LBJ Library.

32. Unidentified lawyer, quoted in Wallace Westfeldt, "Communities in Strife," in *With All Deliberate Speed*, ed. Shoemaker, 38; also in Bardolph, 382.

33. Robert A. Leflar and Wylie H. Davis, "Devices to Evade or Delay Desegregation," in *Desegregation and the Supreme Court*, ed. Benjamin Munn Ziegler (Boston: Heath, 1958), 96–100; see also Blaustein and Ferguson, 252–267; Patrick E. McCauley, "Be It Enacted," in *With All Deliberate Speed*, ed. Shoemaker, 130–134; Powell, "What's Happening in

School Integration?" *Congressional Record* 103 (May 16, 1957): 7115. For a discussion of state legislators and the measures taken to uphold segregation, see Sarratt, chapter 2.

34. Peters, 190.

35. McMillen, 103; *Report of the United States Commission on Civil Rights, 1959* (Washington, D.C.: Government Printing Office, 1959), 201.

36. William H. Jones, "Desegregation of Public Education in Texas— One Year Afterward," *Journal of Negro Education* 24 (1955): 350–351.

37. Jimmy Banks, *Money, Marbles, and Chalk: The Wondrous World of Texas Politics* (Austin: Texas Publishing Company, 1971), 259; George Norris Green, *The Establishment in Texas Politics: The Primitive Years, 1938–1957* (Westport, Connecticut: Greenwood Press, 1979), 135; D. B. Hardeman, "Shivers of Texas: A Tragedy in Three Acts," *Harper's Magazine* 212–213 (1956): 50–51. For an in-depth biography of Allan Shivers, see Sam Kinch and Stuart Long, *Allan Shivers: The Pied Piper of Texas Politics* (Austin: Shoal Creek Publishers, 1973).

38. Unidentified Austin capitol reporter, in Hardeman, "Shivers of Texas," 51.

39. Unidentified Shivers observer, in ibid.

40. Hardeman, "Shivers of Texas," 51–52; for a description of several of Allan Shivers' tactics, see Green, chapter 10.

41. Yarborough, in William G. Phillips, *Yarborough of Texas* (Washington, D.C.: Acropolis Books, 1969), 34.

42. Ralph W. Yarborough interview with RDL, Austin, Texas, October 9, 1992 (Yarborough was an attorney and judge in Austin in the late 1940s and early 1950s. He ran for Texas governor in 1952, 1954, and 1956. He became a United States senator from Texas serving from 1957 to 1971); Bartley, 49–52; Phillips, 35; Hardeman, "Shivers of Texas," 53; Ashmore, *Epitaph for Dixie*, 139; J. A. Hendrix, "The Shivercrat Rebellion: A Case Study in Campaign Speaking Strategies," *Southern Speech Journal* 33 (1968): 289–290; Parmet, 133; O. Douglas Weeks, *Texas One-Party Politics in 1956* (Austin: Institute of Public Affairs, University of Texas, 1957), 7–8.

43. Yarborough to RDL, October 9, 1992; James G. Dickson Jr., *Law and Politics: The Office of the Attorney General in Texas* (Manchaca, Texas: Sterling Swift, 1976), 65–66; Banks, 261; Kinch and Long, 64, 99.

44. Green, 166–169; Dickson, 66; for a concise discussion of the controversies and scandals of Shivers' years in office, see Kinch and Long, chapters 18–19.

45. Ibid.; Yarborough to RDL, October 9, 1992.

46. Allan Shivers to Dwight D. Eisenhower, Letter, July 16, 1953, in James C. Duram, *A Moderate among Extremists: Dwight D. Eisenhower and the School Desegregation Crisis* (Chicago: Nelson-Hall, 1981), 60; Herbert Brownell to RDL, Letter, November 23, 1992. Brownell was the United States attorney general under President Eisenhower from 1953 to 1957. See also Duram, "Whose Brief?" 43; Burk, *The Eisenhower Administration*, 134–135.

47. *Austin American*, May 18, 1954; see also Jones, "Desegregation of Public Education in Texas," 352.

48. *Dallas Morning News*, May 19, 1954; see also Leonard B. Murphy, "A History of Negro Segregation Practices in Texas, 1865–1958," (M.A. thesis, Southern Methodist University, 1958), 160; Duram, *Moderate among Extremists*, 90–91.

49. First quote Shivers, in *Houston Post*, May 18, 1954; second quote Shivers, in *Houston Post*, May 19, 1954; see also LBJ Papers, United States Senate Files, 1949–1961, General Files, Folder: Segregation, Box 568, LBJ Library.

50. *Southern School News*, September 1954; Jones, "Desegregation of Public Education in Texas," 352–353; *Report of the United States Commission on Civil Rights, 1959*, 201; "Segregation and the Public Schools," *Texas School Board Journal* 1–2 (June 1954): 2–3, 24.

51. Sarratt, 278; *Southern School News*, October 1954.

52. Shivers, in Green, 156, see also 155; Jones, "Desegregation of Public Education in Texas," 353; Ashmore, *Epitaph for Dixie*, 142; Bartley, 73–74; Weeks, 7–8.

53. Shivers, in *Dallas Morning News*, July 16,1954; and, in Edward Lee McMillan, "Texas and the Eisenhower Campaigns" (Ph.D. dissertation, Texas Tech University, 1960), 231. For an example of a Shivers campaign ad, see *Mansfield News*, August 13, 1954.

54. Shivers quote explained, in Yarborough to RDL, October 9, 1992; and McMillan, 229–230; see also Herbert M. Baggarly, *The Texas Country Editor*, ed. Eugene W. Jones (New York: World Publishing, 1966), 121; Kinch and Long, 159; Bartley, 73–74; Ashmore, *Epitaph for Dixie*, 142.

55. Yarborough, in *Southern School News*, September 1954.

56. Yarborough to RDL, October 9, 1992; see also Green, 155; Baggarly, 121.

57. Yarborough, in Phillips, 38–39.

58. Weeks, 8; *Southern School News*, October 1954.

59. Shepperd, in *Southern School News*, October 1954; Murphy, 162.

60. Shepperd, in Jones, "Desegregation of Public Education in Texas," 355.

61. Shepperd, in Kluger, 734.

62. Shepperd, in Jones, "Desegregation of Public Education in Texas," 355.

63. Shivers, in Jones, "Desegregation of Public Education in Texas," 356, and see 353; quote also discussed, in *Southern School News*, February 1955; Murphy, 161; Harry K. Wright, *Civil Rights U.S.A.: Public Schools Southern States, 1963, Texas* (Washington, D.C.: United States Civil Rights Commission, Government Printing Office, 1964), 3.

64. Weeks, 8–9; *Southern School News*, July 1955; Jones, "Desegregation of Public Education in Texas," 353.

65. Governor Allan Shivers Press Memorandum, May 31, 1955, Allan Shivers Papers (hereafter referred to as Shivers Papers), Folder: Segregation

Miscellaneous, Box 1977/8-464, TSA; see also *Southern School News,* June 1955.

66. *Southern School News,* June 1955.

67. Ibid.

68. *Texas Poll,* Report 528, April 7, 1955, in Alan Scott, "Twenty-Five Years of Opinion on Integration in Texas," *Southwestern Social Science Quarterly* 48 (September 1967): 155, 160; Weeks, 9.

69. McMillen, 103; *Southern School News,* June, July, August, September, October 1955; *Report of the United States Commission on Civil Rights, 1959,* 266; Wright, 3–4.

70. *Southern School News,* September, Carlton, quoted in October, and see December 1955; see also McMillen, 104–105; Routh and Anthony, "Southern Resistance Forces," 57–58; Bartley, 97–98; Weeks, 9; *Dallas Morning News,* July 23, 29, November 12, 13, 1955.

71. *Southern School News,* September, and Shepperd, quoted in October 1955; see also Weeks, 9.

72. Governor Allan Shivers Press Memorandum, July 27, 1955, and Shivers statement to Texas Advisory Committee on Segregation, Shivers Papers, Folder: Segregation and Miscellaneous, Box 1977/8-464, TSA; see also *Race Relations Law Reporter* 1 (February 1956): 1077; Green, 187; Bartley, 79, 140; Weeks, 9; Wright, 11; *Report of the United States Commission on Civil Rights, 1959,* 235; *Southern School News,* September 1955.

73. *R. E. McKinney et al. v. W. C. Blankenship et al.,* Supreme Court of Texas, October 12, 1955, 282 S.W. 2d 691 (hereafter referred to as *McKinney v. Blankenship*); see also *Race Relations Law Reporter* 1 (February 1956): 77–81; Weeks, 9; Wright, 5; *Southern School News,* September, October, November 1955.

74. Governor Allan Shivers Press Memorandum, October 12, 1956, Shivers Papers, Folder: Segregation Miscellaneous, Box 1977/8-464, TSA.

75. Bartley, 138–140; Green, 187; see also *Southern School News,* February, March, April 1956.

76. Governor Allan Shivers Press Memorandum, Shivers to George W. Sandlin, Letter, and Shivers to Will Crews Morris, Letter, all dated February 23, 1956, all attached as one, Shivers Papers, Folder: Segregation Miscellaneous, Box 1977/8-464, TSA; the doctrine of interposition defined by Yarborough to RDL, October 9, 1992; see also *Southern School News,* February, March 1956.

77. Bartley, 139; *Southern School News,* February, March 1956.

78. "From Address of Governor Shivers, March 1, 1956," Shivers Papers, Folder: Segregation Miscellaneous, Box 1977/8-464, TSA; Shivers' plan was reiterated in a Press Memorandum, April 12, 1956, Shivers Papers, Folder: April 1956, Box 1977/81-532, TSA.

79. Banks, 123; Hendrix, "The Shivercrat Rebellion," 290–291; Bartley, 138–140; Green, 171–173. For a discussion of Shivers' political strategy and the events surrounding his attempt to gain leadership and "favorite son" status in 1956, see Weeks, chapters 3–4; Kinch and Long, chapter 20.

For a letter seeking voters' support, see also Shivers to Fellow Democrats, Letter, LBJ Papers, United States Senate Files, 1949–1961, Office Files of George Reedy, 1956–1957, Box 418, LBJ Library.

80. Ibid.; Hardeman, "Shivers of Texas," 53–55; see also "Governor Allan Shivers to Fellow Texans on Texas State Network," May 3, 1956, LBJ Papers, United States Senate Files, 1949–1961, Office Files of George Reedy, 1956–1957, Reedy: Convention 1956 Folder, Box 418, LBJ Library.

81. Herbert Brownell to RDL, Letter, November 23, 1992.

82. Ibid.

83. Ibid.; Archer Fullingim, "The Printer Fires Both Barrels," reprinted in the *Congressional Record*, August 6, 1957, Appendix, A6362; *Texas Observer*, April 25, 1956, see editorial same issue; Kinch and Long, 185; *Austin American*, April 21, 1956; see also Allan Shivers Press Memorandum, April 16, 1956, Shivers Papers, Folder: Shivers/April 1956, Box 1977/81-532, TSA.

84. Brownell to RDL, Letter, November 23, 1992.

85. Hendrix, "The Shivercrat Rebellion," 294–295; Bartley, 98, 139–140; Green, 171–173; for a concise discussion of Shivers in the 1956 political campaigns, see Weeks, chapter 4.

86. *Southern School News*, April, May, July 1956; Weeks, 37–38; Bartley, 98, 140; Fuermann, 196; Kinch and Long, 186.

87. *Texas Poll*, in *Southern School News*, July 1956; see also Fuermann, 197.

88. *Southern School News*, July 1956.

89. Ibid., August 1956; these numbers are reported higher, but with approximately the same ratio of difference, in Weeks, 38.

90. Bartley, 140.

91. Quote from Yarborough to RDL, October 9, 1992; see also Green, 174–175.

92. Yarborough to RDL, October 9, 1992; see also Green, 174–176; Weeks, 35–37; see also Kinch and Long, 186 (the authors stated Shivers took no part in the 1956 campaign for governor).

93. Weeks, 37; Bartley, 117n.

94. Shivers and Eisenhower are discussed in Weeks, chapter 6; see also Kinch and Long, 189; Green, 172; Bartley, 166.

95. *Southern School News*, September 1956; see also Muse, 87.

96. Pressley to RDL, October 5, 1992.

97. Ibid.

98. Griffin and Freedman, 3.

4. Taking a Stand on School Integration: The Dilemma of President Dwight David Eisenhower during His First Term

1. Sherman Adams, *Firsthand Report: The Story of the Eisenhower Administration* (New York: Popular Library, 1962), 327; Duram, *A Moderate among Extremists*, 53, 105, 119–120.

2. Dwight D. Eisenhower, *Waging Peace: The White House Years,*

1956–1961 (New York: Doubleday, 1965), 150; see also Duram, *A Moderate among Extremists*, 108–109.

3. For a discussion of the Little Rock crisis, see Duram, *A Moderate among Extremists*, chapter 9; see also Emmet John Hughes, *The Ordeal of Power: A Political Memoir of the Eisenhower Years* (London: Macmillan, 1963), 241–245; Adams, chapter 16.

4. Duram, *A Moderate among Extremists*, 109, 130; Peters, 242.

5. Peters, 242.

6. Robert L. Branyan and Lawrence H. Larsen, *The Eisenhower Administration, 1953–1961: A Documentary History* (New York: Random House, 1971), 1049; Rodgers and Bullock, 414–415; Duram, *A Moderate among Extremists*, 106.

7. Ashmore, *Epitaph for Dixie*, 182.

8. Peltason, 48–50.

9. Kluger, 753; Peltason, 46–47; Adams, 334. Eisenhower referred to "the foolish extremists on both sides" in a letter to Billy Graham, March 30, 1956, DDE Papers, Ann Whitman Files, Name Series, Box 8, DDE Library.

10. Burk, *The Eisenhower Administration*, 143.

11. Duram, *A Moderate among Extremists*, 106–108; Burk, "Dwight D. Eisenhower and Civil Rights Conservatism," 53.

12. Finch, 196–197; see also discussions of Eisenhower's reaction to the Southern Manifesto, in Eisenhower, *Waging Peace*, 150; Muse, 74–75; Duram, *A Moderate among Extremists*, 126–127.

13. Arthur Larson, *Eisenhower: The President Nobody Knew* (New York: Charles Scribner's Sons, 1968), 126–127.

14. Hughes, 200–201.

15. Frederic E. Morrow, *Black Man in the White House* (New York: Coward-McCann, 1963), 48.

16. Adams, 330–331; see also Branyan and Larsen, 1049; Duram, *A Moderate among Extremists*, 251–252.

17. Eisenhower, in Parmet, 438; and, in Duram, *A Moderate among Extremists*, 110–111.

18. Ibid. In his later memoirs, published in 1965, Eisenhower declared his support for the Supreme Court's school integration decision in *Brown I*. He stated, "I definitely agreed with the unanimous decision." No explanation was given for his changed opinion. See Eisenhower, *Waging Peace*, 150.

19. Larson, 124.

20. Eisenhower quoted, in Hughes, 201; also, in Sitkoff, 25.

21. Ann Whitman Diary Entry, August 14, 1956, DDE Papers, Ann Whitman File, Ann Whitman Diary Series, Box 8, DDE Library; also in Duram, *A Moderate among Extremists*, 132.

22. Eisenhower to Brownell, Telephone Call, August 19, 1956, DDE Papers, Ann Whitman File, Ann Whitman Diary Series, Box 8, DDE Library; see also Duram, *A Moderate among Extremists*, 133.

23. Eisenhower to Graham, Letter, March 30, 1956, DDE Papers, Ann

Whitman File, Name Series, Box 16, DDE Library; also in Duram, *A Moderate among Extremists*, 129; see also Eisenhower, *Waging Peace*, 151–152.

24. Parmet, 439; Larson, 12–14, 124–129; Herbert Brownell to RDL, Letter, November 23, 1992; Duram, *A Moderate among Extremists*, 71, 218–219, 250–253; Woodward, 139.

25. Duram, *A Moderate among Extremists*, 70–71, 252–253; Parmet, 439; Larson, 124–127; Woodward, 139; Ronald Schlundt, "Civil Rights Policies in the Eisenhower Years" (Ph.D. dissertation, Rice University, May 1973), 130.

26. Ed Edwin, "Interview with James Hagerty," March 2, 1967, Oral History Research Office, Columbia University, New York, OH-91, DDE Library.

27. Eisenhower quoted, in Duram, *A Moderate among Extremists*, 54. For another example of Eisenhower's distaste of extremes and the use of superlatives, see Larson, 5.

28. Duram, *A Moderate among Extremists*, 63, 115; Duram, "Whose Brief?" 45; Adams, 332; Michael S. Mayer, "With Much Deliberation and Some Speed: Eisenhower and the *Brown* Decision," *Journal of Southern History* 52 (1986): 44–45.

29. Quote, in Larson, 12–14; Duram, *A Moderate among Extremists*, 250–251.

30. Larson, 12–14; Parmet, 310; Duram, *A Moderate among Extremists*, 63; Duram, "Whose Brief?" 45–46; see also John Luter, "Interview with Allan Shivers," September 23, 1969, Columbia Oral History Project, Columbia University, OH-238, DDE Library.

31. *Brown II*; Eisenhower, *Waging Peace*, 151; Duram, *A Moderate among Extremists*, 131–132, 218–219.

32. Brownell to RDL, Letter, November 23, 1992; for an in-depth description of the Eisenhower administration during this time, see Herbert Brownell and John P. Burke, *Advising Ike: The Memoirs of Attorney General Herbert Brownell* (Lawrence: University Press of Kansas, 1993).

33. *Brown I*; Brownell to RDL, Letter, November 23, 1992; Eisenhower, *Waging Peace*, 150; Duram, "Whose Brief?" 43; Duram, *A Moderate among Extremists*, 59.

34. Eisenhower, in Duram, *A Moderate among Extremists*, 62.

35. Brownell to RDL, Letter, November 23, 1992; quote, in Eisenhower, *Waging Peace*, 150; Duram, *A Moderate among Extremists*, 61–62; Lee, 257; Mayer, "With Much Deliberation," 48–49.

36. Brownell to RDL, Letter, November 23, 1992; Duram, *A Moderate among Extremists*, 60; Burk, *The Eisenhower Administration*, 134–135.

37. Eisenhower, in Duram, *A Moderate among Extremists*, 60–61; also in Mayer, "With Much Deliberation," 49–50.

38. Duram, *A Moderate among Extremists*, 63–64, 109–110; Duram, "Whose Brief?" 45–46. Eisenhower also asked Brownell what would happen if the South abolished the public school systems; for a discussion, see Mayer, "With Much Deliberation," 56; and Burk, *The Eisenhower Administration*, 137.

39. Eisenhower, in Mayer, "With Much Deliberation," 54, and for a more in-depth view of the selection process, see 51–53; and also Burk, *The Eisenhower Administration,* 140; Kluger, 657–667; Lee, 254–256.

40. Eisenhower, in Mayer, "With Much Deliberation," 55.

41. The Justice Department's oral arguments before the Supreme Court, December 1953, in Hill and Greenberg, 114; see also Kelly, 265–266; Burk, *The Eisenhower Administration,* 138. For a discussion of the preparation of the brief and oral presentation, see Mayer, "With Much Deliberation," 56–58; see also Schlundt, 133.

42. Eisenhower, in Duram, *A Moderate among Extremists,* 64, 68; Burk, *The Eisenhower Administration,* 137–138.

43. *Brown I*; Eisenhower, *Waging Peace,* 150; Lee, 258–259; Parmet, 438.

44. Hughes, 200.

45. *Brown I*; Mayer, "With Much Deliberation," 68–69; Burk, *The Eisenhower Administration,* 148–149; Kluger, 726–727.

46. Wilhoit, 43; Duram, *A Moderate among Extremists,* 118–119; Goldman, 110; Schlundt, 134.

47. Brownell to RDL, Letter, November 23, 1992; see also Mayer, "With Much Deliberation," 67; Burk, *The Eisenhower Administration,* 148–149; Kluger, 726–727.

48. Justice Department brief, in Mayer, "With Much Deliberation," 66.

49. Quote, in Kluger, 727; also in Peltason, 50.

50. Ibid.

51. First quote, Sobeloff's oral arguments, April 13, 1955, in Peltason, 17; and also, in Burk, *The Eisenhower Administration,* 150; second quote, Sobeloff's oral arguments, April 13, 1955, in Peltason, 17; and also, in Mayer, "With Much Deliberation," 72–73.

52. Warren, in Duram, *A Moderate among Extremists,* 130.

53. Burk, *The Eisenhower Administration,* 152–153; Parmet, 440–441.

54. Burk, *The Eisenhower Administration,* 155, 159–160; Muse, 51–54; Finch, 197; Duram, *A Moderate among Extremists,* 122–124; Parmet, 440–442; John Weir Anderson, *Eisenhower, Brownell, and the Congress: The Tangled Origins of the Civil Rights Bill of 1956–1957* (Tuscaloosa: University of Alabama Press, 1964), 30–31; Roy Wilkins, *Standing Fast: The Autobiography of Roy Wilkins,* with Tom Mathews (New York: Viking Press, 1982), 228–231. For a description and discussion of Autherine Lucy and the riots at the University of Alabama, see also "How Miss Lucy Upset Alabama U.," *Ebony* 12 (March 1957): 51–54.

55. Ibid.; first quote and second quote, Eisenhower, in Duram, *A Moderate among Extremists,* 122; second quote, Eisenhower, also in Parmet, 442; and in Adams, 334; Justice Department Directives, in Burk, *The Eisenhower Administration,* 153.

56. Eisenhower, *Waging Peace,* 4; Burk, *The Eisenhower Administration,* 154.

57. Sitkoff, 33–34; Parmet, 444–445.

58. Herbert Brownell Jr., "Statement of Attorney General Herbert

Brownell Jr., on Civil Rights," March 9, 1956, DDE Papers, Ann Whitman File, Cabinet Series, Box 6, DDE Library; see also Edelsberg and Brody, *Civil Rights in the 84th Congress, 1955–1956,* October 29, 1956, LBJ Papers, United States Senate Files, 1949–1961, Office Files of George Reedy, 1956–1957, Reedy: Convention 1956 Folder, Box 418, LBJ Library; Parmet, 444–446; Burk, *The Eisenhower Administration,* 156.

59. Dwight David Eisenhower, "The State of the Union," *Vital Speeches,* 22 (February 1, 1956): 232–233; see also Eisenhower, *Waging Peace,* 153; Adams, 330.

60. J. Edgar Hoover, "Racial Tension and Civil Rights," March 9, 1956, DDE Papers, Ann Whitman File, Cabinet Series, Box 6, DDE Library; summarized in Minutes of Cabinet Meeting, March 9, 1956, DDE Papers, Ann Whitman File, Cabinet Series, Box 6, DDE Library; see also Eisenhower, *Waging Peace,* 152; Adams, 331; Burk, *The Eisenhower Administration,* 160–161; Duram, *A Moderate among Extremists,* 124–127; Taylor Branch, *Parting the Waters: America in the King Years, 1954–1963* (New York: Simon and Schuster, 1988), 181–183.

61. Herbert Brownell Jr., "Statement of Attorney General Herbert Brownell Jr., on Civil Rights," and attachments, March 9, 1956, DDE Papers, Ann Whitman File, Cabinet Series, Box 6, DDE Library; summarized in Minutes of Cabinet Meeting, March 9, 1956, DDE Papers, Ann Whitman File, Cabinet Series, Box 6, DDE Library; see also Branch, 181–183; Burk, *The Eisenhower Administration,* 160–161; Parmet, 444–445; Duram, *A Moderate among Extremists,* 125–127; Adams, 332; Anderson, 36.

62. Ibid.; the last statement was not taken down verbatim in the meeting and cannot be considered a direct quote.

63. Gerald D. Morgan, "Memorandum for Ann Whitman," March 24, 1956, DDE Papers, White House Central Files, Confidential 1953–1961, Subject Series, Box 61, DDE Library.

64. Herbert Brownell Jr. to Richard M. Nixon, Letter, April 9, 1956, LBJ Papers, United States Senate, 1953–1961, Office Files of George Reedy, 1956–1957, Reedy: Convention 1956 Folder, Box 418, LBJ Library; see also Branyan and Larsen, 1085.

65. Edelsberg and Brody, *Civil Rights in the 84th Congress, 1955–1956,* LBJ Papers, United States Senate Files, 1953–1961, Office Files of George Reedy, 1956–1957, Reedy: Convention 1956 Folder, Box 418, LBJ Library; see also Burk, *The Eisenhower Administration,* 163; Parmet, 448.

66. Ibid.

67. Morrow, 85–86; also in Parmet, 448.

68. Edelsberg and Brody, *Civil Rights in the 84th Congress, 1955–1956,* LBJ Papers, United States Senate Files, 1953–1961, Office Files of George Reedy, 1956–1957, Reedy: Convention 1956 Folder, Box 418, LBJ Library; see also Parmet, 442–443; Duram, *A Moderate among Extremists,* 216–235; Burk, *The Eisenhower Administration,* 158, 164.

69. Ann Whitman Diary Entry, March 21, 1956, DDE Papers, Ann Whitman File, DDE Diary Series, Folder: 1955–1956/1, Box 9, DDE Library; see also Adams, 333; Burk, 162–163; Duram, *A Moderate among*

Extremists, 127–130. For a concise article on Billy Graham's convictions, his meeting with Eisenhower, and his church meetings in the South, see Billy Graham, "Billy Graham Makes Plea for an End to Intolerance," *Life* 41 (October 1, 1956): 138, 140, 143–144, 146, 151.

70. Billy Graham to Dwight D. Eisenhower, Letter, March 27, 1956, DDE Papers, Ann Whitman File, Name Series, Box 16, DDE Library.

71. Billy Graham to Dwight D. Eisenhower, Letter, June 4, 1956, DDE Papers, Ann Whitman File, Name Series, Box 16, DDE Library.

72. Pre-Press Conference Briefing, August 8, 1956, DDE Papers, Ann Whitman File, Ann Whitman Diary Series, Box 8, DDE Library; and Dwight D. Eisenhower to Herbert Brownell, Telephone Call, August 19, 1956, DDE Papers, Ann Whitman File, Ann Whitman Diary Series, Box 8, DDE Library.

73. Dwight D. Eisenhower, Notes, August 21, 1956, DDE Papers, Ann Whitman File, Draft Series, Box 3, DDE Library; although the notes are not signed, the handwriting was determined to be that of Eisenhower by the archivists at the DDE Library. According to DDE Library Records, Eisenhower left Washington for San Francisco on August 21, 1956.

74. Dwight D. Eisenhower, "Acceptance Speech of the President at the Republican National Convention," August 23, 1956, DDE Papers, United States White House Official Reporter, Records of Jack Romagna, Speeches 1956, Folder: Pre-Election Speeches (1956), 1, Box 17, DDE Library; also in *Vital Speeches* 22 (September 1, 1956): 685–689.

5. The Mansfield School Integration Case: *Jackson v. Rawdon*

1. *Brown I;* Mansfield's NAACP branch and area are identified in "Writ of Temporary Injunction," September 1956, State of Texas vs. NAACP Records, Case Proceedings and Undated, Folder: Affidavits and Subpoenas, Box 3N156, BTHC; T. M. Moody is identified as Mansfield's NAACP branch president in "1955–1956: Texas State Conference of Branches, NAACP Officers and Branch Roster," State of Texas vs. NAACP, Folder 4: 1955–1956 and Undated, Box 3N161, BTHC.

2. Lawson to RDL, January 5, 1993; see also Davis to RDL, October 6, 1992.

3. Ibid.; see also Floyd Moody Sr. to RDL, October 6, 1992; Griffin and Freedman, 4–5; Gillette, "The NAACP in Texas," 263.

4. Lawson to RDL, January 5, 1993; Davis to RDL, October 6, 1992; see also "Texas State Conference of Branches," lists Davis as Chairman, Area 9, State of Texas vs. NAACP Records, Folder 4: 1955–1956 and Undated, Box 3N161, BTHC; Gillette, "The NAACP in Texas," 263.

5. Information from a consensus of those interviewed; Davis to RDL, October 6, 1992; Lawson to RDL, January 5, 1993; Griffin and Freedman, 4; Gillette, "The NAACP in Texas," 263.

6. Information from a consensus of those interviewed; Davis to RDL, October 6, 1992; Lawson to RDL, January 5, 1993; Floyd Moody Sr. to RDL, October 6, 1992; Griffin and Freedman, 4–5; see also Wright, 7–8.

7. *Brown II;* "Directives to the Branches Adopted by Emergency South-wide NAACP Conference," *Crisis* 62 (June–July 1955): 339–340, 380; Marshall described this meeting and its purpose in "Testimony of Thurgood Marshall," October 18, 1956, State of Texas vs. NAACP Records, Folder: Case Proceedings, 1956–1957 and Undated, Box 3N151, BTHC. The directives are also discussed in Bartley, 82–83.

8. Ibid.; *Brown I.*

9. Davis to RDL, October 6, 1992; see also Lawson to RDL, January 5, 1993; Griffin and Freedman, 4–5.

10. *Brown I; Brown II;* information from a consensus of those interviewed; Davis to RDL, October 6, 1992; Lawson to RDL, January 5, 1993; Briscoe to RDL, October 5, 1992; Floyd Moody Sr. to RDL, October 6, 1992. Last quotation is a phrase used by Walter White to describe the civil rights movement as a drive forward for African Americans with no regression, see White, *A Man Called White,* chapter 17.

11. MISD, School Board Meeting Minutes, July 26, 1955; see also Wright, 8; Griffin and Freedman, 5; Gillette, "The NAACP in Texas," 263.

12. "Texas State Conference of Branches Memorandum to All Education Committees," August 8, 1955, State of Texas vs. NAACP Records, Investigations of Texas Branches 1956, Folder: 4, Box 3N158, BTHC; also in "Edwin C. Washington Memorandum to All Education Committees," August 8, 1955, Possible Exhibit No. 4, Attorney General's Records, Folder: Unnamed, see yellow sheets, Box 1991/17-1, TSA.

13. "Testimony of J. E. Moody, Floyd Moody, and Charles Moody," Court of Inquiry, September 27, 1956, State of Texas vs. NAACP Records, Investigations of Texas Branches 1956, Folder: 8, Box 3N158, BTHC; Davis to RDL, October 6, 1992; Lawson to RDL, January 5, 1993. Tate also testified to meeting with Davis and the parents of the plaintiffs in Davis' office though no date is given in "Oral Testimonies," vol. 10, State of Texas vs. NAACP Records, Case Proceedings, 1956–1957 and Undated, 2405–2406, Box 3N156, BTHC.

14. "Testimony of J. E. Moody, Floyd Moody, and Charles Moody," Court of Inquiry, September 27, 1956, State of Texas vs. NAACP Records, Investigations of Texas Branches 1956, Folder: 8, Box 3N158, BTHC; Floyd Moody Sr. to RDL, October 6, 1992; Davis to RDL, October 6, 1992; Lawson to RDL, January 5, 1993. This meeting is also reported in Bob Bray, "Texas School Told to Integrate," *Texas Observer,* August 1, 1956, although this article claims the meeting took place in September 1955; Gillette, "The NAACP in Texas," 263.

15. Ibid.; see also Muse, 88–89.

16. MISD, School Board Meeting Minutes, August 22, 1955.

17. Information from a consensus of those interviewed; Davis to RDL, October 6, 1992; Lawson to RDL, January 5, 1993; see also description of steps taken by possible plaintiffs, in Muse, 78.

18. Davis to RDL, October 6, 1992; Tate, in "Oral Testimonies," vol. 10, State of Texas vs. NAACP Records, Case Proceedings, 1956–1957 and Undated, 2406, Box 3N156, BTHC; see also investigation notes about Tate's

involvement in the Mansfield school integration case, in Attorney General's Records, Folder: Number of Exhibits, Box 1991/17-1, TSA.

19. See Charles Moody's testimony in "Testimony of J. E. Moody, Floyd Moody, and Charles Moody," Court of Inquiry, September 27, 1956, State of Texas vs. NAACP Records, Investigations of Texas Branches 1956, Folder: 8, Box 3N158, BTHC.

20. Information from a consensus of those interviewed; Floyd Moody Sr. to RDL, October 6, 1992; Davis to RDL, October 6, 1992; Lawson to RDL, January 5, 1993; Briscoe to RDL, October 5, 1992.

21. Griffin and Freedman, 3; Dodge, "Black Like Me Now," *Dallas Observer*, September 6, 1990.

22. Davis to RDL, October 6, 1992.

23. Floyd Moody Sr. to RDL, October 6, 1992.

24. Davis to RDL, October 6, 1992.

25. *Nathaniel Jackson, a minor, et al. v. O. C. Rawdon, et al.*, United States District Court, Northern District, Texas, Civ. No. 3152, November 21, 1955, 135 F. Supp 936. Information and testimony on the original trial is also found in *Nathaniel Jackson, a minor, by his father and next friend, W. D. Jackson, et al. v. O. C. Rawdon, as President of the Board of Trustees, Mansfield Independent School District, et al.*, United States Court of Appeals, Fifth Circuit, June 28, 1956, Civ. No. 15927 (hereafter also referred to as *Jackson v. Rawdon* and the Mansfield school integration case); also in *Race Relations Law Reporter* 1 (February 1956): 75–77, 655–658; *Southern School News*, November 1955, August 1956; see also Griffin and Wright, 5.

26. MISD, School Board Meeting Minutes, October 5, 1955.

27. Information from a consensus of those interviewed; Meeks to RDL, October 6, 1992; Davis to RDL, October 6, 1992; Pigg to RDL, October 6, 1992; Sheila Taylor, "Jim Crow Revisited," *Texas Observer*, June 9, 1979, 6–7; Emory Cantey identified in *Fort Worth Star-Telegram*, September 2, 1956. The *Fort Worth Star-Telegram* cited is the Morning–Five Star, final run edition, unless otherwise indicated.

28. *Jackson v. Rawdon*; Davis to RDL, October 6, 1992.

29. Information from a consensus of those interviewed; Davis to RDL, October 6, 1992; Floyd Moody Sr. to RDL, October 6, 1992; Meeks to RDL, October 6, 1992; Pigg to RDL, October 6, 1992.

30. Beard quoted, in *Mansfield News*, October 27, 1955; also reported in Bray, "Texas School Told to Integrate," *Texas Observer*, August 1, 1956.

31. Ibid.

32. Jones, West, and Beard, quoted in ibid.

33. Joiner, quoted in ibid., November 3, 1955.

34. Ibid., see weekly editions for November 1955 through October 1956; see also Griffin and Freedman, 3, 9–10; Herbert Wey and John Corey, *Action Patterns in School Desegregation: A Guidebook* (Bloomington, Indiana: Phi Delta Kappa, 1959), 36.

35. *Jackson v. Rawdon*; also in *Race Relations Law Reporter* 1 (February 1956): 75–77, 655–658; see also *Brown I*; *Brown II*; *McKinney v. Blankenship*.

36. *Jackson v. Rawdon;* also in *Race Relations Law Reporter* 1 (February 1956): 75–77, 655–658.

37. Davis and Huffman, quoted in ibid.

38. Gibson, quoted in ibid.

39. Wilshire, quoted in ibid.

40. Ibid.

41. Ibid., 75–77; see also description and commentary in Blaustein and Ferguson, 191–193; reported in *Southern School News,* December 1955.

42. Ibid.; see also Peltason, 110–111.

43. Ibid.

44. Ibid.; *Brown I; Brown II; McKinney v. Blankenship.*

45. *Jackson v. Rawdon;* also in *Race Relations Law Reporter* 1 (February 1956): 75–77; see also Peltason, 144; Griffin and Freedman, 5; Wright, 8.

46. Davis to RDL, October 6, 1992; Floyd Moody Sr. to RDL, October 6, 1992.

47. MISD, School Board Meeting Minutes, November 8, 1955; Meeks to RDL, October 6, 1992.

48. *Mansfield News,* November 10, 17, 1955.

49. Ibid., see weekly editions for November 1955 through October 1956; see also Griffin and Freedman, 3, 9–10; Wey and Corey, 36.

50. Information is a consensus of those interviewed; Pressley to RDL, October 5, 1992; Meeks to RDL, October 6, 1992; Pigg to RDL, October 6, 1992.

51. Ibid.

52. Unidentified radical segregationist leader in Mansfield, quoted in Griffin and Freedman, Appendix III, 13–15; this interview is not included in all printings of the pamphlet. Appendix III is found in NAACP Records, Mansfield Files, Library of Congress.

53. U. Simpson Tate to Thurgood Marshall, Letter, November 10, 1955, Attorney General's Records, Folder: Location 302–347, Box 1991/17-4, TSA.

54. U. Simpson Tate to Thurgood Marshall, Letter, December 6, 1955, State of Texas vs. NAACP, Folder 7: Case Preparation, 1939–1957 and Undated, State's Exhibit #42, Box 3N159, BTHC.

55. "Texas State Conference of Branches NAACP, Special Executive Board Meeting," February 11, 1956, Austin, Texas, Attorney General's Records, Folder: Location 302–307, Box 1991/17-4, TSA. This report is also found in State of Texas vs. NAACP Records, Folder: 5, Box 3N161, BTHC.

56. Davis to RDL, October 6, 1992.

57. *Jackson v. Rawdon;* also in *Race Relations Law Reporter* 1 (February 1956): 655–658; *Plessy v. Ferguson;* see also *Legislative History of the United States Circuit Courts of Appeals and the Judges Who Served during the Period 1801 through March 1958* (Washington, D.C.: Government Printing Office, 1958), fold-out chart between pages 88 and 89; Kenneth N. Vines, "The Role of Circuit Courts of Appeal in the Federal Judicial Process: A Case Study," *Midwest Journal of Political Science* 7 (November 1963): 310–311; Wasby et al., 169–170.

58. Ibid.; *Brown I; Brown II; McKinney v. Blankenship.*

59. *Jackson v. Rawdon;* a "true copy" of the decree is in Richard M. Morehead Papers, Box 4Ze233, BTHC; also in *Race Relations Law Reporter* 1 (February 1956): 655–658; see also "What's New in the Law: Public Schools . . . Segregation," *American Bar Association Journal* 42 (1956): 960; *Southern School News,* August 1956; Peltason, 111, 144; Wright, 8–9.

60. Ibid.

61. Ibid.

62. MISD, School Board Meeting Minutes, April–July 1956, quote in Minutes, July 6, 1956; see also Meeks to RDL, October 6, 1992.

63. Meeks to RDL, October 6, 1992.

64. "Report of U. Simpson Tate, Regional Counsel, NAACP Legal Defense and Educational Fund, Inc., Southwest Region, June and July, 1956," Attorney General's Records, Folder: Location 302–347, Box 1991/17-4, TSA; see also Davis to RDL, October 6, 1992; Lawson to RDL, January 5, 1993.

65. *Jackson v. Rawdon,* United States District Court, Northern District, Texas, August 27, 1956, Civ. No. 3152; also in *Race Relations Law Reporter* 1 (February 1956): 884–885.

66. Ibid.; meeting discussed in U. S. Tate, "Press Release," August 27, 1956, NAACP Records, Mansfield Files, Library of Congress; also in "Report of U. Simpson Tate, Regional Counsel, NAACP Legal Defense and Educational Fund, Inc., Southwest Region, August, 1956," Attorney General's Records, Folder: Location 302–347, Box 1991/17-4, TSA; see also Wright, 8–9.

67. Ibid.

68. U. S. Tate, "Press Release," August 27, 1956, NAACP Records, Mansfield Files, Library of Congress; also in "Report of U. Simpson Tate, Regional Counsel, NAACP Legal Defense and Educational Fund, Inc., Southwest Region, August, 1956," Attorney General's Records, Folder: Location 302–347, Box 1991/17-4, TSA.

69. Meeks to RDL, October 6, 1992; see also Bray, "Texas Schools Told to Integrate," *Texas Observer,* August 1, 1956.

70. *Fort Worth Star-Telegram,* August 9, 1956.

71. J. L. Curry and unidentified businessman, quoted in ibid., August 7, 1956.

72. J. E. Moody, quoted in Bray, "Texas School Told to Integrate," *Texas Observer,* August 1, 1956; see also Floyd Moody Sr. to RDL, October 6, 1992; Taylor, "Jim Crow Revisited," 6–7.

73. Lawson to RDL, January 5, 1993; *Austin American,* August 30, 1956; Griffin and Freedman, 5; see also Sarratt, 158; Muse, 88–89; Gillette, "The NAACP in Texas," 264.

6. A Collision Course: The Crisis at Mansfield High School

1. *Brown I; Brown II; Texas Observer,* August 29, 1956; *Dallas Morning News,* August 28, 1956; *Austin American,* August 28, 1956; *Southern School News,* September 1956.

2. Information is a consensus of those interviewed; Davis to RDL, October 6, 1992; Floyd Moody Sr. to RDL, October 6, 1992; Lawson, January 5, 1993; Wright, quoted in *Dallas Morning News*, September 2, and see September 4, 1956; see also Griffin and Freedman, 5; Gillette, "The NAACP in Texas," 264.

3. *Fort Worth Star-Telegram*, August 28, 29, 1956. The *Fort Worth Star-Telegram* cited is the Morning–Five Star, final run edition, unless otherwise indicated. *Dallas Morning News*, August 29, 30, 1956; *Austin American*, August 28, 1956; see also F. Ross Peterson, "Prelude to Little Rock: The Eisenhower Administration and Mansfield, Texas," Department of History, Utah State University, unpublished article in author's possession with written permission to use, 2.

4. *Fort Worth Star-Telegram*, August 28, 29, 1956.

5. Wright, quoted in ibid., August 30, 1956; *Dallas Morning News*, August 30, 1956; Cannon, quoted in *Austin American*, August 30, 1956; a picture of the effigy is in "The Halting and Fitful Battle for Integration," *Life* 41 (September 17, 1956): 34; see also Wright, 9; Muse, 89; Peterson, "Prelude to Little Rock," 3; Cannon reported leaving town, in Griffin and Freedman, 5; Green, 189; Peltason, 145.

6. *Fort Worth Star-Telegram*, August 30, 1956; *Dallas Morning News*, August 30, 1956; Griffin and Freedman, 5–6.

7. Griffin and Freedman, 5–6; see also Pressley to RDL, October 5, 1992; Meeks to RDL, October 6, 1992.

8. *Fort Worth Star-Telegram*, August 31, 1956, see also Morning–Three Star edition for same date; Muse, 89.

9. Ibid.; *Dallas Morning News*, August 31, 1956; *Texas Observer*, September 5, 1956; Griffin and Freedman, 6–7; Peterson, "Prelude to Little Rock," 3; two photos of the effigy appear in R. C. Hickman, *Behold the People: R. C. Hickman's Photographs of Black Dallas, 1949–1961* (Austin: Texas State Historical Association, 1994), 118–119.

10. *Fort Worth Star-Telegram*, August 31, 1956, see also Morning–Three Star edition for same date; *Austin American*, August 31, 1956; Wright, 9.

11. Pressley to RDL, October 5, 1992.

12. Photograph of J. T. and Willard Pressley attempting to take the effigy down and story, in *Fort Worth Star-Telegram*, August 31, 1956; Pigg quoted in *Dallas Morning News*, August 31, 1956; Green, 189; Sarratt, 158; Peltason, 145; Dodge, "Black Like Me Now," *Dallas Observer*, September 6, 1990. For a description of the crowd, see Meeks to RDL, October 6, 1992; and Pigg to RDL, October 6, 1992; Pressley to RDL, October 5, 1992; see also young teenager's quote, in William Manchester, *The Glory and the Dream: A Narrative History of America, 1932–1972* (Boston: Little, Brown, 1973), 739. Signs and placards quoted are in several of the citations listed in this note. Capitalization on the signs is quoted exactly for accuracy.

13. Wright, quoted in *Fort Worth Star-Telegram*, Morning–Three Star edition, August 31, 1956; Pigg to RDL, October 6, 1992; Pressley to RDL, October 5, 1992; Owen Metcalf identified as leader in article as O. M.

Metcalf in the *Dallas Morning News*, August 31, 1956, but a slightly different conversation is recorded; see also the *Texas Observer*, September 5, 1956 (Owen Metcalf is identified as a leader, and the story is retold with a third series of different quotations); also in Peterson, "Prelude to Little Rock," 4.

14. *Dallas Morning News*, August 31, 1956; Griffin and Freedman, 7; Gillette, 264.

15. *Fort Worth Star-Telegram*, August 31, 1956; Pigg to RDL, October 6, 1992.

16. Tate discusses this hearing in Report of U. Simpson Tate, Regional Counsel, NAACP Legal Defense and Educational Fund, Inc., Southwest Region, August, 1956, Attorney General's Records, Folder: Location 302–347, Box 1991/17-4, TSA; *Fort Worth Star-Telegram*, August 31, 1956; Tate, Gooch, and Estes, quoted in the *Dallas Morning News*, August 31, 1956; another version of the quotation, in Griffin and Freedman, 6; see also Peterson, "Prelude to Little Rock," 2.

17. Fender, quoted in *Fort Worth Star-Telegram*, August 31, 1956; *Dallas Morning News*, August 31, 1956; *Austin American*, August 31, 1956; Griffin and Freedman, 7.

18. City of Mansfield Records, City Commission Meeting Minutes, August 30, 1956; Halbert reported leaving town, in Griffin and Freedman, 5; Green, 189; and Peltason, 145.

19. L. Clifford Davis to Honorable Allan Shivers, Governor of Texas, Telegram, August 31, 1956, NAACP Records, Mansfield Files, Library of Congress; Tate discusses this telegram in "Report of U. Simpson Tate, Regional Counsel, NAACP Legal Defense and Educational Fund, Inc., Southwest Region, August, 1956," Attorney General's Records, Folder: Location 302–347, Box 1991/17-4, TSA; and also in a letter, U. Simpson Tate to Roy Wilkins, Executive Secretary, NAACP, August 31, 1956, NAACP Records, Mansfield File, Library of Congress; sections of the telegram are printed in *Fort Worth Star-Telegram*, August 31, 1956, although not quoted exactly from the text; also partially quoted, in *Dallas Morning News*, August 31, 1956; *Austin American*, August 31, 1956; and Peterson, "Prelude to Little Rock," 3–4; *Dallas Express*, September 8, 1956.

20. *Fort Worth Star-Telegram*, August 31, 1956; *Dallas Morning News*, August 31, 1956; *Dallas Express*, September 8, 1956; Griffin and Freedman, 7.

21. Ibid.

22. Pressley to RDL, October 5, 1992; *Fort Worth Star-Telegram*, September 1, 1956; *Dallas Morning News*, September 1, and see the photograph of the effigy hanging from the high school building September 2, 1956, Focus section; *Texas Observer*, September 5, 1956; Griffin and Freedman, 7. A photograph of the effigy hanging from the high school building is also in *Austin American*, September 4, and reported on September 1, 1956; a third photograph of the effigy on the school building, in "The South: Fury and Progress," *Time* 68 (September 17, 1956): 32. The scene at the high school is also described in the *New York Times*, Septem-

ber 1, 1956; and in "Report of U. Simpson Tate, Regional Counsel, NAACP Legal Defense and Educational Fund, Inc., Southwest Region, August, 1956," Attorney General's Records, Folder: Location 302–347, Box 1991/ 17-4, TSA.

23. Huffman, quoted in *Fort Worth Star-Telegram*, September 1, 1956; and *Texas Observer*, September 5, 1956; also in Peltason, 145; Wey and Corey, 158; Robert Sherill, *Gothic Politics in the Deep South* (New York: Grossman, 1968), 88; see also *Austin American*, September 1, 1956.

24. *Fort Worth Star-Telegram*, September 1, 1956; *Dallas Morning News*, September 1, 1956; *New York Times*, September 1, 1956; see also Gillette, "The NAACP in Texas," 267.

25. Pressley to RDL, October 5, 1992; a picture of Hight and the crowd appears on the front page of the *New York Times*, September 1, 1956; the unidentified radical segregationist from the group encountering Hight is quoted in the same edition; Metcalf, quoted in *Fort Worth Star-Telegram*, September 1, 1956; and in *Austin American*, September 1, 1956; see also *Dallas Morning News*, September 1, 1956; *Texas Observer*, September 5, 1956; also reported in a United Press Release, August 31, 1956, in Mansfield Historical Society Records, Mansfield, Texas; each newspaper reports a slightly different version of the confrontation.

26. *Fort Worth Star-Telegram*, September 1, 1956; *Dallas Morning News*, September 1, 1956; *Austin American*, September 1, 1956; *New York Times*, September 1, 1956; and *Texas Observer*, September 5, 1956.

27. Ibid.; Peterson, "Prelude to Little Rock," 6.

28. *Dallas Morning News*, September 1, 1956; Meeks to RDL, October 6, 1992.

29. "Report of U. Simpson Tate, Regional Counsel, NAACP Legal Defense and Educational Fund, Inc., Southwest Region, August, 1956," Attorney General's Records, Folder: Location 302–347, Box 1991/17-4, TSA; Tate discusses this visit in a letter to Roy Wilkins, Executive Secretary, NAACP, August 31, 1956, NAACP Records, Mansfield File, Library of Congress.

30. Governor Allan Shivers, Press Memorandum, Office of the Governor, August 31, 1956, Shivers Papers, Folder: Segregation 1956—Mansfield, Box 1977/81-532, TSA; also reported in *Fort Worth Star-Telegram*, September 1, 1956.

31. Governor Allan Shivers, Press Memorandum, Office of the Governor, Statement, August 31, 1956, Shivers Papers, Folder: Segregation 1956—Mansfield, Box 1977/81-532, TSA; also reported in Wright, 9–10; Peltason, 145; Gillette, "The NAACP in Texas," 265–266; Green, 189; Muse, 89–90; Sarratt, 158–159; Bartley, 146–147; United Press Release, August 31, 1956, in Mansfield Historical Society Records, Mansfield, Texas; *Southern School News*, September 1956; *Dallas Morning News*, September 1, 1956; *Austin American*, September 1, 1956; *Texas Observer*, September 5, 1956; *New York Times*, September 3, 1956; *Christian Science Monitor*, September 1, 1956.

32. Governor Allan Shivers, Press Memorandum, August 31, 1956,

Shivers Papers, Folder: Segregation 1956—Mansfield, Box 1977/81-532, TSA; also reported in Wright, 9–10; Peltason, 145–146; Bartley, 147; United Press Release, August 31, 1956, in Mansfield Historical Society Records, Mansfield, Texas; *Southern School News*, September 1956; *Dallas Morning News*, September 1, 1956; *Austin American*, September 1, 1956; and *Texas Observer*, September 5, 1956.

33. Ibid.; Kinch and Long, 188–189; Sarratt, 158–159; see also editorials in *Texas Observer*, September 5, 1956; and *Fort Worth Star-Telegram*, September 2, 1956.

34. Ibid.; Sherill, 88; Wilhoit, 47.

35. Ibid.; *Brown I*; *Brown II*.

36. Ibid.; quotation, in letter to Governor Allan Shivers, September 4, 1956, Shivers Papers, Folder: Segregation 1956—Mansfield, Box 1977/81-532, TSA; see also Anderson, 128–129.

37. Pressley to RDL, October 5, 1992.

38. *New York Times*, September 1, 1956.

39. *Fort Worth Star-Telegram*, September 1, 1956; *Dallas Morning News*, September 1, 2, 1956; *New York Times*, September 1, 1956; *Christian Science Monitor*, September 1, 1956.

40. *Dallas Morning News*, September 1, 2, 1956; *Austin American*, September 1, 1956; *New York Times*, September 1, 1956; MISD, School Board Meeting Minutes, August 31, 1956; Meeks to RDL, October 6, 1956.

41. *Fort Worth Star-Telegram*, September 1, 1956.

42. L. Clifford Davis to R. L. Huffman, Telegram, August 31, 1956, NAACP Records, Mansfield File, Library of Congress; also in "Report of U. Simpson Tate, Regional Counsel, NAACP Legal Defense and Educational Fund, Inc., Southwest Region, August, 1956," Attorney General's Records, Folder: Location 302–347, Box 1991/17-4, TSA; see also U. Simpson Tate to Roy Wilkins, Executive Secretary, NAACP, Letter, August 31, 1956, NAACP Records, Mansfield File, Library of Congress; Huffman, quoted in *Dallas Morning News*, September 1, 1956; see also *Austin American*, September 1, 1956; *New York Times*, September 1, 1956; *Texas Observer*, September 5, 1956.

43. *Fort Worth Star-Telegram*, Morning–Three Star edition, September 1, 1956; *Austin American*, September 1, 1956; *New York Times*, September 1, 1956.

44. *Fort Worth Star-Telegram*, Morning–Three Star edition, September 1, 1956; *Austin American*, September 1, 3, 1956; *Texas Observer*, September 5, 1956; *New York Herald-Tribune*, September 3, 1956; *Dallas Express*, September 8, 1956; see also Gillette, "The NAACP in Texas," 268.

45. Telegram to Governor Allan Shivers, August 31, 1956, Shivers Papers, Folder: Segregation 1956—Mansfield, Box 1977/81-532, TSA.

46. Floyd Moody Sr. to RDL, October 6, 1992; *Dallas Express*, September 8, 15, 1956; same article, in *Houston Informer*, September 15, 1956.

47. *Fort Worth Star-Telegram*, September 1, 1956.

48. L. Clifford Davis to United States Attorney Herbert Brownell, Telegram, August 31, 1956, NAACP Records, Mansfield Files, Library of

Congress; see also "Report of U. Simpson Tate, Regional Counsel, NAACP Legal Defense and Educational Fund, Inc., Southwest Region, August, 1956," Attorney General's Records, Folder: Location 302–347, Box 1991/ 17–4, TSA; see also U. Simpson Tate to Roy Wilkins, Executive Secretary, NAACP, Letter, August 31, 1956, NAACP Records, Mansfield File, Library of Congress.

49. *Dallas Morning News*, September 1, 1956; *New York Times*, September 1, 1956; *Texas Observer*, September 5, 1956; Gillette, "The NAACP in Texas," 265.

50. Dates for Brownell's trip, in Herbert Brownell's Personal Appointment Book, Herbert Brownell Papers, 1877–1988, Subject Series, Folder: Appointment Books Pocket Size, 1955–1956, Box 265, DDE Library; *Dallas Morning News*, August 26, 27, 28, 29, 1956.

51. Brownell to RDL, November 23, 1992.

52. Official White House Transcript of Dwight David Eisenhower Press Conference, August 31, 1956, DDE Papers, Ann Whitman File, Press Conference Series, Box 5, DDE Library; also reported in *Dallas Morning News*, September 1, 1956; *New York Times*, September 1, 1956.

53. State Representative Joe Pool to Governor Allan Shivers, Telegram, August 31, 1956, Shivers Papers, Folder: Segregation 1956—Mansfield, Box 1977/81-532, TSA; *Fort Worth Star-Telegram*, September 1, 1956; see also Gillette, "The NAACP in Texas," 268.

54. *Fort Worth Star-Telegram*, September 2, 3, 4, 1956; *New York Times*, September 2, 1956.

55. Ibid.

56. *Fort Worth Star-Telegram*, September 2, 3, 1956; Floyd Moody Sr. to RDL, October 6, 1956.

57. Metcalf and Beard, quoted in *Fort Worth Star-Telegram*, September 2, 1956.

58. Cantey, quoted in *Fort Worth Star-Telegram*, September 2, see also September 3, 1956; *Austin American*, September 2, 1956; *Dallas Morning News*, September 2, 1956; *New York Times*, September 2, 1956; *Christian Science Monitor*, September 1, 1956.

59. *Fort Worth Star-Telegram*, September 3, 1956; *Dallas Morning News*, September 2, 1956.

60. *Fort Worth Star-Telegram*, September 4, 1956; Gillette, "The NAACP in Texas," 267.

61. Curry, quoted in *Fort Worth Star-Telegram*, September 4, 1956.

62. A copy of this report is in the possession of Michael Lowery Gillette, Director, Center for Legislative Archives, National Archives, Washington, D.C.; Gillette cites the report—E. J. Banks to Homer Garrison Jr., October 8, 1956, Bureau of Intelligence Case No. 64921, Texas Department of Public Safety Files, Austin; Gillette discusses and quotes the report, in Gillette, "The NAACP in Texas," 284, n. 17; repeated efforts by this author to receive a copy of the report from the Texas Rangers and the Texas Department of Public Safety proved futile. After several inquiries, these agencies believe the report and file under this case number or any other

designation no longer exists. It was explained to the author that files are burned after a certain period of time. Gillette received his copy prior to 1984. A brief letter written to Colonel Homer Garrison with copies to Shivers and Crowder corroborates the report of several Texas Rangers being dispatched to Mansfield on September 4, see in Jerry A. McNeill, Staff Photographer, United Press, to Colonel Homer Garrison, Director, Department of Public Safety, Letter, September 7, 1956, Shivers Papers, Public Safety Texas Rangers, Box 1977/81-93, TSA. McNeill wrote, "We want to take this opportunity to express our appreciation for the wonderful cooperation extended to us by Captain Bob Crowder, Sgt. Jay Banks, and all the other Rangers that were on duty at Mansfield. These men extended to us every courtesy."

63. *Fort Worth Star-Telegram*, Morning–Three Star edition, September 5, 1956; *Dallas Morning News*, September 5, 1956; *New York Times*, September 5, 1956; *Christian Science Monitor*, September 4, 1956. A photograph of a Texas Ranger leaning against a tree with the school building and effigy in the background is in "The South: Fury and Progress," *Time* 68 (September 17, 1956): 32. The same photograph is also in "Negro Progress in 1956," *Ebony* 12 (January 1957): 59.

64. Ibid.; photographs of the monkey in "The Halting and Fitful Battle for Integration," *Life* 41 (September 17, 1954): 34; and in *Fort Worth Star-Telegram*, Morning–Three Star edition, September 5, 1956.

65. Clark, Curry, and Metcalf, quoted in *Fort Worth Star-Telegram*, Morning–Five Star and Morning–Three Star editions, September 5, 1956; *Dallas Morning News*, September 5, 1956; *New York Times*, September 5, 1956; *Christian Science Monitor*, September 4, 1956; see also Griffin and Freedman, 8; Sarratt, 271; Peterson, "Prelude to Little Rock," 8–9. For a picture of the Reverend Mr. Clark leaving the crowd, see "A Round Table Has Debate on Christians' Moral Duty," *Life* 41 (October 1, 1956): 162.

66. "Jesus Christ" to R. L. Huffman, Letter with Attachments, August 31, 1956, Shivers Papers, Folder: Federal Segregation, Mansfield 1956, Box 1977/81-87, TSA.

67. Ibid.

68. Ibid.

69. "Jesus Christ" to Dwight D. Eisenhower, Telephone Call on Telephone Memorandum, September 4, 1956, 10:28 A.M., White House Office Files, Telephone Logs, May 1, 1956, to September 30, 1956, Box 10, DDE Library.

70. "Jesus Christ" to R. L. Huffman, Letter with Attachments, August 31, 1956, Shivers Papers, Folder: Federal Segregation, Mansfield 1956, Box 1977/81-87, TSA.

71. *Fort Worth Star-Telegram*, September 6, 1956.

72. Ibid., September 5, 1956.

73. Ibid., and see Morning–Three Star edition, September 6, 1956; *Dallas Morning News*, September 5, 1956; Peterson, "Prelude to Little Rock," 8.

74. *Fort Worth Star-Telegram*, September 5, 1956; *Dallas Morning News*, September 5, 1956; *New York Times*, September 5, 1956.

75. Davis' first quote in *Fort Worth Star-Telegram*, September 5, 1956; Davis' second quote in *Dallas Morning News*, September 5, 1956; *Austin American*, September 5, 1956; *New York Times*, September 5, 1956; Peterson, "Prelude to Little Rock," 9.

76. Quotation, in *Mansfield News*, September 6, 1956; *Fort Worth Star-Telegram*, Morning–Three Star edition, September 6, 1956; *New York Times*, September 6, 1956.

77. Official Transcript of Dwight D. Eisenhower Press Conference, September 5, 1956, DDE Papers, Ann Whitman File, Press Conference Series, Box 5, DDE Library; see also *New York Times*, September 6, 7, 1956; *Fort Worth Star-Telegram*, Morning–Three Star edition, September 6, 1956; *Dallas Morning News*, September 6, 1956; *Austin American*, September 6, 1956; Sarratt, 57; Muse, 90–92; Bartley, 147; Peltason, 51.

78. Ibid.; see also Peterson, "Prelude to Little Rock," 10–11; Gillette, "The NAACP in Texas," 266–267; Charles C. Alexander, *Holding the Line: The Eisenhower Era, 1952–1961* (Bloomington: Indiana University Press, 1975), 118.

79. Ibid.

80. Ibid.

81. Ibid.

82. Brownell to RDL, November 23, 1992.

83. *Brown II*; see editorial in *Dallas Morning News*, September 7, 1956.

84. Shivers, quoted in *Dallas Morning News*, September 7, 1956; see also *Fort Worth Star-Telegram*, September 7, 1956; *Austin American*, September 7, 1956; *New York Times*, September 7, 1956; *Southern School News*, October 1956.

85. *New York Times*, September 7, 1956.

86. John Morsell, "Statement Given to the Associated Press, Re: School Integration Disturbances—NAACP Action and Policy," September 7, 1956, NAACP Records, Mansfield File, Library of Congress.

87. Wilkins, quoted in *Dallas Express*, September 15, 1956.

88. Marshall, quoted in *Austin American*, September 6, 1956.

89. Press Release from the Office of the Attorney General, John Ben Shepperd, August 6, 1956, Shivers Papers, Folder: Segregation 1956—Mansfield, Box 1977/81-532, TSA; see also *Southern School News*, October 1956.

90. Ibid.

91. Thurgood Marshall to Dwight D. Eisenhower, Letter, August 6, 1956, DDE Papers, White House Central Files, General Files: Schools and or School Decisions, G 124-A-1, Folder 1, Box 916, DDE Library; see also Durham, *A Moderate among Extremists*, 134–135; Burk, *The Eisenhower Administration*, 168.

92. Ibid.

93. Norman Thomas to Dwight D. Eisenhower, Letter, August 6, 1956, DDE Papers, White House Central Files, General Files: Schools and or School Decisions, G 124-A-1, Folder 1, Box 916, DDE Library. This letter also appeared in Thomas' syndicated column.

94. Ibid.

95. *Brown II;* Official Transcript of Dwight D. Eisenhower Press Conference, September 11, 1956, DDE Papers, Ann Whitman File, Press Conference Series, Box 5, DDE Library; *Fort Worth Star-Telegram,* September 12, 1956; *New York Times,* September 12, 1956.

96. *Fort Worth Star-Telegram,* Morning–Three Star edition, September 18, 1956.

97. *Austin American,* September 26, 1956; *New York Times,* September 26, 1956.

98. *United States Reports* 352 (October Term 1956), Cases Adjudged in the Supreme Court (Washington, D.C.: United States Government Printing Office, 1957), 925.

99. Information is a consensus of those interviewed; Davis to RDL, October 6, 1992; Floyd Moody Sr. to RDL, October 6, 1992; Lawson to RDL, January 5, 1993; Briscoe to RDL, October 5, 1992. The Mansfield parents sincerely feared for their children's welfare. This fear was not unfounded or uncommon. For a chilling account of the threats and fears experienced by the Little Rock teenagers and their parents, see Melba Pattillo Beals, *Warriors Don't Cry: A Searing Memoir of the Battle to Integrate Little Rock's Central High* (New York: Simon and Schuster, 1994).

7. The Mansfield School Integration Case and Crisis: A Significant Aftermath

1. Stillwell, quoted in Muse, 88; also in *Austin American,* September 8, 1956; Banks, quoted in Sarratt, 158–159; see also Peltason, 143; Bartley, 146–147.

2. U. Simpson Tate to President Dwight D. Eisenhower, Telegram, September 10, 1956, DDE Papers, Central Files, Official File 142-A, Negro Matters, Folder: 142A-5-1, Box 731, DDE Library; see also *Dallas Express,* September 15, 1956; *Austin American,* September 11, 1956.

3. Dwight D. Eisenhower to U. Simpson Tate, Letter, September 17, 1956, DDE Papers, Central Files, Official File 142-A, Negro Matters, Folder: 142A-5-1, Box 731, DDE Library.

4. Ibid.; Sarratt, 158–159.

5. Allan Shivers, "Statement of the Governor," September 18, 1956, Republican National Committee Records, 1932–1965, News Clippings, Folder: Texas Democrats, Shivers, Allan (Governor), 5/1/51–10/1/56, Box 190, DDE Library; see also *Austin American,* September 19, 1956.

6. Chandler and Clement, quoted in Sarratt, 156–158; *Austin American,* September 3, 9, 10, 11, 13, 1956; *Dallas Express,* September 15, 1956; Peltason, 151–155; Muse, 32–33, 92–104, 157; see also Thurgood Marshall interviewed in *Newsweek* 48 (September 17, 1956): 36–37. Marshall discusses the difference in Clement's and Shivers' handling of the school integration crises in their states.

7. Dwight David Eisenhower, *Public Papers of the Presidents of the United States: Dwight David Eisenhower, 1956* (Washington, D.C.:

United States Government Printing Office, 1958), 779–788, Eisenhower, quoted in 780–781.

8. For an example of Eisenhower's speeches with references to racial equality and civil rights between September 1956 and September 1957, see Dwight D. Eisenhower, "Remarks at the Republican Campaign Picnic at the President's Gettysburg Farm," September 12, 1956, 771–774, "People Ask the President," Television Broadcast, October 12, 1956, 912–913, in *Public Papers of the Presidents of the United States, Dwight D. Eisenhower, 1956*; see also Dwight D. Eisenhower, "The State of the Union: The Cost of Peace," January 10, 1957, *Vital Speeches* 23 (February 1, 1957): 226–229.

9. For a concise discussion of Eisenhower's role in Little Rock, see Duram, *A Moderate among Extremists*, chapter 9; see also Adams, 339–354. For a day-to-day account, see Muse, chapter 10; Lee, 259–261; Sarratt, 57–59.

10. Brown and Faubus, quoted in McMillen, 271; see also Chandler Davidson, *Biracial Politics: Conflict and Coalition in the Metropolitan South* (Baton Rouge: Louisiana State University Press, 1972), 166; Green, 189. Governors George and Lurleen Wallace of Alabama used Shivers' precedent of enforcement in Mansfield in their state in 1964 and 1965, respectively; for a discussion, see Sherill, 285.

11. Adams, 339–354; Duram, *A Moderate among Extremists*, 144–159; Muse, 128–145; Lee, 260–261.

12. John Luter, "Interview with Allan Shivers," September 23, 1969, Oral History Research Office, Columbia University, New York, OH-238, DDE Library.

13. Ibid.

14. For an in-depth discussion, see Duram, *A Moderate among Extremists*, chapter 9; see also Adams, chapter 16; Muse, chapter 10; Lee, 259–261; Sarratt, 57–59.

15. Herbert Brownell to Dwight D. Eisenhower, Letter, November 7, 1957, in *Official Opinions of the Attorney General of the United States Advising the President and Heads of Department in Relation to Their Official Duties, volume 41, ed. Vida Ord Alexander* (Washington, D.C.: United States Government Printing Office, 1963), 313–332, quote in 332.

16. Ibid., 327.

17. Ibid., 327–328.

18. Ibid., 332.

19. Eisenhower, quoted in Adams, 338, see also 335–339; Lee, 262–263; Duram, *A Moderate among Extremists*, 143, 182–183; Peltason, 54; Hughes, 242–243; Burk, *The Eisenhower Administration*, 171–173.

20. *Austin American*, September 11, 1956; *Southern School News*, October 1956.

21. Ibid.

22. *Race Relations Law Reporter* 1 (February 1956): 1077–1091; *Southern School News*, October 1956; Wright, 11; see also Fuermann, 217–218; *Texas Observer*, October 3, 1956.

23. *Race Relations Law Reporter* 1 (February 1956): 1077–1080.

24. Ibid., 1080–1086.

25. Ibid., 1086–1088; *Southern School News*, October 1956; Wright, 11.

26. *Race Relations Law Reporter* 1 (February 1956): 1088–1089.

27. Ibid., 1086–1088; *Southern School News*, October 1956; Wright, 11.

28. Walter F. Murphy, "The South Counterattacks: The Anti-NAACP Laws," *Western Political Quarterly* 12 (1959): 371–390; Aldon D. Morris, *The Origins of the Civil Rights Movement: Black Communities Organizing for Change* (New York: Collier Macmillan, 1984), 30–35.

29. Davis Grant to J. A. Gooch, Letter, September 13, 1956, Attorney General's Records, Folder: Miscellaneous Material/Joe McMinn NAACP, Box 1991/57-29, TSA. The same letter is found in State of Texas vs. NAACP, General Correspondence, 1950–1957, Folder: 1, Box 3N158, BTHC; Morrow's activities are discussed in *Austin American*, September 14, 1956.

30. "Investigation Report Possible Barratry Activities of Clifford Davis," Attorney General's Records, Folder: Location 302–347, Box 1991/17-4, TSA. The same report is found in State of Texas vs. NAACP, Investigation of Texas Branches 1956, Folder: 8, Box 3N158, BTHC.

31. John Ben Shepperd to NAACP Officers, Letter, September 18, 1956, Attorney General's Records, Folder: Unnamed, Box 1991/17-1, TSA; see also *Austin American*, September 15, 1956.

32. L. B. Murphy, 176; Shepperd, quoted in *Austin American*, September 22, 1956; and in *Texas Observer*, September 26, 1956; for a discussion on barratry and the NAACP, see October 3, 1956; see also Peltason, 69; *Southern School News*, October 1956.

33. Marshall, quoted in *Texas Observer*, September 26, 1956; also in *Austin American*, September 24, 1956.

34. "Testimony of J. E. Moody, Floyd Moody, and Charles Moody," Court of Inquiry, September 27, 1956, State of Texas vs. NAACP Records, Investigations of Texas Branches 1956, Folder: 8, Box 3N158, BTHC.

35. These testimonies were acknowledged on September 27, 1956, by J. E. Moody, in "Testimony of J. E. Moody, Floyd Moody, and Charles Moody," Court of Inquiry, September 27, 1956, State of Texas vs. NAACP Records, Investigations of Texas Branches 1956, Folder: 8, Box 3N158, BTHC; but a search by the author at the BTHC, TSA, and through inquiries at the Library of Congress for the transcripts proved futile. A request to the U.S. Department of Justice, Civil Rights Division, under the Freedom of Information Act, to release the Mansfield File kept by the department after the crisis was denied. The files were sealed in 1970 to protect the privacy of the Mansfield Public School System.

36. "Testimony of J. E. Moody, Floyd Moody, and Charles Moody," Court of Inquiry, September 27, 1956, State of Texas vs. NAACP Records, Investigations of Texas Branches 1956, Folder: 8, Box 3N158, BTHC; Davis to RDL, October 6, 1956; see also Griffin and Freedman, 8–9.

37. "Testimony of J. E. Moody, Floyd Moody, and Charles Moody,"

Court of Inquiry, September 27, 1956, State of Texas vs. NAACP Records, Investigations of Texas Branches 1956, Folder: 8, Box 3N158, BTHC.

38. Ibid.

39. Investigation notes on Tate in Attorney General's Records, Folder: Number of Exhibits, Box 1991/17-1, TSA.

40. Case officially designated *The State of Texas v. The National Association for the Advancement of Colored People, a corporation, et al.,* District Court, 7th Judicial District, Smith County, Texas, May 8, 1957, No. 56-649; Tate and Durham quoted from testimony, in "Oral Testimonies," vol. 10, State of Texas vs. NAACP Records, Folder: Case Proceedings, 1956–1957 and Undated, Box 3N156, 2406, BTHC; see also "Oral Testimonies," vol. 4, State of Texas vs. NAACP Records, Folder: Case Proceedings, 1956–1957 and Undated, Box 3N151, 538–540, 544–547, BTHC; Marshall's testimony on Mansfield, in "Oral Testimonies," October 18, 1956, State of Texas vs. NAACP Records, Folder: Case Proceedings, 1956–1957 and Undated, Box 3N153, 17–26, BTHC.

41. Marshall, quoted in *Texas Observer*, October 31, 1956.

42. *Race Relations Law Reporter* 2 (1957): 678–681; *Southern School News*, November 1956; Murphy, 176–177; Peltason, 69–70.

43. Dunagan, quoted in *Texas Observer*, October 24, 1956; and in Ronnie Dugger, "Confessions of a White Liberal," in *Black, White, and Gray: Twenty-One Points of View on the Race Question*, ed. Daniel Bradford (New York: Sheed and Ward, 1964), 236; Yellow carbon receipt of letter to T. M. Moody is filed with other branch receipts in Attorney General's Records, Folder: Sheriff's return on Writ, Box 1991/57-29, TSA.

44. Allan Shivers, "Address of Governor Allan Shivers to 55th Legislature," January 10, 1957, Shivers Papers, Folder: Message to 55th Legislature, 1957, Box 1977/81-538, TSA; also in *Senate Journal, Texas, 55th Legislature, 1957*, January 10, 1957, 28–32, Shivers quoted on 29.

45. Green, 189–190; Wright, 12.

46. Wright, 12–14; Green, 190; for an official recognition of several of the proposed bills and their paths through the Texas Legislature, see *Journal of the House of Representatives of the Regular Session of the 55th Legislature of the State of Texas*, 106, 3750, 3776–3777; *Senate Journal, Texas, 55th Legislature, 1957*, 1717; and *Vernon's Texas Statutes, 1958 Supplement: Including General and Permanent Laws, of the 55th Legislature, Regular Session and 1st and 2nd Called Sessions* (Kansas City, Missouri: Vernon Law Books, 1958), 274–278.

47. Green, 190; Article 2901a, quoted in *Vernon's Texas Statutes*, 276–277, see also 275–278; and in Wright, 13–14; S. Larry Roush, "A Summary of Southern States' Legislative Reactions to School Desegregation," *Texas School Board Journal* 3–7 (September 1957): 7.

48. Ibid.

49. *Vernon's Texas Statutes*, 278–281; Wright, 14–15; Green, 190.

50. Wright, 14–17.

51. Ibid.

52. Griffin and Freedman, 9; see also Beverly Frank, "John Howard Griffin" (M.A. thesis, University of Texas at Arlington, 1989), 132–133. Griffin is best known for writing *Black Like Me* (Boston: Houghton-Mifflin, 1961). To write this book, Griffin chemically dyed his skin dark brown and spent several weeks living in the South as an African American and recording his observations and experiences.

53. Griffin and Freedman, 10; Frank, 133.

54. Briscoe to RDL, October 5, 1992.

55. Ibid.; Floyd Moody Sr. to RDL, October 6, 1992; Taylor, "Jim Crow Revisited," *Texas Observer*, June 9, 1979.

56. Davis to RDL, October 6, 1992; *Austin American-Statesman*, September 9, 1956.

57. Marian Wright Edelman, "Southern School Desegregation, 1954–1973: A Judicial-Political Overview," *Annals of the American Academy of Politics and Social Sciences* 405–407 (May 1973): 35–38; Wasby et al., 212–214; Greg Olds, "Integration in Texas: Some Gains Made, but Substantial Problems Remain," *Texas Observer*, October 28, 1966.

58. MISD, School Board Meeting Minutes, January 26, 1965; Pigg to RDL, October 6, 1992.

59. Pigg, quoted in Olds, "Integration in Texas," *Texas Observer*, October 28, 1966; the peaceful 1965 school integration is discussed in the following interviews: Pigg to RDL, October 6, 1992; Meeks to RDL, October 6, 1992; Pressley to RDL, October 5, 1992; Briscoe to RDL, October 5, 1992.

60. Marshall, quoted on the "Today Show: Documentary on Thurgood Marshall," January 26, 1993, National Broadcasting Company.

61. Quote, in White, *How Far the Promised Land?* 103.

Bibliography

Primary Sources

1. Archival Collections

Abilene, Kansas. Dwight David Eisenhower Library.
  Brownell, Herbert, Jr., Papers, 1877–1988.
  Eisenhower, Dwight David. Papers as President of the United States, 1953–1961; Ann Whitman Files: Ann Whitman Diary Series, Cabinet Series, Draft Series, Dwight David Eisenhower Diary Series, Name Series, Press Conference Series.
  ———. Records as President. White House Central Files, 1953–1961: Confidential, 1953–1961 Subject Series, General Files, Official Files 142-A.
  Republican National Committee. News Clippings and Publications, 1932–1965.
  White House Office. Office of the Official Reporter Jack Romagna, 1953–1961: Speeches, 1956.
  White House Office. Telephone Office Records, 1953–1961.
Austin, Texas. Lyndon Baines Johnson Library.
  Johnson, Lyndon Baines. United States Senate Files, 1949–1961: General Files, Office Files of George Reedy.
Austin, Texas. Texas State Archives.
  Attorney General's Records.
  Shivers, Governor Allan, Papers.
Austin, Texas. Barker Texas History Center at the Center for American History, University of Texas.
  Morehead, Richard M., Papers. 1903, 1946–1979.
  State of Texas versus NAACP Case Records. 1911, 1945–1961.
Washington, D.C. Library of Congress.
  National Association for the Advancement of Colored People Records, Mansfield Files. NAACP; MSS Division. Group III; Cont. #A106; ff "Desegregation—School—Texas, 1956-1957," Mansfield, Texas. Group III; Cont. #A99; ff "Desegregation—School—Cases Decided since 1956," p. 7 of Segregation Report, *Jackson v. Rawdon.*

2. Oral History

Columbia Oral History Project, Columbia University.
   Hagerty, James. OH-91, March 2, 1967.
   Shivers, Allan. OH-238, September 23, 1969.

3. Interviews

Briscoe, Maggie. Mansfield, Texas. October 5, 1992.
Davis, L. Clifford. Fort Worth, Texas. October 6, 1992. Telephone Interview, December 17, 1992.
Lawson, John F. Fort Worth, Texas. Telephone Interview, January 5, 1993.
Meeks, Melvin M. Mansfield, Texas. October 6, 1992.
Moody, Floyd, Sr. Fort Worth, Texas. October 6, 1992.
Pigg, Willie. Mansfield, Texas. October 6, 1992.
Pressley, Kenneth. Mansfield, Texas. October 5, 1992.
Steward, Willie. Mansfield, Texas. Telephone Interview, December 8, 1992.
Yarborough, Ralph W. Austin, Texas. October 9, 1992.

4. Correspondence

Brownell, Herbert, Jr., to author, November 23, 1992.

5. Legal Cases

Belton v. Gebhart, 87 A. 2d 862 (Del. Ch. 1952), 91 A. 2d 137 (1953), 347 U.S. 483 (1954).
Bolling v. Sharpe, 347 U.S. 497 (1954), 74 S. Ct. 693, 98 L.Ed. 884.
Briggs v. Elliott, 98 F. Supp. 529 (1951), 103 F. Supp. 920 (1952), 347 U.S. 497 (1954), 132 F. Supp. 776 (1955).
Brown v. Board of Education, United States Supreme Court, May 17, 1954, 347 U.S. 483, 74 S. Ct. 686, 98 L.Ed. 873.
Brown v. Board of Education, United States Supreme Court, May 31, 1955, 349 U.S. 294, 75 S. Ct. 753.
Davis v. County School Board, 103 F. Supp. 337 (1952), 347 U.S. 483 (1954).
Gaines v. Canada, 305 U.S. 337 (1937).
Jackson v. Rawdon, United States District Court, Texas, Civ. No. 3152, November 21, 1955, 135 F. Supp. 936; United States Court of Appeals, Fifth Circuit, June 28, 1956, Civ. No. 15927.
Henderson v. United States, 339 U.S. 816 (1950).
Matthews v. Launius, United States District Court, Western District, Arkansas, October 4, 1955, 134 F. Supp. 684.
McKinney v. Blankenship, Supreme Court of Texas, October 12, 1955, 282, S.W. 2d 691.
McLaurin v. Oklahoma, 339 U.S. 637, rev'g 87 F. Supp. 528 (1950).

Plessy v. Ferguson, United States Supreme Court, 163 U.S. 537 (1896).

Rawdon v. Jackson, U.S. Reports 352 (October Term, 1956), 925, December 3, 1956, C. A. 5th Circuit Certiorari denied. 235 F. 2d 93.

Sipuel v. Oklahoma State Regents, 332 U.S. 631, rev'g 180 P. 2d. 135 (Oklahoma, 1948).

State of Texas v. The National Association for the Advancement of Colored People, District Court, 7th Judicial District, Smith County, Texas, May 8, 1957, No. 56-649.

Sweatt v. Painter, 339 U.S. 629, rev'g 210 S.W. 2d 442 (1950).

6. *United States Official Documents and Reports*

Alexander, Vida Ord, ed. *Official Opinions of the Attorney General of the United States Advising the President and Heads of Department in Relation to Their Official Duties.* Vol. 41. Washington, D.C.: U.S. Government Printing Office, 1963.

Eisenhower, Dwight David. *Public Papers of the Presidents of the United States: Dwight David Eisenhower, 1956.* Washington, D.C.: U.S. Government Printing Office, 1958.

Legislative History of the United States Circuit Courts of Appeals and the Judges Who Serve during the Period 1801 through March 1958. Washington, D.C.: U.S. Government Printing Office, 1958.

Powell, Adam Clayton. "What's Happening in School Integration?" House of Representatives. *Congressional Record* 103 (May 16, 1957): 7112–7117.

Report of the United States Commission on Civil Rights, 1959. Washington, D.C.: U.S. Government Printing Office, 1959.

United States Reports. Vol. 352. Washington, D.C.: Government Printing Office, 1957.

Wright, Harry K. *Civil Rights U.S.A.: Public Schools Southern States, 1963, Texas.* Washington, D.C.: U.S. Government Printing Office, 1964.

7. *Texas State Documents and Reports*

Journal of the House of Representatives of the Regular Session of the 55th Legislature of the State of Texas.

Senate Journal, Texas, 55th Legislature, 1957.

Texas Department of Public Safety, Bureau of Intelligence Case No. 64921. Austin, Texas. Copy in possession of Michael L. Gillette, National Archives, Legislative Division, Washington, D.C. Original may no longer exist.

8. *Mansfield, Texas, Records*

City of Mansfield Records. City Commission Meeting Minutes. 1956.
City of Mansfield Planning and Zoning Offices.
Mansfield Chamber of Commerce. "Welcome to Mansfield." No date.

Mansfield Historical Society. *Historic Mansfield, Texas.* Pamphlet. Mansfield, Texas: City of Mansfield, 1992.
Mansfield Historical Society Records.
Mansfield Independent School District. School Board Meeting Minutes. 1950–1965.

9. Books

Adams, Sherman. *Firsthand Report: The Story of the Eisenhower Administration.* New York: Popular Library, 1962.
Ashmore, Harry S. *An Epitaph for Dixie.* New York: Norton, 1957.
———. *The Negro and the Schools.* Chapel Hill: University of North Carolina Press, 1954.
Baggarly, Herbert M. *The Texas Country Editor.* Ed. Eugene W. Jones. New York: World Publishing, 1966.
Beals, Melba Pattillo. *Warriors Don't Cry: A Searing Memoir of the Battle to Integrate Little Rock's Central High.* New York: Simon and Schuster, 1994.
Boyle, Sarah Patton. *The Desegregated Heart: A Virginian's Stand in the Time of Transition.* New York: William Morrow, 1962.
Brownell, Herbert, and John P. Burke. *Advising Ike: The Memoirs of Attorney General Herbert Brownell.* Lawrence: University Press of Kansas, 1993.
Dabbs, James McBride. *The Southern Heritage.* New York: Alfred A. Knopf, 1958.
Eisenhower, Dwight David. *Waging Peace: The White House Years, 1956–1961.* New York: Doubleday, 1965.
Fuermann, George. *Reluctant Empire.* New York: Doubleday, 1957.
Golden, Harry. *Only in America.* New York: World Publishing, 1958.
Greenberg, Jack. *Race Relations and American Law.* New York: Columbia University Press, 1959.
Griffin, John Howard. *Black Like Me.* Boston: Houghton-Mifflin, 1961.
Hickman, R. C. *Behold the People: R. C. Hickman's Photographs of Black Dallas, 1949–1961.* Austin: Texas State Historical Association, 1994.
Hill, Herbert, and Jack Greenberg. *Citizen's Guide to Desegregation: A Study of Social and Legal Change in American Life.* Westport, Connecticut: Greenwood Press, 1955.
Hughes, Emmet John. *The Ordeal of Power: A Political Memoir of the Eisenhower Years.* London: Macmillan, 1963.
Kelly, Alfred H. "The School Desegregation Case." In *Quarrels That Shaped the Constitution.* Ed. John Arthur Garraty. 243–267. New York: Harper and Row, 1964.
Kilpatrick, James Jackson. *The Southern Case for School Segregation.* New York: Crowell-Collier, 1962.
———. *The Sovereign States: Notes of a Citizen of Virginia.* Chicago: Henry Regnery, 1957.
Larson, Arthur. *The President Nobody Knew.* New York: Scribners, 1968.

Lasch, Robert. "Along the Border." In *With All Deliberate Speed: Segregation—Desegregation in Southern Schools.* Ed. Don Shoemaker. New York: Harper, 1957.

Leflar, Robert A. "Law of the Land." In *With All Deliberate Speed: Segregation—Desegregation in Southern Schools.* Ed. Don Shoemaker. New York: Harper, 1957.

Leflar, Robert A., and Wylie H. Davis. "Devices to Evade or Delay Desegregation." In *Desegregation and the Supreme Court.* Ed. Benjamin Munn Ziegler. Boston: Heath, 1958.

Martin, John Bartlow. *The Deep South Says "Never."* New York: Ballentine Books, 1957.

McCauley, Patrick E. "Be It Enacted." In *With All Deliberate Speed: Segregation—Desegregation in Southern Schools.* Ed. Don Shoemaker. New York: Harper, 1957.

Morrow, Frederick E. *Black Man in the White House.* New York: Coward-McCann, 1963.

Myrdal, Gunnar, Richard Sterner, and Arnold Rose. *An American Dilemma: The Negro Problem and Modern Democracy.* New York: Harper, 1944.

Peters, William. *The Southern Temper.* New York: Doubleday, 1959.

Rose, Arnold. *The Negro in America.* New York: Harper, 1948.

Vernon's Texas Statutes, 1958 Supplement: Including General and Permanent Laws, of the 55th Legislature, Regular Session and 1st and 2nd Called Sessions. Kansas City, Missouri: Vernon Law Books, 1958.

Warren, Robert Penn. *Segregation: The Inner Conflict in the South.* New York: Random House, 1956.

Weeks, O. Douglas. *Texas One-Party Politics in 1956.* Austin: Institute of Public Affairs, University of Texas, 1957.

Westfeldt, Wallace. "Communities in Strife." In *With All Deliberate Speed: Segregation—Desegregation in Southern Schools.* Ed. Don Shoemaker. New York: Harper, 1957.

Wey, Herbert, and John Corey. *Action Patterns in School Desegregation: A Guidebook.* Bloomington, Indiana: Phi Delta Kappa, 1959.

White, Walter. *A Man Called White.* New York: Arno Press, 1969.

———. *How Far the Promised Land?* New York: Viking Press, 1955.

Wilkins, Roy, with Tom Mathews. *Standing Fast: The Autobiography of Roy Wilkins.* New York: Viking Press, 1982.

Woodward, C. Vann. *The Strange Career of Jim Crow.* New York: Oxford University Press, 1955.

Workman, W. D., Jr. "The Deep South." In *With All Deliberate Speed: Segregation—Desegregation in Southern Schools.* Ed. Don Shoemaker. New York: Harper, 1957.

10. Pamphlet/Report

Griffin, John Howard, and Theodore Freedman. *Mansfield, Texas: A Report of the Crisis Situation Resulting from Efforts to Desegregate the*

School System. New York: Anti-Defamation League of B'nai B'rith, 1957.

11. Articles

Bennett, Lerone. "The South and the Negro: Rev. Martin Luther King Jr., Alabama Desegregationist, Challenges Talmadge." *Ebony* 12 (April 1957): 77, 79, 81.

Brisbane, Robert. "Interposition: Theory and Fact." *Phylon* 17 (1956): 12–16.

"Directives to the Branches Adopted by Emergency Southwide NAACP Conference." *Crisis* 62 (June–July 1955): 339–340, 381.

Eisenhower, Dwight David. "Acceptance Speech." *Vital Speeches* (September 1, 1956): 685–689.

———. "The State of the Union." *Vital Speeches* 22 (February 1, 1956): 226–233.

———. "The State of the Union: The Cost of Peace." *Vital Speeches* 23 (February 1, 1957): 226–229.

Ervin, Sam J., Jr. "The Case of Segregation." United States Senate. *Congressional Records* 102 (March 22, 1956): 5349–5350.

Fleming, Harold C. "Resistance Movements and Racial Desegregation." *Annals of the American Academy* 304 (1956): 44–52.

Fullingim, Archer. "The Printer Fires Both Barrels." *Congressional Records*. Appendix (August 6, 1957), A6362.

Graham, Billy. "Billy Graham Makes Plea for an End to Intolerance." *Life* 41 (October 1, 1956): 138, 140, 143–144, 146, 151.

"The Halting and Fitful Battle for Integration." *Life* 41 (September 17, 1954): 34–37.

Hardeman, D. B. "Shivers of Texas: A Tragedy in Three Acts." *Harper's Magazine* 212–213 (1956): 50–56.

"How Miss Lucy Upset Alabama U." *Ebony* 12 (March 1957): 51–54.

Hyman, Herbert H., and Paul B. Sheatsley. "Attitudes toward Desegregation." *Scientific American* 195 (December 1956): 35–39.

Jones, William H. "Desegregation of Public Education in Texas—One Year Afterward." *Journal of Negro Education* 24 (1955): 350–351.

Leflar, Robert A., and Wylie H. Davis. "Segregation in the Public Schools." *Harvard Law Review* 67 (January 1954): 377–435.

Marshall, Thurgood. "A Policy of 'Gradualism' in Integration. . . . Top Negro Says 'I Invented It.'" Interviewed by Joseph Carter. *Newsweek* 48 (September 17, 1956): 36–37.

Marshall, Thurgood, and Roy Wilkins. "Interpretation of Supreme Court Decision and the NAACP Program." *Crisis* 62 (June–July 1955): 329–333.

Morrison, Allan. "The South and the Negro: Senator Herman Talmadge, Georgia Segregationist, Defends 'Southern Way.'" *Ebony* 12 (April 1957): 76, 78, 80.

Murphy, Walter F. "The South Counterattacks: The Anti-NAACP Laws." *Western Political Quarterly* 12 (1959): 371–390.

"Negro Progress in 1956." *Ebony* 12 (January 1957): 58–59, 61–62.

Race Relations Law Reporter 1 (February 1956): selected cases and reports.

Race Relations Law Reporter 2 (1957): selected cases and reports.

"A Round Table Has Debate on Christians' Moral Duty." *Life* 41 (October 1, 1956): 139–140, 143, 145–146, 151–152, 154, 159–160, 162.

Roush, S. Larry. "A Summary of Southern States' Legislative Reactions to School Desegregation." *Texas School Board Journal* 3–7 (September 1957): 3–7.

Routh, Frederick B., and Paul Anthony. "Southern Resistance Forces." *Phylon* 18 (1957): 50–58.

"Segregation and the Public Schools." *Texas School Board Journal* 1–2 (June 1954): 2–3, 24.

"The South: Fury and Progress." *Time* 68 (September 17, 1956): 32–33.

Waring, Thomas R. "The Southern Case: Against Desegregation." *Harper's Magazine* 212–213 (January 1956): 39–45.

"What's New in the Law: Public Schools . . . Segregation." *American Bar Association Journal* 42 (1956): 960.

Wilkins, Roy. "Desegregation: North and South." *Current History* 32–33 (May 1957): 283–287.

12. Newspapers

American Statesman. Selected articles. 1956.

Austin American. Selected articles. 1956.

Christian Science Monitor. Selected articles. 1956.

Dallas Express. Selected articles. September 1956.

Dallas Morning News. Selected articles. 1955–1956.

Fort Worth Star-Telegram. Selected articles. 1956.

Houston Informer. September 1956.

Houston Post. May 1954.

Mansfield News. Selected articles. 1953–1956.

New York Herald-Tribune. September 1956.

New York Times. Selected articles. 1956.

Southern School News. Selected articles. 1954–1956.

Texas Observer. Selected articles. 1956–1966.

Bray, Bob. "Texas School Told to Integrate." *Texas Observer,* August 1, 1956.

13. Television Documentary

Marshall, Thurgood. "Today Show: Documentary on Thurgood Marshall." New York: National Broadcasting Company, January 26, 1993.

Secondary Sources

1. Books

Alexander, Charles C. *Holding the Line: The Eisenhower Era, 1952–1961.* Bloomington: Indiana University Press, 1975.

Anderson, John Weir. *Eisenhower, Brownell, and the Congress: The Tangled Origins of the Civil Rights Bill of 1956–1957.* Tuscaloosa: University of Alabama, 1964.

Banks, Jimmy. *Money, Marbles, and Chalk: The Wondrous World of Texas Politics.* Austin: Texas Publishing, 1971.

Bardolph, Richard, ed. *The Civil Rights Record: Black Americans and the Law, 1849–1970.* New York: Thomas Y. Crowell, 1970.

Barr, Alwyn. *Black Texans: A History of Negroes in Texas, 1528–1971.* Austin: Jenkins, 1973.

Barr, Alwyn, and Robert A. Calvert, eds. *Black Leaders: Texans for Their Times.* Austin: Texas State Historical Association, 1985.

Bartley, Numan V. *The Rise of Massive Resistance: Race and Politics in the South during the 1950's.* Baton Rouge: Louisiana State University Press, 1969.

Blaustein, Albert, and Clarence Clyde Ferguson, Jr. *Desegregation and the Law: The Meaning and Effect of the School Segregation Cases.* New Brunswick: Rutgers University Press, 1957.

Blaustein, Albert, and Robert L. Zangrando. *Civil Rights and the American Negro: A Documentary History.* New York: Trident Press, 1968.

Branch, Taylor. *Parting the Waters: America in the King Years, 1954–1963.* New York: Simon and Schuster, 1988.

Branyan, Robert L., and Lawrence H. Larsen. *The Eisenhower Administration, 1953–1961: A Documentary History.* New York: Random House, 1971.

Brooks, Thomas R. *Walls Come Tumbling Down: A History of the Civil Rights Movement, 1940–1970.* Englewood Cliffs, New Jersey: Prentice-Hall, 1974.

Burk, Robert F. "Dwight David Eisenhower and Civil Rights Conservatism." In *Dwight David Eisenhower: Soldier, President, Statesman.* Ed. Joann P. Krieg. Westport, Connecticut: Greenwood Press, 1987.

———. *The Eisenhower Administration and Black Civil Rights.* Knoxville: University of Tennessee Press, 1984.

Davidson, Chandler. *Biracial Politics: Conflict and Coalition in the Metropolitan South.* Baton Rouge: Louisiana State University Press, 1972.

Dickson, James G., Jr. *Law and Politics: The Office of the Attorney General in Texas.* Manchaca, Texas: Sterling Swift, 1976.

Dugger, Ronnie. "Confessions of a White Liberal." In *Black, White, and Gray: Twenty-One Points of View on the Race Question.* Ed. Daniel Bradford. New York: Sheed and Ward, 1964.

Duram, James C. *A Moderate among Extremists: Dwight D. Eisenhower and the School Desegregation Crisis.* Chicago: Nelson-Hall, 1981.

———. "Whose Brief? Dwight David Eisenhower, His Southern Friends, and the School Segregation Cases." In *Dwight David Eisenhower: Soldier, President, Statesman.* Ed. Joann Krieg. Westport, Connecticut: Greenwood Press, 1987.

Finch, Minnie. *The NAACP: Its Fight for Justice.* Metuchen, New Jersey: Scarecrow Press, 1981.

Gillette, Michael Lowery. "Heman Marion Sweatt: Civil Rights Plaintiff." In *Black Leaders: Texans for Their Times.* Ed. Alwyn Barr and Robert A. Calvert. Austin: Texas State Historical Association, 1985.

Goldfield, David R. *Black, White, and Southern: Race Relations and Southern Culture, 1940 to the Present.* Baton Rouge: Louisiana State University Press, 1990.

Goldman, Roger L. *Thurgood Marshall, Justice for All.* New York: Carroll and Graf, 1992.

Green, George Norris. *The Establishment in Texas Politics: The Primitive Years, 1938–1957.* Westport, Connecticut: Greenwood Press, 1979.

Johnson, Guy B. "Freedom, Equality, and Segregation." In *Integration versus Segregation.* Ed. Hubert Humphrey. New York: Thomas Y. Crowell, 1964.

Kinch, Sam, and Stuart Long. *Allan Shivers: The Pied Piper of Texas Politics.* Austin: Shoal Creek Publishers, 1973.

Kluger, Richard. *Simple Justice: The History of Brown v. Board of Education and Black America's Struggle for Equality.* New York: Alfred A. Knopf, 1975.

Lee, R. Alton. *Dwight D. Eisenhower, Soldier and Statesman.* Chicago: Nelson-Hall, 1981.

Manchester, William. *The Glory and the Dream: A Narrative History of America, 1932–1972.* Boston: Little, Brown, 1973.

Marable, Manning. *Race, Reform, and Rebellion: The Second Reconstruction in Black America, 1945–1982.* Jackson: University Press of Mississippi, 1984.

McMillen, Neil R. *The Citizens' Council: Organized Resistance to the Second Reconstruction, 1954–1964.* Chicago: University of Illinois Press, 1971.

Mitau, G. Theodore. *Decade of Decision: The Supreme Court and the Constitutional Revolution, 1954–1964.* New York: Charles Scribner's Sons, 1967.

Morris, Aldon D. *The Origins of the Civil Rights Movement: Black Communities Organizing for Change.* New York: Collier Macmillan, 1984.

Muse, Benjamin. *Ten Years Prelude: The Story of Integration since the Supreme Court's 1954 Decision.* New York: Viking Press, 1964.

Parmet, Herbert S. *Eisenhower and the American Crusades.* New York: Macmillan, 1972.

Peltason, Jack Walter. *Fifty-Eight Lonely Men: Southern Federal Judges and School Desegregation.* New York: Harcourt, Brace and World, 1961.

Phillips, William G. *Yarborough of Texas.* Washington, D.C.: Acropolis Books, 1969.

Sarratt, Reed. *The Ordeal of Desegregation: The First Decade.* New York: Harper and Row, 1966.
Sherill, Robert. *Gothic Politics in the Deep South.* New York: Grossman, 1968.
Sitkoff, Harvard. *The Struggle for Black Equality, 1954–1980.* New York: Hill and Wang, 1981.
Travelstead, Chester C. "Southern Attitudes toward Racial Integration." In *The Countdown on Segregated Education.* Ed. William W. Brinkman and Stanley Lehrer. New York: Society for the Advancement of Education, 1960.
Wasby, Stephen L., Anthony A. D'Amato, and Rosemary Metrailer. *Desegregation from Brown to Alexander: An Exploration of Supreme Court Strategies.* Carbondale: Southern Illinois University Press, 1977.
Webb, Walter Prescott. *The Great Plains.* Lincoln: University of Nebraska Press, 1931.
Wilhoit, Francis M. *The Politics of Massive Resistance.* New York: George Braziller, 1973.
Wilkinson, J. Harvie, III. *From Brown to Bakke: The Supreme Court and School Integration, 1954–1978.* New York: Oxford University Press, 1979.

2. Unpublished Theses and Dissertations

Frank, Beverly. "John Howard Griffin." M.A. thesis, University of Texas at Arlington, 1989.
Gillette, Michael Lowery. "The NAACP in Texas, 1937–1957." Ph.D. dissertation, University of Texas, 1984.
McMillan, Edward Lee. "Texas and the Eisenhower Campaigns." Ph.D. dissertation, Texas Tech University, 1960.
Murphy, Leonard B. "A History of Negro Segregation Practices in Texas, 1865–1958." M.A. thesis, Southern Methodist University, 1958.
Schlundt, Ronald. "Civil Rights Policies in the Eisenhower Years." Ph.D. dissertation, Rice University, 1973.

3. Articles

Amaker, Norman C. "The 1950s: Racial Equality and the Law." *Current History* 56–57 (November 1969): 275–280, 300–301.
Baker, Liva. "With All Deliberate Speed." *American Heritage* 24 (February 1973): 42–48.
Edelman, Marian Wright. "Southern School Desegregation, 1954–1973: A Judicial-Political Overview." *Annals of the American Academy of Political and Social Sciences* 405–407 (May 1973): 32–42.
Hendrix, J. A. "Shivercrat Rebellion: A Case Study in Campaign Speaking Strategies." *Southern Speech Journal* 33 (1968): 289–295.
Mayer, Michael S. "With Much Deliberation and Some Speed: Eisenhower and the Brown Decision." *Journal of Southern History* 52 (1986): 43–76.

McCain, R. Ray. "Reactions to the United States Supreme Court Decision of 1954." *Georgia Historical Quarterly* 52 (December 1968): 371–387.

Rodgers, Harrell R., Jr., and Charles S. Bullock III. "School Desegregation: A Policy Analysis." *Journal of Black Studies* 2 (June 1972): 409–437.

Scott, Alan. "Twenty-Five Years of Opinion on Integration in Texas." *Southwestern Social Science Quarterly* 48 (September 1967): 155–163.

Vines, Kenneth N. "The Role of Circuit Courts of Appeal in the Federal Judicial Process: A Case Study." *Midwest Journal of Political Science* 7 (November 1963): 305–319.

4. Unpublished Articles

Peterson, F. Ross. "Prelude to Little Rock: The Eisenhower Administration and Mansfield, Texas." Unpublished article in author's possession. Written permission to use and quote.

5. Newspapers

Dodge, Tom. "Black Like Me Now." *Dallas Observer*, September 6, 1990.

Olds, Greg. "Integration in Texas: Some Gains Made, but Substantial Problems Remain." *Texas Observer*, October 28, 1966.

Taylor, Sheila. "Jim Crow Revisited." *Texas Observer*, June 9, 1979.

Index